COMPUTER METHODS

FOR LITERARY RESEARCH

COMPUTER METHODS

for Literary Research

Robert L. Oakman

The University of Georgia Press

Athens

Copyright © 1980, 1984 by Robert L. Oakman

All rights reserved

Published in 1984 in a revised, paperback edition by the
University of Georgia Press, Athens, Georgia 30602

Manufactured in the United States of America

88 87 86 85 84   5 4 3 2 1

The paper in this book meets the guidelines for permanence
and durability of the Committee on Production Guidelines
for Book Longevity of the Council on Library Resources.

Library of Congress Cataloging in Publication Data

Oakman, Robert L., 1941–
Computer methods for literary research.

Bibliography: p.
Includes index.
1. Literary research—Data processing. I. Title.
PN73.024 1983   802'.85   83-9273
ISBN 0-8203-0686-X (pbk.)

To Betsy, who was there from the inception, and to Jeffrey and Jonathan, without whose unexpected double arrival this book might have been finished a year earlier

CONTENTS

PREFACE TO THE FIRST EDITION

COMPUTER APPLICATIONS IN LITERATURE are now two decades old, the Reverend John W. Ellison's computerized concordance to the Revised Standard Version of the Bible having been completed in 1957. The first decade saw the production of several fine concordances and tentative moves into other areas of literary application—stylistics, authorship identification, and textual collation. Also typical of these years was a rash of glowing predictions that the computer would revolutionize the discipline of literary scholarship and even effect a marriage between the much-discussed "two cultures" of the scientist and the humanist. Indeed, Ephim G. Fogel in a special computer studies issue of *Shakespeare Newsletter*, published at the end of 1965, looked forward to a day in the near future when every large humanities department would contain a "creative computer-oriented professor" and a "literary data-processing fellowship" for a deserving graduate student, as well as a humanities expert in every university computer center.[1] Speaking glowingly of the "limitless examples and statistics" which computers would provide literary scholarship, Louis Marder even suggested that "ignorance may become impossible"—a forecast indicative of the naive understanding of those devoted early to computers and, moreover, ignorant of the world in general.[2]

[1] Ephim G. Fogel, "The Humanist and the Computer," *Shakespeare Newsletter*, 15 (1965), 51.

[2] Louis Marder, "Computer Scholarship in Shakespearean and Related Studies," *Shakespeare Newsletter*, 15 (1965), 52.

The second ten years of literary computing have fortunately seen a decline in such wild generalizations and the installment of a few computer humanists in university departments. Several pioneering volumes of essays document respectable results, and a selection of journals and an international society have sprung up to publicize new findings. Yet computing in literature is a long way from being the way of the future predicted in 1965. One reason may be the lack of a single reference source giving an overview of the field to the literary student or scholar without computer experience. Besides programming manuals for particular computer languages and several collections of papers, there is not at present a book to survey the field from the unifying perspective of one observer.

Intended to fill this gap, this book has a double focus, computer fundamentals and literary applications, in order to convey two kinds of information to the humanist with little or no computer experience. The first several chapters discuss in a nontechnical way concepts common to all machine applications: basic elements of computer systems, input/output methods and equipment, and structuring textual materials for their efficient analysis with computer programs. Throughout these pages, illustrations and examples are chosen with literary possibilities in mind. Building on these central foundations, the bulk of the book focuses on specific, detailed discussion of important literary applications: concordances, automated bibliography, lexicography, textual collation, disputed authorship, and content and stylistic analysis. The final chapter assesses available textual archives in computer form and general-purpose programs suitable for literary use, before considering prospects for the future. Overall, the book intends a synthetic and critical survey of computer applications in literature at the present time. If successful, it will show the kinds of jobs a computer does well, along with the limitations and compromises it places on literary scholarship.

This book, one man's view of the possibilities, pitfalls, and potentials of literary computing today, is designed for the general literary scholar or student unfamiliar with the machine and the ways it can be made to do respectable literary tasks like textual collation and stylistic analysis. After reading the book, he should have a clearer perspective about the machine as a research tool. It is not, however, a programming textbook. To pursue his own computer project, the scholar will be ready either to learn programming for himself or to converse intelligently with an expert in his local computer center about his needs. Chances are the computer consultant will have no idea of the scholar's concerns or interests; too often there is a communications gap between these two cultures of letters and science on opposite sides of the campus. If this book helps to alleviate some of these communications problems, it will have served one of its main purposes.

The text discusses a large representative sample of applications but is not an exhaustive catalog of all projects. Specific areas of application are analyzed and accompanied with annotated bibliography by chapter. With a few exceptions, the year 1976 was the cutoff date for bibliographical references; occasionally a reference from 1977 is given for an article which follows up earlier work already represented in the text. The selected proceedings of the Third International Conference on Computing in the Humanities held at the University of Waterloo, Ontario,[3] appeared in August, 1977, too late for treatment in the manuscript. As the fifth set of conference papers connected with the Association for Literary and Linguistic Computing, this volume is as various and informative as the earlier collections, which are referenced frequently in the book, and worth the attention of scholars pursuing further topics.

[3] Serge Lusignan and John S. North, eds., *Computing in the Humanities* (Waterloo, Ontario: University of Waterloo Press, 1977).

ACKNOWLEDGMENTS

THE LIST OF PEOPLE to whom I owe acknowledgment of assistance, encouragement, and information vital to this undertaking is very long. Original impetus and assistance in getting started can be credited to my two department chairmen for summer research and sabbatical leaves, the late John Welsh in English and William J. Eccles in Mathematics and Computer Science. Subsequent chairmen, William H. Nolte in English and Robert M. Stephenson, Jr., in Mathematics and Computer Science, offered support for the final stages of writing with summer research leave in 1977. Colleagues in both departments contributed valuable information and suggestions throughout the preparation of the manuscript: Robert L. Cannon, Howard Eisenstein, Michael Farringdon, Trevor Howard-Hill, Raymond K. O'Cain, and G. Ross Roy. Students Veronica McNulty and David Pitre offered bibliographical help, and secretaries in both departments typed drafts of the manuscript in various stages of its development. Librarians at McKissick and Thomas Cooper Libraries of the University of South Carolina were always willing to order specialized books and serials and to seek out materials from all over the world on interlibrary loan. Special thanks go to the humanities and science librarians, Jean Rhyne and Carolyn Stanley, and their staffs, as well as to the Director of Libraries, Kenneth E. Toombs, for providing a research study in Cooper Library for the last writing year.

In the spring of 1975, my wife and I enjoyed a long sabbatical research trip to Britain to gather materials for the book. Under the kind auspices of the British Council, we visited major universities throughout the realm and shared insights about literary computing with important scholars and friends. Special thanks for their courtesy, hospitality, and other assistance during our visits are due our hosts: Roy Wisbey and Colin Day in London, John Dawson at Cambridge, John Horden at Leeds, A. J. Aitken at Edinburgh, Joan Smith at Manchester, Susan

Hockey at Oxford, Michael Farringdon at Swansea, Robert Church-house at Cardiff, and Eveline Wilson at Kent. Britons offering special assistance at later stages of the project include Peter Smith and Michael Farringdon for running the ALGOL68R program in Chapter 4 at Swansea; A. J. Dickson for bibliographical sleuthing under trying circumstances; and Alan Jones and D. E. Ager for providing opportunities to discuss aspects of the work at ALLC symposia in Oxford and Birmingham.

Numerous other scholars on both sides of the Atlantic corresponded or discussed their computer work with me and often generously sent copies of their papers. In this category I owe special thanks to Richard Bailey, David Bellos, Todd Bender, Terry Crawford, Kate Crennell, Andrew Crosland, Joseph Donohue, Penny Gilbert, John Griffith, Neil Hamilton-Smith, John Jolliffe, Kenneth Kemp, Geir Kjetsaa, Angus McIntosh, Sidney Michaelson, A. Q. Morton, Wilhelm Ott, James Peavler, Eric Poole, Joseph Raben, Lawrence Schiffman, Ben Schneider, Sally and Walter Sedelow, David Shaw, Ellen Spolsky, Richard Venezky, Steve Waite, and Ruth Widmann.

Portions of Chapters 4, 5, and 6 appeared first in somewhat different forms in the following articles: "Concordances from Computers: A Review," *Proof*, 3 (1973), 411–25; "A Computerized Bibliography of Scottish Poetry," in *Computers in the Humanities*, ed. J. L. Mitchell (Edinburgh: Edinburgh University Press, 1974), pp. 168–74; "The Present State of Computerized Collation: A Review Article," *Proof*, 2 (1972), 333–48; and "Textual Editing and the Computer," *Costerus*, 4 (1975), 79–106. I am grateful to editors and publishers of these journals and book for granting permission to adapt and republish the materials here. Research travel for this work was supported in part by a grant from the University of South Carolina Research and Productive Scholarship Fund.

Finally, continuing gratitude is owed to my wife, Betsy, who lived through all the years that this book was in process with grace and good humor.

Robert L. Oakman
Columbia, South Carolina, 1978

INTRODUCTION

SINCE I COMPLETED THE MANUSCRIPT for the first edition of this book in early 1978, computer developments have continued to expand in ways that few humanists and not even many computer scientists would have predicted. The microcircuitry of silicon chips has exploded the computer world, bringing small, inexpensive, powerful machines within the financial range of most Americans. Now, in 1983, people can go down to their local personal-computer store and purchase a machine for under a hundred dollars which has far more power than the Remington Rand UNIVAC of 1951, the first commercially produced machine. When UNIVAC appeared, predictions were that the potential market for computers, envisioned as large machines with military and government applications, would be about six such machines.[1] The shortsightedness of such projections has always been typical of forecasts about the growth and characteristic trends of the computer revolution.

Parents at school PTA meetings now routinely discuss what microcomputer (in layman's terminology, microcomputer = personal computer = home computer) to buy for their children's "computer literacy," and national commissions recommend orientation to and familiarity with computers for all students before they finish high school. Educators from kindergarten through secondary school are scrambling around trying to decide how to show young people in their classrooms that the personal computer is more than the colored action toy they are proficient at playing in the video arcade or on their home television set. Discussions of 32K of RAM (random-access memory), floppy disks read by dual-disk drives, word processing with WordStar, and machines based on the popular CP/M operating system are becoming commonplace in university humanities departments.

[1] Reported by Robert M. Baer, *The Digital Villain* (Reading, Mass.: Addison-Wesley, 1972), p. 37.

With this accelerating pace of growth and presence of some form of computers in every area of daily life, I feel that trying to bring my book up to date is almost like trying to tame a whirlwind. Yet many scholars and students of literature still think of computers in terms which predate the microcomputer phenomenon. In fact, many of the large-scale literary projects discussed in this book—concordances or collation projects, for example—still require the large memory size and full-scale programming facilities of big computer systems typical of most larger colleges and universities.

Moreover, the knowledge of what the microcomputer or word processor can and cannot do for literary computing remains puzzling to many scholars. At a recent conference on computers in the humanities, a speaker discussed the development of large machine-searchable data banks of information in the same terms as ten to twenty years ago. The materials were being encoded into the machine at terminals, and the results were spit out for offset printing on printout paper. The hardware, programs, and principles of textual analysis being described were no more innovative than projects from 1970 included in the first edition of this book. Although the specific application was new to computer processing, the scholar spent more time describing well-tried techniques of input and processing than he did in discussing the unique possibilities for analysis of his special text materials. The computing itself had all been done before. As one wry critic has commented about such performances: "The reinvention of the wheel, and its proud presentation at international symposia, is a familiar event."[2] There is still an audience out there for the basic lessons of literary computing that this book addresses.

Publications about computing in the humanities are keeping pace with the growth of computing everywhere. The two major international professional societies devoted to this field, the Association for Literary and Linguistic Computing (ALLC) and the newer Association for Computers and the Humanities (ACH), have continued to host symposia, usually alternating with each other every other year and on opposite sides of the Atlantic. Most of these meetings have published selected proceedings, from which a scholar can get a good feel for the kinds of work being done today in humanistic computing. Since the Third International Conference on Computing in the Humanities (ICCH/3) at the University of Waterloo, Ontario, conferences have been held as follows:

[2] L. D. Burnard, "At Home with the Hardware," *TLS*, 9 May 1980, p. 533.

1978. ALLC/5. University of Aston, Birmingham, England. Papers: D. E. Ager, F. E. Knowles, and Joan Smith, eds., *Advances in Computer-Aided Literary and Linguistic Research* (Birmingham: University of Aston, Department of Modern Languages, 1979).

1979. ICCH/4. Dartmouth College, Hanover, New Hampshire. No published papers.

1979. International Conference on Literary and Linguistic Computing. Tel Aviv, Israel. Papers: Zvi Malachi, ed., *Proceedings* (Tel Aviv: Tel Aviv University, Katz Research Institute for Hebrew Literature, 1979).

1980. ALLC/6. University of Cambridge, England. Selected papers published in the first four issues of the *ALLC Journal*: 1, Nos. 1–2 (Summer and Autumn 1980); 2, Nos. 1–2 (Summer and Autumn 1981).

1981. ICCH/5. University of Michigan, Ann Arbor. Papers: Richard W. Bailey, ed., *Computing in the Humanities* (New York: North-Holland, 1982).

1982. ALLC/7. University of Pisa, Italy. Papers in press.

North Carolina State University at Raleigh is serving as host to the 1983 ICCH/6 Symposium, and the next ALLC Conference in Europe will be at the Catholic University of Louvain-la-Neuve, Belgium, in April 1984.

Two other general reference books deserve special mention. Very similar in outlook and tone with this book is Susan Hockey's fine survey: *A Guide to Computer Applications in the Humanities* (Baltimore: Johns Hopkins University Press, 1980). Despite the title, most of the techniques and scholarship discussed are literary or linguistic in nature; in fact, Mrs. Hockey does not cover computer applications in music and the visual arts. She works for the Oxford University Computing Service, one of the best-equipped university centers for literary computing; and the book grew out of her courses there to introduce humanities students to computer methods. The book discusses several topics related to literary research in somewhat more detail than here—vocabulary counts, dialectology, and computational linguistics—illustrated with many results in the form of graphs and computer printout. Certainly anyone who finds this book helpful will also want to consult the Hockey book.

Computing in the Humanities, edited by Peter C. Patton and Renée A. Holoien (Lexington, Mass.: Lexington Books, 1981), represents a different approach, a sort of case study of computer applications being carried out by faculty members in the humanities at one institution, the

University of Minnesota. Only one of four sections of the book is especially devoted to analysis of language and literature, including studies of the Greek New Testament, the Anglo-Saxon chronicles, and troubadour poets in Occitan. Literary scholars may perhaps find useful suggestions for their own research in the other three parts of the book, devoted to archaeology and history, the visual arts, and computer-assisted instruction. Taken as a whole, the book belongs on the same shelf with the proceedings of the conferences listed earlier. It shares with them the lack of a single, unifying perspective and a mixed quality of research results described.

Certainly the emergence of the personal computer represents the most dramatic computing development in the past few years. Literary scholars have begun to use these machines for their scholarly work, especially for word processing (discussed below), computer-assisted instruction, and applications that fall into the general realm of information retrieval (see Chapter 6). Ned Davison at the University of Utah has even argued for doing simple stylistic analyses like theme searches and poetic patterning with interactive text-editor programs appropriate for small computer systems.[3]

Recommending an introduction to the hardware and software of microcomputers is a tough task; a visit to any corner bookstore these days typically presents a large choice of titles, often written for specific models, manufacturers, or software packages. No particular one has garnered unanimous raves of approval in reviews. For a general, entertaining first book, a novice may find the well-known *Personal Computer Book* by Peter A. McWilliams a popular choice (Los Angeles: Prelude Press, 1982, with regular updated editions). In a breezy, witty, informal style, McWilliams—a computer user, not a computer professional—defines the terminology of home computers; analyzes their possible uses; and gives his own openly opinionated evaluations of the burgeoning, even bewildering choice of machinery. The several articles comprising a special report on choosing a personal computer in the November 1982 issue of *Money* magazine offer some of the best concise, descriptive discussions that I have seen on such topics as microcomputer fundamentals and jargon, word processing, and brand-name comparisons for different applications and pocketbooks. Obviously the editorial staff invested a lot of time studying hardware, interviewing salesmen and

---

[3] Ned Davison, "Nursery Rhymes to Shakespeare: Using an Editor to Look at Literature," *Creative Computing*, 7 (October 1981), 110–18 passim.

users, and digesting the information for their literate but non-technical readers.

The development of word processing has probably the most far-reaching potential effect on scholars in all disciplines of any computer innovation since 1978. In this area, the place to start a search for information should be William Zinsser's apologia, *Writing with a Word Processor* (New York: Harper and Row, 1983). A successful professional writer, and author of the well-received *On Writing Well*, 2nd ed. (New York: Harper and Row, 1980), Zinsser approached the machine, and the IBM corporate mind behind it, with the innate resistance, even snobbery, of the humanist about turning over his writing to a computer. He feared the loss of his typed drafts with his penciled revisions "in the electricity," as he put it. The first time he began composing at his IBM Displaywriter exactly that event happened, because of a faulty program diskette. Nevertheless, he eventually came to appreciate the flexibility of his machine, described in full detail for other inquirers. Two fine chapters describe how Zinsser merged his writing methods with the capacities of the word processor and how other writers have adapted the machine's abilities to their own practices. In the end, Zinsser, like Ben Schneider in *Travels in Computerland* (see Chapter 2), became a convert to the new technology; and he describes in humorous, feeling detail all the pitfalls and triumphs along the way. I predict that Zinsser's easy-to-follow personal narrative will lead many other humanists with fears about the machine down the road to word processing behind him.

For more information about what word processors are and what they do, again Peter McWilliams may be a good choice: *The Word Processing Book: A Short Course in Computer Literacy* (Los Angeles: Prelude Press, 1982). Included are comparisons of different equipment and software programming packages to carry out the usual functions of word processing: input of text; automatic hyphenation; deletions and additions to the text as a part of editing and revision; reformatting of text after changes; automatic pagination; and printing of the final edited revision of the text, often with footnotes. Various programs to check for misspelled words are also available; when the errors have been found, the scholar uses the "search and replace" operation at his word processor to find and correct them directly at a terminal.[4]

[4] Wayne Holder in "Software Tools for Writers," *BYTE*, 7 (July 1982), 138–63 passim, discusses additional program packages such as readability formulas and syllabic counting that can be helpful for composing and editing.

The word processor, like the typewriter before it, will surely change the way we write in the future. Two recent references address this relationship between word processing and the writing process: Paula Nancarrow, Donald Ross, and Lillian Bridwell, eds., *Word Processing and the Writing Process: An Annotated Bibliography* (Minneapolis: University of Minnesota, Department of English, 1982); and John Lawlor, ed., *Computers in Composition Instruction* (Los Alamitos, Calif.: SWRL Educational Research and Development, 1982), papers and responses from a 1982 research conference in California. From these sources scholars may get valuable suggestions for their own work or for teaching composition to students.

The most intriguing programs I have encountered in the past five years with implications for literary scholarship, word processing, and stylistic analysis were developed outside academia at Bell Telephone Laboratories in New Jersey. Calling their handiwork the Writer's Workbench, the designers set out to create a system of interrelated programs which run on machines with the popular UNIX operating system to aid professional staff to write clear, more forceful technical reports and documents. None of the main developers was in English; team members were trained in psychology, reading research, mathematics, computer science, and computational linguistics.

They started with a general consensus about what constituted good writing: it must be grammatically correct, correctly spelled, and not overly wordy. William Strunk, Jr., and E. B. White (*The Elements of Style*, 3rd ed. [New York: Macmillan, 1979]), added some refinements: cut out passive verbs, use short concrete diction, and prefer verbs to nouns made from them ("orient your employees" rather than "have an orientation for them"). With these simple guidelines, the creators of Writer's Workbench wrote computer programs to carry out all of the following analyses on English prose, among others: checking spelling and obvious punctuation, finding overly abstract diction, calculating readability levels, keeping statistics on sentence length and type, noting passive constructions, flagging *be* verbs and split infinitives, and even marking suspect sexist language. Not only do the programs note these and other surface features of the prose for the author interactively at a terminal, but they suggest ways to revise and make the writing clearer, more concise, and more vibrant.[5]

Granted that the Writer's Workbench may not be a panacea for

[5] For a comprehensive survey of the philosophy and content of the Writer's Workbench project with bibliography, see two articles in *IEEE Transactions on Communications* (January 1982): Lorinda Cherry, "Writing Tools," pp. 100–105; and Nina H. Mac-

improving all levels of writing, it does hold several valuable lessons for literary scholars concerned with the state of the written word in English. It includes several features that the stylistic analyses and packages described in Chapters 7 and 8 have not tried; it would be worthwhile to see what kinds of insights it would suggest about literary prose. Because it is written for UNIX, it can run on many current large and medium-size computer systems with no headaches of implementation. Moreover, forecasters predict that UNIX operating systems will soon be available for personal computers. Perhaps the most far-reaching implication of this development is the extent to which it embodies the practical *modus operandi* of computer people. Without philosophizing about reader response or genre distinctions, they took a few well-known generalizations about good writing capable of analysis in surface features of English prose and went ahead developing their programs. Users of the Writer's Workbench report seeing improvement in their writing and a heightened awareness of stylistic possibilities available to them. The message for stylistic researchers and writing teachers is clear: if we do not address issues of analyzing writing with computers, others without our background are going to do it on their own, without seeking our advice or approval, because it needs to be done.

Among recent hardware developments, the Kurzweil Data Entry Machine (KDEM) is a welcome addition for literary computing. Its capacities address directly the biggest headache and bottleneck of large-scale literary processing: the encoding of texts into machine-readable form easily and accurately. This optical scanning device can learn to read any font of Roman, Greek, or Cyrillic alphabets directly from the printed page into a magnetic tape file. Before it starts to read a book in a typefont it does not already "understand," an operator trains the KDEM machine to recognize each printed character of the new typefont by its shape—its angles, curves, and lines. KDEM can process books with clear distinctions between black type and white background or typescript from an electric typewriter with a dark, uniform strike. The printed page is scanned while it is lying on a glass screen like a copy machine, and an operator monitors the automatic reading to correct errors noticed in the scanning process. At present three universities in Britain (Oxford, Birmingham, and Glasgow) and at least one American university (Brigham Young) have Kurzweil machines. Having used the machine myself at Oxford, I can testify to its wonderful advantages; it is

---

donald, Lawrence T. Frase, Patricia S. Gingrich, and Stacey A. Keenan, "The Writer's Workbench: Computer Aids for Text Analysis," pp. 105–10.

much faster and less prone to error than any of the older methods of typing texts into the computer, all of them liable to mistakes in the keying process. [6]

Of the areas of literary application treated in the first edition of this book, scholarly editing and textual criticism seem to have been the most active in recent years in terms of innovation. No doubt the enormous developments in computer typesetting and photocomposition have had a major effect on this activity. In Europe, Wilhelm Ott's pioneering work in collation and typesetting by machines (see Chapter 6) has been adapted by Hans Walter Gabler at the University of Munich for what promises to be one of the most significant editing projects of the 1980s—a comprehensive scholarly edition of James Joyce's *Ulysses* with its very complex textual history (see Gabler, "Computer-Aided Critical Edition of *Ulysses*," *ALLC Bulletin*, 8 [1981], 232–48).

Two American textual projects suggest other important trends for the future. The work of Thomas C. Faulkner and his associates at Washington State University in preparing an edition of Robert Burton's *Anatomy of Melancholy* represents one approach. These scholars have assembled a number of computer programs and techniques developed elsewhere—WYLBUR for text editing, WATCON for concordancing, SPIRES for information retrieval, and Donald Knuth's TEX system for computer typesetting—and configured them into their own complete editing system (for details, see Faulkner's article, "Computer Applications for an Edition of Robert Burton's *The Anatomy of Melancholy*: A System for Scholarly Publishing," *CHum*, 15 [1981], 163–82). On the other hand, Peter and Miriam Shillingsburg have amassed considerable practical experience working out on their own PL/I collation processes for editions of W. M. Thackeray and Washington Irving (for fullest details about this work, see Miriam J. Shillingsburg, "Computer Assistance to Scholarly Editing," *Bulletin of Research in the Humanities*, 81 [Winter 1978], 448–63). Having encoded six editions of *Vanity Fair* at a terminal, the Shillingsburgs ran their programs to find variants in texts compared two at a time; and the computer spit out all the differences between the texts. Some of these were true variants, while others resulted from typing errors introduced into the computer versions of the

---

[6] Susan Hockey (Oxford University Computing Service, 13 Banbury Road, Oxford OX2 6NN, England) has had the most experience with employing the Kurzweil scanner in literary computing; at ICCH/5 she reported on their experiences at Oxford in training operators to use the machine efficiently to read literary texts in a great variety of languages (paper not published). See also Patricia Galloway, "Hardware Review: The Kurzweil Data Entry Machine," *CHum*, 15 (1981), 183–85.

texts at the terminal keyboard. A second run on the cleaned-up text files presented the actual variants ready for scholarly inspection.

Editing the *Papers of Henry Laurens*, David Chesnutt and his colleagues at the University of South Carolina have created two important programs for computerized editing, CINDEX for assistance in scholarly indexing and CACTUS for dropping computer typesetting codes into machine-readable files of the critical text and footnotes. Automating the old manual method of index cards, CINDEX allows the scholar to remain in control of the process, including creation of index terms and cross references. The computer can prepare an index of one volume of a scholarly edition and later merge these separate indexes into a collected cumulative one. The distinguishing feature of the CACTUS programs is their ability to ready a computer-readable document or text for typesetting by automatically dropping into the file appropriate codes for typefont, spacing, margins, format, etc. The Laurens text processing system set out to be comprehensive in scope: from input of documents at a word processor through editing and production of notes to creation of the scholarly index and preparation of computer tapes of the texts with inserted typesetting codes ready for photocomposition of galley proofs. This "computer systems" approach has isolated areas where scholarly editors can use the capabilities of the machine to best advantage within the framework of their usual work, and the results have already been adopted by several other scholarly editions. For a full discussion of the philosophy and methods of the Laurens Project, see Chesnutt's two-part article: "Comprehensive Text Processing and the Papers of Henry Laurens," *Newsletter of the Association for Documentary Editing*, 2, No. 2 (May 1980), 12–14; 2, No. 3 (September 1980), 3–5.

Archives of literary texts in computer-readable form have continued to expand in recent years. The Oxford Archive (see Chapter 8) remains the largest repository of English-language texts with greatly augmented holdings; it also has some texts in most other ancient and modern languages, including Arabic, French, German, Greek, Hebrew, Italian, Latin, Sanskrit, and such exotic languages as Malay and Serbo-Croatian. The recently published catalog—*Oxford Text Archive* (Oxford: Oxford University Computing Service, 1983)—gives a complete listing of Oxford texts and addresses of thirteen other large archives. In a survey of computer activities in German research, David Chisholm (*CHum*, 11 [1978], 279–87) describes the major holdings of German materials. The Institut für Deutsche Sprache at Mannheim (Postfach 5409, D-6800 Mannheim, West Germany) acts as a clearinghouse of information about German texts. Many Celtic texts in Welsh, Breton, and Cornish are now becoming available; for a complete list with locations, see A. C. V. Hawke, *ALLC Bulletin*, 10 (1982), 60–63.

Besides this survey of trends in computing research in the humanities, the annotated bibliographic entries for further reading at the end of each chapter have been updated for this edition with new references. In addition, I have corrected errors noticed in the original printing. Otherwise, the text survives as it first appeared.

I owe a number of people thanks for assistance. Among colleagues at the University of South Carolina who have contributed to making this revision possible, I owe a debt of gratitude to Phil H. Sawyer, Jr., of the Instructional Services Center; Jerry Allen of Computer Services; Trevor Howard-Hill, Mark Harris and Bruce Castner of the English Department; David Chesnutt of History; and James Hardin of Foreign Languages. My secretary, Carolyn Cobia, has deciphered difficult handwriting and typed all these new sections with speed and efficiency. Instrumental in encouragement that a second edition was warranted were Earle Jackson and Cindy Miller of the University of South Carolina Press, and Lyn Hensel of the University Legal Department handled the assignment of copyright agreement of the original edition. Karen Orchard of the University of Georgia Press has been from the first a staunch supporter and trusted advisor in this transfer of publishers.

Many colleagues on both sides of the Atlantic are responsible for various aspects of this work. For information about their research, I acknowledge Peter and Miriam Shillingsburg, Philip H. Smith, Jr., and Rudy Spraycar. For encouragement following the first edition, thanks to Todd Bender, Ned Davison, Louis Milic, David Nordloh, Joseph Raben, Don Ross, and Ben Schneider. Marshall Hayes, editor of *Book Forum*, thought enough of the first edition to excerpt a portion of it in his journal [5, No. 1 (1979), 122–26]. For opportunities to discuss this research in public forums, I thank Joan Smith and Ellen Spolsky. For current information about A. Q. Morton's continuing research into stylistic clues of authorship, I thank Thomas Merriam. For hospitality and stimulating conversation in England and Europe in 1982 about topics of mutual interest, special thanks are due to Susan Hockey in Oxford; Peter Freeman, Michael Greenhalgh, and Andrew Parkin in Leicester; Christian Delcourt in Liège; Hans Walter Gabler in Munich; Wilhelm Ott in Tübingen; and Horst Drescher in Germersheim.

Finally, to my family and friends in Columbia who have supported me all along the way, I offer my fondest regards.

Robert L. Oakman
Columbia, South Carolina, 1983

ABBREVIATIONS OF FREQUENTLY CITED SOURCES

BOOKS:

Aitken   Aitken, A. J., R. W. Bailey, and N. Hamilton-Smith, eds. *The Computer and Literary Studies*. Edinburgh: Edinburgh University Press, 1973.

Jones and Churchhouse   Jones, Alan, and R. F. Churchhouse, eds. *The Computer in Literary and Linguistic Studies*. Cardiff: University of Wales Press, 1976.

Mitchell   Mitchell, J. L., ed. *Computers in the Humanities*. Edinburgh: Edinburgh University Press, 1974.

Wisbey   Wisbey, Roy A., ed. *The Computer in Literary and Linguistic Research*. Cambridge: Cambridge University Press, 1971.

JOURNALS:

ALLC Bulletin   Association for Literary and Linguistic Computing Bulletin

CHum   *Computers and the Humanities*

CSHVB   *Computer Studies in the Humanities and Verbal Behavior*

ICRH Newsletter   *Newsletter* of the Institute for Computer Research in the Humanities, New York University (ceased with Vol. 4 in 1969)

R.E.L.O. Revue   *Revue* de l'Organisation internationale pour l'Etude des Langues anciennes par Ordinateur

SIGLASH Newsletter   *Newsletter* of the Special Interest Group on Language Analysis and Studies in the Humanities, Association for Computing Machinery

PART I

Fundamentals of Literary Computing

CHAPTER 1

Computers for
Information Processing

■

WHEN MOST PEOPLE VISUALIZE A COMPUTER, they think of a gigantic "mechanical" brain, quickly and silently calculating their electric bills or scrutinizing their income tax returns for inadmissible deductions. Normally they view the machine as a calculating device, primarily designed for scientific or business applications. They assume that its secret workings can be appreciated only by highly trained mathematical wizards or engineering graduates. Because they lack specialized knowledge, they cannot expect to understand the mysteries of the monster machine. Leave that to its attendants, people familiar with the binomial theorem, circuit design, and the special jargon of computer science: throughput, software, and real-time solutions (as opposed to "unreal" time?).

Often accompanying this attitude is a general feeling of dismay and suspicion about the intrusion of computers into modern life. Technology and its henchmen are mucking up the world; they should stay out of hallowed fields like the humanities. Anyone who has been billed erroneously for a purchase that was returned for credit the day after it was bought knows the frustration of trying to communicate with a computerized billing system. The first month he dutifully returns the punch-card bill—not to be folded, spindled, or mutilated—with a note that the purchase was returned, only to be dunned the next month for the same amount plus a service charge for interest on the unpaid account. His patience is rapidly exhausted; he will not pay what he does not owe. But he cannot make the machine understand the error of its ways. To get satisfaction, he often has to phone the company long distance at his own expense, then mail a duplicate copy of the credit voucher to verify his innocence. Time and money are expended in needless bother because "the computer made a mistake." Of course, situations like this one alienate the ordinary, nontechnical public from the ubiquitous machine. Yet it is the people working with the computer that are at fault, not the machine itself. If the hand is crippled, the brain cannot feed itself. The mechanical drudge is blamed because the clerk opening the original bill forgot to notice the note of explanation.

Besides their widespread blame for human errors, two other misconceptions about computers are present in the preceding remarks. There is nothing mysterious or revolutionary in their workings that the average person cannot understand. Computers are large, fast, and accurate machines, able to carry out hundreds of thousands of simple operations in a single second. Perhaps their phenomenal speed and reliability make it difficult for people to conceive of their nature. A man might easily make a clerical error in balancing a checkbook after six months of accumulation. But a computer can do the job effortlessly and flawlessly in less than a minute. Computers, then, do ordinary things in extraordinary ways, relative to man's abilities.

Indeed, computers are tools to increase man's capacities to do things he has always waited or needed to do. Why should they not aid the literary scholar if they can? A great many computer applications are not quantitative in nature. The widespread notion that these machines are large numerical calculators, used only by businessmen, mathematicians, and engineers, is embodied unfortunately in the connotations of the English word *computer*, which suggests numerical computation as endemic to the machine. The literary scholar needs to know that the computer is much more than a glorified calculating machine. It is a device for manipulating all types of symbolic information, including literary texts. The French term for computer—*ordinateur*—more accurately conveys this broader connotation of processing all kinds of symbols. Coined in the 1960s from the Latin verb, *ordinō* (to order), *ordinateur* indicates the general sense of arranging information or setting it in order appropriate to a computer. The machine can rearrange the words of a sonnet into alphabetical order as readily as it can add up a column of sales figures or extract the square root of 2. It is, thus, a general-purpose device capable of handling all kinds of symbolic materials.

Everyone knows that the computer is an electrical machine. In order to process all kinds of symbolic information, computer designers require some electronic means to represent this data. The principle is, in fact, elementary, familiar from high school science. Electric current is represented by a flow of positive and negative charges in a conducting wire. These are the only two states of electricity, positive and negative, which we shall call *binary* conditions. A light switch is also a binary device with only two possible states, on and off; similarly a column on a punchcard either has holes punched in it or not. We are familiar with many other binary states—yes and no, stop and go, left and right, true and false. The twofold nature of electricity determines the computer as a binary device.

To see how information is stored in binary representation, let us symbolize the two states of positive and negative charge by the digits 0 and 1, usually called *bits*, an amalgam of *binary* and *digit*. These are the elements of the binary coding system out of which all symbols stored in computers are composed. Strings made up only of these two bits represent a variety of symbols used by man—letters, numbers, musical notes, etc. To illustrate, suppose we agree that capital A will be represented inside the computer by the combination of binary digits 1010, B by 1011, and C by 1100. Would there be enough combinations of four binary digits, either 0 or 1, to symbolize, or *encode*, all the letters of the alphabet in uppercase? In other words, what are all the possible, unique codes using only combinations of four binary symbols? Experiment yields the following list:

0000	0100	1000	1100
0001	0101	1001	1101
0010	0110	1010	1110
0011	0111	1011	1111

Since there exist no more beside these sixteen combinations, we would have codings for only sixteen of the capital letters with four bits.

If we increase the code to five digits, we shall double the possibilities to thirty-two, more than enough to encode all the uppercase letters.[1] The thirty-two codes can be written down from the preceding list by putting a 0 in front of the sixteen codes, then putting a 1 in front of them. Notice that we have no other choices, since we have only these two symbols to use for binary representation. As we have demonstrated, adding another slot to be filled by one of the binary digits doubles the number of possible symbols. In fact, there are sixty-four distinct codes possible with a six-digit binary code. Inductively we have developed an important relationship essential to understanding the coding scheme of a binary device like the computer. We can state the principle as follows:

If there are n slots to be filled with binary digits, symbolized by 0 and 1, there are 2^n possible, different, and unique symbols to fill them.

[1] For students of literature, let it be noted that the age of computers has no monopoly on the idea of a five-digit coding scheme using two symbols to represent the letters of the English alphabet. Sir Francis Bacon proposed such a system, called a "Bilateral Alphabet," for writing coded messages in his *Advancement of Learning* (Book VI, Chapter 1), published in 1605. (I am indebted to Michael Farringdon for this interesting reference.)

Since $2^6 = 2 \times 2 \times 2 \times 2 \times 2 \times 2$, we calculate that sixty-four symbols can be created out of six binary digits.

Early computing devices were designed on the principle of the six-digit binary code. The following illustrates thirty-six of the assigned symbols out of sixty-four possibilities:

26 uppercase letters: ABCDE . . . Z
10 decimal digits: 0123456789

The other twenty-eight symbolic codes were assigned to several other categories of symbols: punctuation marks (. , ; " : ( )), mathematical operators (+ − = /), and other special-purpose signs ($ % * # @ etc.). Because most early computing activities were scientific or business oriented, these original codes displayed a bias toward special symbols such as the equal sign or the dollar mark. One set of roman letters, all uppercase, seemed sufficient. As literary data processing applications were developed, a need arose for the uppercase and lowercase roman letters, as well as nonroman alphabets like Greek and Cyrillic. Gradually an eight-bit binary coding scheme has been replacing the six-digit standard. By the formula, eight digits allow 256 different codes, more than enough for all the Western alphabets and all of the possible symbols needed in business, the sciences, and the arts.

There is nothing unfamiliar about using a coding scheme for representing letters and punctuation marks. In his essay called "Nature" (1836), Ralph Waldo Emerson said that the words of men are "signs of natural facts": language itself is symbolic of events in the real world. Its component letters represent natural sounds or phonemes. A few years later, Emerson's contemporary, Samuel Morse, invented the telegraph code, another symbolization of the codes of language. Just as a string of dots and dashes stands for the letters and numbers in Morse code, a string of electrical charges, represented by the bits 0 and 1, symbolizes these elements of human communication inside the computer. Based on the four-bit code suggested above, the word CAB consists of twelve bits: 1100 1010 1011. Similarly eighteen bits would be required with a six-bit code and twenty-four using eight bits per letter.

The computer can, therefore, be defined as a general-purpose electronic digital machine for information processing. Any kind of data that can be symbolized by a code can be represented in the computer's binary digits. It can then be manipulated in a great variety of ways at the incredibly fast speed of electricity flowing in a conducting wire. It makes little difference that the letter we know as A, represented by one symbol in print, is actually a combination of six or eight bits inside the machine.

These several digits can be moved around and processed several thousand times by the machine in the same amount of time it would take us to write down the one symbol on paper.

The computer is probably the most powerful and versatile tool man has ever invented for increasing his capacity to assimilate and control the world. Its devices simulate the functions of man's hand, eye, and brain. To see what functions the computer must serve, let us examine a simple literary problem and the way a scholar might solve it. Let us test Gerard Manley Hopkins' common practice of alliteration with his sonnet, "Hurrahing in Harvest." Given an authoritative text of the poem, we begin by rearranging the words of each line into several lists. All words beginning with the same letter will be on the same list. Every letter that begins a word in a line will determine a list. For instance, the first line of the poem, "Summer ends now; now, barbarous in beauty, the stocks arise," will be sorted into seven lists, for the letters S (2 words), E, N (2 words), B (2 words), I, T, and A. After each line is analyzed, only the letter lists for consonants are needed to check alliteration. Those containing two or more words signal alliteration: S, N, and B in this case. If more than half the lines show such alliteration, we may decide that we have successfully demonstrated one of Hopkins' common stylistic habits. A table of alliterations per line can be prepared to prove the point.

At least five functions built into any general computer system are involved in this simple poetic analysis. To begin with, we must have an accurate text of the poem. It is the *input* data for the problem, probably a printed copy from a book or a manuscript version. Line by line, we dissect the poem into lists of words with the same first letter. These are copied on paper, an interim storage medium or kind of *memory*. We use this aid to memory, so that we are not forced to remember the lists in our heads.

Several mental activities can be classified as *processing*. Reading the words and deciding on what list they belong is done without effort, though not without thinking. After each line has been dissected, only the lists for consonants are examined for more than one word. In fact, the vowels are probably omitted from consideration as the lists are being prepared. We keep a count of lines with two or more alliterative consonants, perhaps jotting it down on our tablet storage device. Finally we check to see if our count exceeds seven, half the number of lines in the sonnet. All of these operations, accomplished almost unconsciously, are ways of processing the data in the Hopkins poem.

Assuming our criterion for alliteration is met, we might draw up a table showing the number of alliterations in each line. This table, a kind of *output* of the experiment, serves as evidence to validate our contention about Hopkins' penchant for alliteration. Writing the results in the table qualifies as more processing.

The most important element of this illustration is the *control* function, handled by the brain, either consciously or involuntarily. Everything takes place in an ordered, logical fashion. We must have a copy of the poem before we can look for alliterations, and we need not make up our final table of proof until we have found at least eight lines of multiple alliteration. The eye and the hand are activated when necessary to read words or make notes on paper. The conscious mind supervises putting words on the proper lists and counting instances of consonantal pairs per line. In a real sense, the whole exercise is organized, orchestrated, and overseen by the brain.

We have discussed the five functions inherent in all rational human activities: input, memory, processing, output, and control. Input information, sensory or otherwise, is stored (often in the mind itself), processed, and released as output in a variety of forms. The brain monitors and controls all the operations. Since the functions are basic to all problem solving, every computer system must have components, hardware devices and programs, to fulfill these five functions. In this sense, the computer is a synthetic, working model for problem solving, with perceiving sensors, processing capabilities, and ways to display its results. It is a kind of mechanical brain, but its operations are limited and usually predictable, when compared to those of the infinitely more flexible human brain. Its ability to carry them out rapidly and accurately makes it the powerful tool that it is.

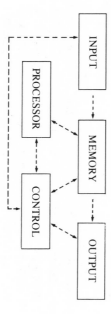

FIGURE 1. The five elements of a general computer system.

Let us examine the relationships among these five functions in terms of Figure 1 in which arrows show directions of flow of information. Notice the supervision of all the components by the control element, which could be a computer program or perhaps a series of circuits in the *central processing unit* (CPU). This basic piece of equipment in all computer systems is usually contained in one or two hardware devices that integrate the main memory of the machine, the circuitry of the processor, and the various control mechanisms. Auxiliary memory and input and output equipment such as card readers and line printers make up other components of the total system. Chapters 2 and 3 will discuss these individual parts of a general system in more detail. For now, a general understanding of the overall design is sufficient.

If the computer were applied to the poetry problem, all five functions would be needed. The text of the poem would be read into the main memory from some piece of input hardware. The processor would dissect the lines of poetry into separate words and sort them into lists by initial letter, although the lists themselves would be stored as intermediate results back in the main memory. Counting would also take place in the processor, often called an *accumulator* or a *register*, from the early days of almost exclusively arithmetic computation. Counts of alliterations per line would be filed for later reference in the memory, along with the running total of lines containing two or more instances of alliteration. Assuming that this total exceeded seven lines after all had been processed, the control unit would cause the results to be printed from the memory onto an output device such as a printer for the scholar's inspection. Throughout the whole process, a computer program oversees and manages the operations, fulfilling the control function.

As this analysis suggests, searching Hopkins' poem for alliteration based on this criterion is a literary processing job for which the computer is well suited. It can simulate the scholar's action, processing the poetic lines, by means of an ordered sequence of operations and the use of several pieces of hardware. Numerous interchanges of information occur between various parts of the computer system. Here the computer's electronic speed and accuracy are necessary to carry out these transfers rapidly with no mistakes. In fact, given the text in a form ready for machine processing, the computer can scan the poem and make a conjecture about Hopkins' poetic style much quicker than the scholar, following the literal-minded process described above. Of course, the man may skip several steps—such as noting everything down on paper—whereas the machine follows a rigorous sequence of explicit instructions. Even so, a nimble-witted scholar would have to hurry to beat the computer's time of a few seconds.

In sum, the computer has wonderful power to aid the literary scholar in his work. Pursuing its job quickly, accurately, and silently, it can produce results worthy of even a skeptic's attention. Yet it is the scholar who ultimately has to assess the computer's findings for critical importance. He is the final authority and arbiter of critical taste. It is not the computer's fault if counting alliterative lines in a Hopkins sonnet is judged an unsatisfactory way to prove his alliterative stylistic habits. An old computer slogan, familiar throughout the world of data processing, is worthy of quotation here: garbage in, garbage out. The computer is a tool and servant of man. Given an ill-conceived plan to carry out, it should not be blamed when it produces suspect or biased results. In this regard, the social scientist Ole R. Holsti sounds appropriate final words of caution for those contemplating computer applications:

Perhaps the single greatest danger in the use of computers is that a misplaced faith may lull us into accepting the validity of findings without a critical consideration of the steps preceding and following machine processing. Computers cannot save a sloppy research design nor will they transform a trivial research problem into an important one. There is no guarantee that they will not be used to inundate us with studies of great precision and little importance.[2]

In later chapters, we shall see both how well and how poorly some scholars have used the computer in their work. Understanding the ways a computer can digest and process literary materials represents a first step in assuring that future projects will be well thought out from the start.

[2] Ole R. Holsti, *Content Analysis for the Social Sciences and Humanities* (Reading, Mass.: Addison-Wesley, 1969), p. 194.

FOR FURTHER READING

Bratley, Paul, and Serge Lusignan. "The Electronic Scriptorium." *CHum*, 13 (1979), 93–103.

A "case study" of how text processing with computers has been incorporated into the humanities at the University of Montreal with realistic advice about how to go about it.

Crowley, Thomas H. *Understanding Computers.* New York: McGraw-Hill Book Company, 1967.

Introduction to computer concepts and basic hardware written for the layman in nontechnical language. Excellent discussion with appropriate examples and illustrations, although somewhat dated on computer devices.

Dorf, Richard C. *Computers and Man.* San Francisco: Boyd and Fraser Publishing Company, 1974.

A recent survey of computers, their applications, and history. Recommended by *Computing Reviews* for the general reader.

Rothman, Stanley, and Charles Mosmann. *Computers and Society.* 2nd ed. Palo Alto, Calif.: Science Research Associates, Inc., 1976.

A competent "computer appreciation" book emphasizing fundamentals and comprehensive discussion of the effect on the individual and his society of the "computer revolution."

Turnbull, J. J., ed. *Computers in Language Studies.* Manchester, England: National Computing Centre, 1973.

Beginner's study guide with bibliography to various areas of computing for languages, including stylistics, concordances, information retrieval, and programming languages.

CHAPTER 2

Getting Literary Materials In and Out of the Machine

■

IN THEIR EARLY DAYS computers were not designed to handle literary problems with large files of textual data. Input, processing, storage, and output posed great problems for the pioneers of literary data processing. Gradually programming languages were developed to make text handling more convenient; and hardware devices, especially for output, have been improved. Input has, however, continued to be a nuisance. Postponing the subject of processing for later consideration, let us focus in this chapter on the problem of *throughput*—from the input of literary data into the machine, through the storage phase in the memory, and out the other end in some form of finished output.

Before he decides on a method of input, the scholar has to think seriously about what kinds of information he wants to submit to the computer. This stage leading up to data preparation is often the most crucial part of data processing. Decisions made here often determine the effectiveness of subsequent operations. The scholar must decide on a form for encoding his materials and on an input device. The first of these tasks, choosing a way to structure the data for his project, depends on the nature of his job. Because preparing data in a form that the computer can use is often neither easy nor convenient, the scholar must think ahead, so that all the information he will ultimately want to examine is included at the start.

The most common kinds of literary data for computer processing are texts, perhaps for making a concordance or doing a stylistic analysis, and bibliographical materials suitable for information retrieval. The job of encoding literary texts requires careful editorial consideration. To begin with, the scholar should choose an authoritative text on which to base his work. If there is no accurate, reliable text, he must decide whether to go ahead and encode possibly faulty materials. If the work is to be concorded, how will the input data be marked with an identifying location? For poetry, the title and line number seem a suitable choice; each line of poetry might be coded with a locational abbreviation as it is prepared.

But line numbers are not usual for prose concordances; perhaps the page number keyed to an edition or a chapter title is all that will be used to identify each section of running prose. A statistical study of alliteration in poetry may not require all this detail about location, so long as the scholar can refer to the passages in question if necessary. His computer output will probably be tables and lists for his own analysis instead of a concordance to the author's text to be published for use by others. In each of these cases, the final use of the text must be taken into account in choosing the kind of locational information to include.

Bibliographical listings do not normally occur as either prose or lined poetry. Entries usually have a standard form, such as the author's name followed by the title and publication information, and are often noted with an identifying number. For instance Pollard and Redgrave's *Short Title Catalogue*, the standard bibliography of books printed in Britain from 1475 to 1640, assigns a bibliographical number to every title that could be included in a computerized data file to identify it uniquely. Every entry might be signaled initially by its code number and concluded with an appropriate punctuation mark like a period. Although the individual entries would contain different information, this format marking their boundaries would be common to all of them. Other information sometimes appropriate for inclusion in the data structures for literary applications include tagging words with their parts of speech for grammatical analysis or encoding text in phonetic spelling for studies of sound patterns.

Having decided on an input format, we are ready to convert our textual materials into the internal binary codes a computer can store and process. Fortunately we do not have to prepare the text directly in binary form. Think of the tedium and the mistakes that would be made in typing a sonnet into eight-digit binary codes; every letter and punctuation mark would require typing eight binary digits from a table of codes. Considering the chances for error with a sonnet, we can imagine the input problems for a writer's complete poetic corpus or a modern novel. If binary coding were necessary for input, there would be no literary data processing or any other kind. In practice, the scholar need not do binary coding of his text. After he decides on the character set, he can get his material into coded form indirectly, by transcribing it on an auxiliary machine (such as a keypunch) which in turn produces a record (such as a punchcard) that is read by another auxiliary device (such as a punchcard reader). These machines, called *peripheral devices* by computer scientists, feed the material into the computer system itself, so that it is automatically translated into binary notation.

In all literary data processing, the most serious obstacle is getting the material into the machine. The amount of material is often quite large; and input is tedious, time-consuming, and costly. At best, the method decided upon is often a compromise choice. Most currently available coding systems have limitations that force the scholar to choose not the perfect system but one that is the least limiting for his purposes. Because many devices do not have a full repertory of characters present in printed literary texts, he will probably have to adapt what is available to the needs of his situation. He may have to resort to expedients that are not only expensive of time and money but also work against ultimate accuracy.

To illustrate the situation, consider the problem of character sets and the keypunch machine. Since the days of the first Cornell concordances to the poems of Arnold and Yeats, by far the most frequently used input device for literary data processing has been the eighty-column punch-card prepared at a keypunch machine.[1] So common is its use that once at a conference a speaker joked that literary scholars seem to think it is the only possible input medium. A modern keypunch machine, like the IBM 029 (Figure 2), produces patterns of holes corresponding to the characters shown across the top of the card (Figure 3). Coding with holes in a punchcard is sometimes called *Hollerith coding*, named for the man who invented the punchcard to tabulate the results of the U.S. Census of 1890. As the card is processed by a reader, the holes are sensed electrically; and the binary codes for the characters are stored in the memory of the machine. The keyboard, which resembles that of the typewriter, contains only sixty-three characters, including the uppercase letters, the ten decimal digits, and the common punctuation marks. No lowercase letters of the roman alphabet, accent marks such as grave for French or umlaut for German, or letters in nonroman alphabets are present. Yet people have used the keypunch machine to code classical Greek, Russian, and even Hebrew Rabbinic texts.

In order to circumvent the limitations of the machine, a set of punch-ing conventions is established, so that all important textual information can be included as the data are being prepared. Many modern computers allow encoding of 256 different characters because of their internal binary code of eight bits. The scholar decides on a character set which covers everything in his literary materials and then develops a series of keypunching codes to fit it. English-language projects sometimes type a dollar sign ($) or asterisk (*) in front of all letters that are to be capital;

[1] The concordance to Arnold's poetry appeared in 1959 and to Yeats' poems in 1963. Both were edited by Stephen M. Parrish and published by Cornell University Press.

Getting Literary Materials In and Out of the Machine

FIGURE 2. A typical keypunch machine. (*Photo by Robert E. Van Keuren, USC Computer Services*)

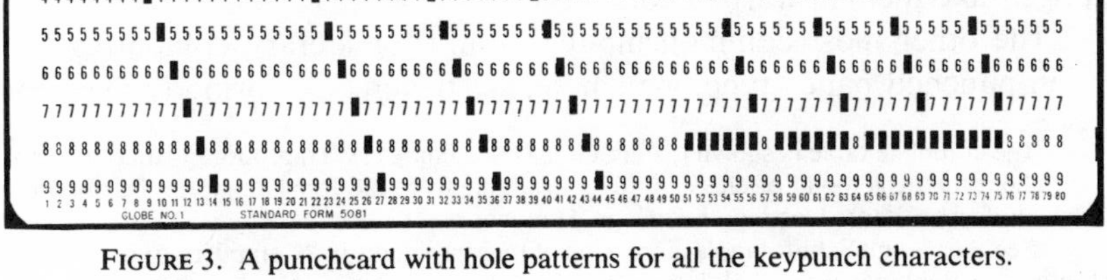

FIGURE 3. A punchcard with hole patterns for all the keypunch characters.

15

by default other letters are lowercase, although they are printed as capitals on the card. Thus, "New York City" might be punched *NEW *YORK *CITY. Similarly accent marks in modern languages are denoted by the inclusion of uncommon textual symbols (#, %, etc.) behind the affected letter. For classical Greek, the Repository of Greek and Latin Texts in Machine-Readable Form, an agency of the American Philological Association administered by Stephen V. F. Waite at Dartmouth, suggests a compact scheme using the characters on the IBM 029 keyboard to encode the Greek alphabet with all accents and diacritical marks. When possible, the nearest English equivalent is used for the Greek letters—A for α, B for β, G for γ, etc.[2]

For Hebrew, Professors David Sarna and Lawrence Schiffmann had to resort to pasting Hebrew letters over the keys of the machine and hiring students with experience in Rabbinic literature as keypunch typists.[3] Even more than classical scholars, they suffered inconvenience in using input equipment whose character set with roman letters bears no resemblance to theirs. Whenever coding conventions or substitutes are needed, the typist has to remember to include them—in essence, has to do a kind of pre-editing—as he is copying the text. As a result, using the keypunch machine for input slows the speed and inevitably decreases the accuracy of punching. Error detection requires careful proofreading or retyping the text a second time on a punchcard *verifier*. This machine, which looks like a keypunch, compares the prepared cards to new keying done by an operator and lights up when a discrepancy appears. Discovering by inspection that the original card is in error, the typist repunches the card. However we do it, error correction of punchcards is a slow and demanding job.

The corrected text encoded on a deck of cards is read by a card reader and usually stored permanently as a long data file on a permanent storage medium like magnetic tape or disk. The cards are then saved as an extra copy of the text in case something happens to the permanent file. After several months these paper cards often become warped because of moisture absorption. If they are needed to reconstruct the permanent file, some may require retyping because the card reader will no longer take them in warped condition.

The other most common input medium for literary computing has been punched paper type, similar to the ticker tape formerly used for

<hr/>

[2] The complete table is shown in *CALCULI* (September 1971) p. 136. Further information about the large body of classical texts available from the Repository can be obtained from Professor Waite, Dartmouth College, Hanover NH 03755.

[3] See Sarna and Schiffmann's discussion of their problems in "Computer-Aided Critical Editions of Rabbinic Texts," *Hebrew Computational Linguistics*, No. 2 (1970), pp. 50–51.

reporting stock market quotations. Paper tape has been particularly popular in Britain; the texts for a variety of computer concordances produced at the Literary and Linguistic Computing Centre at Cambridge, including Middle High German works, the poetry of Edmund Spenser, and the plays of the Dutch dramatist J. V. Vondel, were prepared on paper tape. In several ways, paper tape is more amenable to literary work than cards. A tape punch machine typically incorporates a typewriter or teletype keyboard that can be operated with ease by anyone who can use an electric typewriter. Along with a typescript that can be checked for errors, it produces a running tape with seven channels for coding; consequently, there are 128 ($= 2^7$) codes possible in seven tracks. A shift code for capitalization readily allows both uppercase and lowercase on the tape. In addition, there are codes for the decimal numbers, a full set of punctuation marks, and a wide range of special symbols that can be defined by convention to meet the needs of a particular project. A bibliographer may need the degrees symbol (°) to denote the formats of books (8° for octavo, 4° for quarto, etc.), especially important for those printed before 1800. If his keyboard lacks this character, he can substitute another one that is not found in his text.

Compared to punchcards, paper tape requires less storage space and is not as subject to warping with age. Its major disadvantage is related to its continuous, serial nature. Due to their eighty-column format, punchcards encode serial information in record lengths of eighty characters each. Because of its sequential nature, paper tape is especially suited to the quantity of running text expected with literary processing. Yet it is not as easy to alter or remove erroneous information that has gone onto the tape as it is to replace a bad punchcard. If the thin paper tape gets torn, a whole series of records can be ruined.

To avoid redoing large sections of tape, the typist can counteract errors by inserting error codes in the tape whenever he notices a mistake made in punching. Designers of a project to compile a bibliography of Scottish poetry found two symbols on the keyboard, cents (¢) and percent (%), not significant for their bibliographical purposes. They have used these to denote, respectively, consecutive erroneous characters or an entire faulty record.[4] Let us assume the typist misspells the word *Smith* as *Smmith*. Noting it immediately, he types four cent signs after the word, followed by the correction (the paper tape would now contain the following characters: Smmith¢¢¢¢ith). The four cent signs mean

---

[4] G. R. Roy, R. L. Oakman, and A. C. Gillon, "A Computerized Bibliography of Scottish Poetry," in *Computers in the Humanities*, ed. J. L. Mitchell (Edinburgh: Edinburgh University Press, 1974), p. 170. Articles in this book will hereafter be denoted by Mitchell and their page numbers.

that the four characters immediately preceding them are in error. On the other hand, if he does not discover the mistake until he has typed a full line of text following it, the typist inserts a percent sign in the entry to signal that the whole record is in error and should be deleted. He then retypes the complete entry. In processing the bibliographical data file, the computer is programmed to correct or delete records with mistakes. Based on the conventions assigned to the cent and percent signs, it wipes out either several erroneous characters and the following cent signs or an entire bibliographical entry containing a percent mark. This system incorporates error-correction techniques that are activated by the operator in data preparation to catch both minor and gross mistakes in punching. Letting the computer perform updating and correcting of the data file before its permanent storage alleviates some of the error problem in a serial medium of input like paper tape.

Another key-to-tape input device prepares half-inch magnetic tape directly as the characters are entered on the keyboard. Sometimes called a keytape machine, it has an electric typewriter keyboard with a complete set of characters like a paper tape punch. It bypasses the interim phase of data preparation of the two previous methods: transfer of the data encoded on paper to permanent magnetic tape. As with paper tape, characters are stored serially on the rolls of tape.

Magnetic tape is normally seven or nine tracks wide. Allowing one channel for internal error detection, we come back to our usual six and eight-bit coding schemes, allowing 64 and 256 possible characters, respectively. Essentially the same as tape used by recorders, magnetic tape stores information in codes of positive and negative magnetized spots, another means of representing data in binary form. The characters are coded by standard patterns of these spots magnetized across the channels of tape (Figure 4 illustrates coding of seven-track tape).

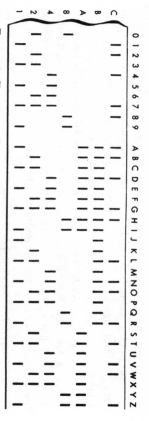

FIGURE 4. Character coding on seven-track magnetic tape. Note the track designations: 1, 2, 4, 8, A, B, and C. (*Courtesy of IBM Corporation*)

FIGURE 5. An operator loading magnetic tape on one of several tape drives. (*Photo by Robert E. Van Keuren, USC Computer Services*)

19

Magnetic tape works well for permanent storage of data because it can hold enormous amounts of information (up to 1600 characters per inch or 46 million characters per 2400-foot roll) and is rarely susceptible to wearing out or becoming unusable. It is advisable to copy valuable magnetic tapes every few months, since they sometimes tend to "fade" and are hard to read. Although more expensive than punchcards or paper tape, magnetic tape has decided advantages over them in speed of readability and storage capacity. Whereas a card reader can process only a few cards in a second, a magnetic tape drive (Figure 5) can sense several hundred thousand characters per second as the tape passes across its reading head. Because internal speeds of computers are measured in billionths of a second, this input medium with faster access is often adopted intermediolly between mechanically read cards and the main computer storage. With key-to-tape equipment, of course, no cards are produced.

All three input methods that have been discussed share two disturbing similarities. They require a typist to prepare the materials at a keyboard, a process bound to introduce error into the computer-readable text not present in the original. Error detection and correction is a frustrating and difficult task. In addition, coding conventions are often necessary in order to encode all the characters present in the source text. Searching for adequate input facilities for a project in machine collation, George Petty and William Gibson tried all three methods and "found them all depressing."[5] They preferred the key-to-tape method only because it permitted skipping the conversion stage from paper to magnetic tape. What is needed is a way to convert the material from its original printed form directly into a machine-readable form. A machine to do *optical character recognition* (OCR) would liberate literary computing by eliminating the bottleneck of input.

Optical scanning is a pioneering area of computer technology. In recent years a few machines have appeared that can theoretically read many character sets or type fonts. With especially designed computer programs and complex optical equipment, engineers "teach" these devices to recognize a particular type font that they will encounter in a text. Such a device is the Scan-Data 300 (Figure 6), which works on the so-called "flying spot" principle. This means that only distinguishing features of each character are scanned. A capital A is not confused with a capital H, although both are made up of two vertical lines and a medial

[5] George R. Petty, Jr., and William M. Gibson, *Project OCCULT: The Ordered Computer Collation of Unprepared Literary Text* (New York: New York University Press, and London: University of London Press, 1970), p. 34.

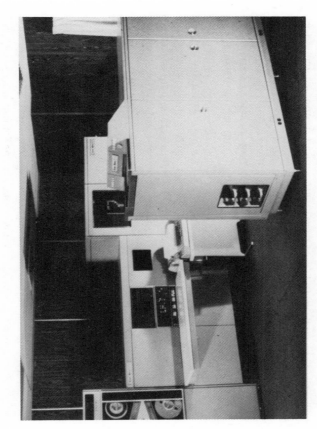

FIGURE 6. An optical character recognition system, the Scan-Data 300. Note the number 7 displayed on the screen as it is being deciphered by the machine. (*Courtesy of Scan-Data Corporation*)

horizontal one. The machine picks out the A because its vertical lines come to a point, whereas they are parallel in the H. With close orthographical analysis of the shapes for each character, machines like this have even been able to decipher Japanese characters. The Scan-Data 300 also allows the user to set a statistical limit to its automatic recognition powers. A character may be somewhat skewed on the printed page and not match exactly any that the machine knows. The user determines how close statistically a character must be to standard before the machine is automatically allowed to read it. When the match is not good enough, the character is displayed on a video screen for visual identification. The operator types in the troublesome character at a keyboard, and the machine continues reading automatically. These machines with learning capacities for new fonts offer the best future hope for input of literary data; but with prices in excess of $400,000, no university has yet been able to afford one. [6]

Several literary data processing projects have adapted the next best alternative form of optical scanning. Hiring a service bureau to do scanning of standard typewriter copy—for instance, that produced by an IBM Selectric Typewriter using any of its character balls—is much less expensive than direct scanning of the text in its original type font. Much OCR equipment is already equipped to read several standard typewriter fonts. If the text is retyped on an electric typewriter, it can then be read with fewer problems. At least two very large data processing projects have chosen this method of input: the *London Stage* Information Bank compiled by Professor Ben R. Schneider, Jr., and the *Thesaurus Linguae Graecae* to put into machine-readable form all Greek literary texts from Homer to A.D. 200, currently being supervised by Professor Theodore F. Brunner. In Schneider's case, the *London Stage 1660–1800* (11 vols., Carbondale: Southern Illinois University Press, 1960–68) lists plays, casts, and related entertainments at Drury Lane and Covent Garden in London from the Restoration to 1800—in all, 21 million characters of information. The *Thesaurus* has a data file many times larger, estimated at 90 million words (not characters!) of Greek literary text. Both projects had grant support (the *Thesaurus* had an initial grant of a million dollars), and both decided on electric typing for optical scanning of their enormous quantities of material. [7]

[6] For more details about characteristics and costs of OCR equipment, consult Richard S. Morgan, "Optical Readers: 1970," *CHum*, 5 (1970), 75–78; P. L. Andersson, "OCR Enters the Practical Stage," *Datamation*, 17 (December 1, 1971), 22–27; and Fonnie H. Reagan, Jr., "Should OCR Be Your Input Medium?" and "A Survey of the OCR Scene," *Computer Decisions*, 3 (June 1971), 19–23.

[7] Information about the current status of the enormous *Thesaurus* project is available from Professor Theodore F. Brunner, T.L.G. Project, University of California, Irvine CA 92664.

The case of the *London Stage* is worth examination in some detail. When he began considering computerizing this dramatic reference book for information retrieval, Ben Schneider was a computer novice. In his witty little book, *Travels in Computerland* (Reading, Mass.: Addison-Wesley, 1974), Schneider describes in delightful, candid detail his growing awareness of the problems of literary input. Over several months he considered at least ten input methods, from keypunching to totally automatic scanning.[8] Because of the quantity of material and the characters it contained, he finally decided on optical scanning of typed sheets of the eleven volumes. He contracted with an inexpensive Chinese company in Hong Kong to do the typing and a service bureau with Scan-Data equipment in London to do the scanning. He chose a European OCRB typewriter ball because its character set included symbols he especially needed, like square brackets. Soon unexpected events began to happen. No one expected the scanner to confuse capital O and zero, a situation that required redesign of these characters on the typing element. Although the 21 million characters were converted more cheaply into machine-readable form by this combination than by other methods (about $11,000—Schneider is never explicit), Schneider's experiences point up the unexpected hitches and frustrations often encountered in large literary data processing applications.

It seems unlikely that many scholars will have the funds, without outside support, to afford optical scanning. Rates for scanning appear to vary widely. In 1971, Schneider was quoted figures of between $0.15 and $0.21 per page (about 2000 characters) and 5 pence (about $0.13) per thousand characters; in the spring of 1975 a friend in England reported to me that she was paying about 13 pence (about $0.35) per thousand characters to a London service bureau with Scan-Data equipment. In both cases the text was being scanned from typed copies of the originals, the scanning figures not including the cost of typing. Of course, the physical process of copying a text on a typewriter introduces unwanted error—a problem inherent in any process involving keystroking.

In a recent assessment of input technology, Professor T. H. Howard-Hill, well known for his computer concordances to Shakespeare, has argued optimistically from Schneider's example for the feasibility of optical scanning with the present generation of OCR equipment.[9] In addition to the Scan-Data 300, he singles out two other machines, Information International's Grafix page reader and the CompuScan 370, that have

---

[8] Schneider compactly summarizes the advantages and disadvantages of all his input options in the following article: "The Production of Machine-Readable Text: Some of the Variables," *CHum*, 6 (1971), 39–47.

[9] T. H. Howard-Hill, "Computer and Mechanical Aids to Editing," *Proof*, 5 (1977), 221–24.

flying spot scanning and multifont capabilities. These last two machines require documents to be submitted on microfilm, already a common format, as Howard-Hill notes, of scholarly access to widely dispersed and valuable manuscripts and texts. Although there will still be some error in scanning—for example with handwritten texts, skewed or broken type, or shadows on the film—Howard-Hill feels that OCR is now practical for literary usage. On the other hand, Robert J. Dilligan's recent experience in having the Twickenham Edition of Pope's poetry scanned from microfilm yields a more pessimistic assessment. Claims of scanner manufacturers to the contrary, the Pope concordance project encountered enough input hangups to suggest that microfilm scanning is still in the developmental stages.[10] There is little question that total optical character recognition, without interim typing, would greatly enhance the growth of literary computing. Theoretically, current machines should be adaptable to any job; practically they still have problems. How soon they will be widely available, sufficiently accurate, and economically feasible to fit into the typical budgetary constraints of academic humanists remains an open question.

Another keyboard method of input apparently more common among North American humanists than their colleagues in Britain offers a choice of characters and the ability to do error correction directly. An operator sits at a keyboard, often called a terminal, connected directly to the computer's internal memory and processor; no interim storage medium like magnetic tape need exist between the typist and the machine. A complicated operating procedure, called *time sharing*, allows a number of terminals to be hooked up on an active, or *on-line*, basis simultaneously. It makes no practical economic sense for a machine whose speed is measured in billionths of a second to be waiting for one person to type in a line of text. If it can be handling jobs from many other terminals, it will not be wasting its expensive time. Because it works so fast, each user seems to have direct access to the machine with little waiting, although actually he is sharing computer time and space with many others (hence, the term *time sharing*). Anyone who has made a reservation at an airline ticket counter has seen time sharing in action; all the airline terminals are connected to a central computer housing a complete list of flights and available seats. In a matter of seconds, the clerk can confirm or deny a request for a reservation.

[10] See the "Technical Preface" to *A Concordance to the Poems of Alexander Pope*, ed. Emmett G. Bedford and Robert J. Dilligan (Detroit: Gale Research Company, 1974), I, xix–xx.

FIGURE 7. Encoding information at a computer terminal. The CRT screen displays it for the user's inspection. (*Photo by Robert E. Van Keuren, USC Computer Services*)

Computer terminals for time sharing have input keyboards—often teletypes or electric typewriters—with an option of uppercase and lowercase for text processing. Facilities for the computer to "talk back" to the operator fall into two general types: the typewriter or a television screen for visual display of characters, called variously a *cathode ray tube* (CRT) terminal (Figure 7), or a *visual display unit* (VDU). Some CRT units are capable of sophisticated graphical applications such as drawing pictures or graphs on the screen in multiple colors as well as displaying ordinary character sets.

The interactive nature of time sharing makes it especially convenient for text processing. Suppose a scholar has a terminal connected to a time-sharing system with text editing facilities. As he discovers mistakes, he can edit them out before submitting his data file to the computer for permanent storage. Yet surprisingly very few literary scholars have taken advantage of terminals for input. Perhaps they were unaware of these possibilities, or their computer centers lacked uppercase/lowercase terminals or text editing programs. A Canadian scholar, Penny Gilbert, did use this method successfully to encode medieval Latin manuscripts for collation by computer.[11] Rejecting punchcards because of error corrections, she prepared her texts with punctuation, capitalization, and locational information at a terminal, then corrected her file with an interactive editing program on the IBM 370 system at the University of Manitoba. The corrected text was then stored permanently on magnetic tape prior to computerized collation. Based on Gilbert's success and that of many time-sharing applications in other fields, entering materials and editing them at a CRT terminal promises to become one of the best available means of input for literary scholars.

More recently the compilers of the *Dictionary of the Old Spanish Language* at the University of Wisconsin have taken advantage of up-dated technology in scanning and editing *off-line*, that is, not connected to a large computer system, to encode 25 million characters from manuscript documents in Old Spanish before 1500. They typed the text with an OCR typing element which prints a bar code under each character on the page of typed material; a page reader manufactured by Datatype Corporation senses the bar codes, which are similar to the vertical lines of the price code on supermarket products, and produces a magnetic tape version of the texts. Sitting at a terminal having its own built-in editing program facilities (in computer jargon, an "intelligent" terminal) the scholars call up segments of text and edit them for errors, then store them on magnetic tape cassettes for eventual feeding into the main university computer memory for further processing. In other words, all the typing and correction phases of the project are handled with stand-alone, relatively inexpensive equipment needing no interaction with a large computer system. The scholars made no compromises on character sets in Old Spanish for the bar code scanning and have not tied up a costly time-sharing system on the main computer with many hours of on-line editing.[12]

---

[11] Penny Gilbert, "Automatic Collation: A Technique for Medieval Texts," *CHum*, 7 (1973), 144.

[12] Further information about the Old Spanish Dictionary Project is available from Professor John J. Nitti, Seminary of Medieval Spanish Studies, University of Wisconsin, Madison WI 53706.

To sum up, the whole problem of input of large literary files continues to be complex and confused. As a practical solution, a scholar should first design a data structure to include all of his essential information, including the character set he will need. Then he should weigh his input choices in terms of the following factors: types of equipment available to him; their suitability for his data structure, including coding conventions; methods of error correction; and comparative costs. Many literary scholars have not known how to examine their alternatives and end up with a hastily chosen and frustrating solution. Although some compromises are probably inevitable, thoughtful consideration of the pros and cons (note the binary choices) of different input methods can help to minimize difficulties at the outset.

Internal storage of the materials in the memory of the computer is not as complicated as the input problem. The scholar has fewer hardware options to consider, and these do not require sacrifice of accuracy. Whatever has been encoded for input, the machine can read, store, and remember with speed and efficiency. Memory devices are of two types, depending on whether the computer accesses their information in a serial or random fashion. All of the input methods we have described have serial access: information is read in the linear order in which it is encoded. Boxes of cards and magnetic tapes are read from front to back; characters encoded at a CRT terminal go in as they are typed.

No matter what input method is used initially, magnetic tapes often provide permanent storage of machine-readable data files. They possess the four qualities desired in a computer memory device: reliable storage over long periods of time, ability to handle large amounts of data in small space, fast speed of access, and inexpensive cost. By these criteria, only in speed do magnetic tapes fall short in comparison to other kinds of internal memory. They must be accessed serially by physically moving the tape across a reading head, and this mechanical process is much slower than the computer's internal, electrical speeds. Nevertheless, they make very good sense for permanent storage. When scholars exchange literary texts in machine-readable form, they usually send duplicate copies of magnetic tapes—size, cost, compatibility, and reliability being key factors in this choice.

The relatively slow access speed with magnetic tapes rules them out as the usual central memory device. We need a storage medium accessible at the speed in which electrical current flows in wires. Magnetic *core memory* sometimes fits the bill or, among newer technologies, miniaturized electrical circuit "chips" called *microcircuits*. As spots of tape magnetized positively and negatively represent binary codes for 0 and 1, tiny circular ferrite rings (or *cores*), the basic elements of core memory, can

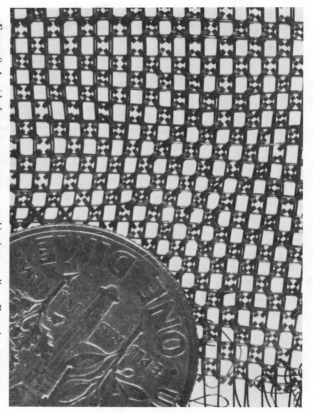

Figure 8. A grid of core memory, compared in size to a dime. Four tiny cores are arranged in an X-shaped pattern with sensor wires passing through them. (*Photo by James M. Huff; USC Instructional Services*)

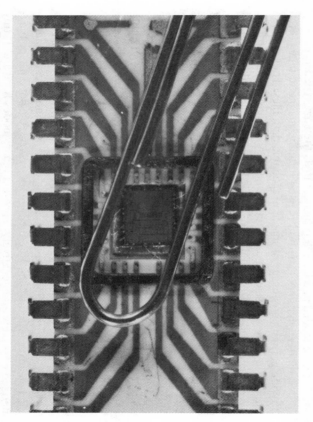

Figure 9. An even smaller "chip" memory (the dark square in the center), dwarfed by a paper clip and the electrical connections attached to it. The chip holds several thousand times more information than a core memory of its size. (*Photo by James M. Huff; USC Instructional Services*)

be magnetized in either a clockwise or counterclockwise direction. Similarly the tiny individual elements of the microcircuit exist in two steady electrical states, representing the two binary codes. In either case we have an electromagnetic phenomenon for symbolizing information in binary form. Magnetic core memories are made up of many wire grids of these tiny cores called core planes. Each core is less than one-eighth inch in diameter and stores one bit of binary data (Figure 8). Each "chip," smaller than the fingernail on a person's little finger, contains literally thousands of spots of binary data (Figure 9). Indeed, microcircuit memories offer very large amounts of storage in very little space.

Random access is one of the most useful characteristics of either kind of central memory, a part of the *central processing unit* (CPU) of all large computers. That is, binary information can be found and retrieved from any portion of the memory device as quickly as from any other. The rate of transfer of information along the electrical wires that make up the grids of core is phenomenal, measured in speeds of millionths of a second. Miniaturization with microcircuits is even faster; in fact, it is pushing the limits on speed of electrical access within such minute distances. Besides speed and small size, central memory devices also are very reliable; even if the power supply goes off, core elements continue to hold their binary charges until remagnetized. For these three reasons, either cores or microcircuits serve as the main memory of most computers.

Closely linked with central storage are two other fast auxiliary magnetic storage devices, disk and drum. Disk packs look like stacks of phonograph records with binary information stored on magnetic spots on each circular plate. Drums store information in a similar way on magnetic locations of a rotating cylindrical tube. In both cases, information is relayed on and off the unit as it passes under a sensory head (a typical disk pack is shown in Figure 10). Speeds of both types of hardware vary among models but are fast enough to consider them random-access devices. Their storage capacities are enormous for their size, running well into millions of bits of information. In fact, in terms of the unit cost per bit, disk and drum storage are less expensive than main memory. But they also have slower access rates to information. Computer scientists putting together a computer memory system usually accept some trade-off of lower speed with lower cost in selecting various pieces of equipment.

A large university computer center will commonly have several disk or drum units connected directly to the central memory for intermediate storage and monitoring input and output. A typical job flow will feed information from serial-access peripheral devices like card readers or terminals into a disk unit. From there it will be transferred into faster-

FIGURE 10. An operator unloading a portable disk pack from a disk drive. The pack itself contains stacked circular disks, which contain the stored information. (*Photo by Robert E. Van Keuren, USC Computer Services*)

access core or "chips" within the CPU when space becomes available. Processing will take place while the data are stored in central memory; then results will be routed back through the disk to the proper output device. Using the disk as an intermediary, or *interface* in computer jargon, saves time and money, since the CPU with its fast memory and processor does not sit idle while information passes in and out from slow peripheral equipment.

Often the large quantities of text common to literary data processing cannot be stored all at one time in the main memory for processing. In the past large projects required machines with huge memories, or texts had to be broken up into sections to be stored and processed on a piece-

30

meal basis. A technique in computer memory allocation, called *virtual memory*, helps to alleviate some of this problem. The user has a "logical" memory available to him much longer than central storage itself. Although physically the logical memory is maintained on auxiliary hardware such as a disk, it can be treated as if it were main memory. In terms of the way a user conceives of this auxiliary storage, it is virtually a central memory. A complex operating program in the machine monitors where information is stored at all times, swapping it in and out of actual central memory as needed for processing. Virtual memory, which greatly enlarges memory size at less cost than buying more central storage, is already making projects with large data files easier to implement than formerly.

Compared to making decisions about data structures and input, the literary scholar need only to be aware of the kinds and characteristics of internal memory devices. Professional staff at a computer center usually are responsible for buying and maintaining this equipment; they should be consulted about the best way to store texts associated with a particular application. All relevant information about character sets or input coding conventions can be retained within memory. The scholar needs little technical knowledge about how this information is being kept or moved around internally; a general understanding about this part of a computer system is sufficient for him to use it to his advantage.

When the machine has completed its tasks, materials stored in memory are ready to be sent to output, the final step in the computer process. Unlike input, methods of output have been greatly improved over the past few years. Hardware now available offers considerable flexibility about medium of presentation, even choice of type. The scholar is no longer limited to the line printer (Figure 11) for getting his information back to analyze or publish it. Just as the keypunch machine lacked lowercase letters and several punctuation marks, so did the early printers that produced the first concordances. The volume for Matthew Arnold's poems was published in 1959 by offset printing of the sheets as they came from the line printer. The final product illustrates the output inadequacies of the past. Lines of poetry are given all in uppercase and with only one punctuation mark, the hyphen. Over the first few years much of the impetus for the development of output equipment with uppercase and lowercase roman letters and the full complement of punctuation marks was due to Stephen Parrish's pioneering series of Cornell concordances. The third one, published in 1964 to the poetry of Emily Dickinson (edited by S. P. Rosenbaum) included all punctuation marks but still had only uppercase letters in the offset printout.

FIGURE 11. A fast line printer that can print out thousands of uppercase and lowercase characters per minute. (*Photo by Robert E. Van Keuren, USC Computer Services*)

By 1969 a new IBM print chain, with 120 standard characters and potential for expansion to 240, was tested by J. B. Bessinger, Jr., and Philip H. Smith, Jr., for production of a Cornell *Beowulf* concordance, although they finally decided on another output device. A more limited device with uppercase and lowercase capabilities was announced for the ICL 1900 series of British machines in 1974.[13]

Only recently have scholars begun publishing by offset printed results of these expanded print chains, with all uppercase and lowercase characters and punctuation marks. Andrew T. Crosland's two 1975 concordances devoted to American literary works, the poems of Stephen Crane and *The Great Gatsby* by F. Scott Fitzgerald (both from Detroit: Gale Research Company), are representative of the handiwork that the IBM print chain can produce. Other scholars have modified this print chain to fit their special character requirements: the Library of Congress decided on 162 characters for printing catalog cards in all roman alphabets and Dutch scholars used 207 for their lexicographic work, including Scandinavian and Gothic characters and German and Dutch ligatures.[14] Well-adjusted, with a clean character set, this modern machine, printing on white unlined paper, yields output up to literary publishing standards.

This printer runs slower than ordinary line printers with uppercase letters and standard punctuation. For the scholar's perusal and analysis, textual output not to be published or in prepublication form might as well be printed on regular line printers common to all general computer systems. In a time-sharing environment, materials can be displayed at a terminal (CRT screen or teletype printer) for the scholar's use. In the meantime, a permanent file of the text containing all of the essential typographical features in coded form may be kept on magnetic tape for later publication, if desired.

Several literary computing projects have chosen the electric typewriter for final output. It allows great flexibility of the character set, with the possibility of designing a special typeball for any particular application. For this reason Bessinger and Smith decided on the typewriter for

[13] See *ALLC Bulletin*, 2, No. 1 (1974), 62.

[14] See Phyllis A. Richmond, "An Extended Character Set for Humanities Computer Output," *CHum*, 4 (1970), 247–50, for discussion of the Library of Congress character set, illustrated in *CHum*, 6 (1972), 159. F. de Tollenaere describes the Dutch set in "Encoding Techniques in Dutch Historical Lexicography," *CHum*, 6 (1972), 147–52.

the *Beowulf* concordance; their typing element incorporated the letters in Old English which subsequently disappeared from the language: ash (æ), thorn (þ), eth (ð), and yogh (ȝ). Roy Wisbey's several excellent word indexes and concordances for Middle High German were also printed from coded paper tape on an electric typewriter; they have underlining for italics and all the diacritical marks that he required.[15]

The main drawback of the typewriter as an output device, whose handiwork can be published by offset lithography, is its slow speed. A computer taken up with routing large quantities of text to a typewriter terminal is wasting its valuable time; even slow line printers are much faster than typewriters. Although now somewhat out of date, comparative figures associated with the *Beowulf* project are revealing: the printer produced a formatted concordance in 90 minutes, whereas typing the same materials took 45 hours.[16] As usual with computer equipment, we seem to be faced with a trade-off of advantage with disadvantage—in this case, between speed and availability of a special character set. To the literary scholar, this delay does not seem as serious as it does to the computer scientist. The scholar is used to waiting years for publication of an article; having to wait several months for a concordance to appear once processing is complete represents no hardship. Transferring the text to auxiliary storage like magnetic tape frees the computer for other jobs. Then final output can be done on peripheral typewriters disconnected from the main system and, thus, not using up expensive machine time.

Three other output possibilities have been adapted in recent years for publication of machine-processed literary materials. One area of computer technology scarcely tested for literary data processing is *computer output microfilm*, designated COM in the ever-expanding jargon of computer acronyms. Literary scholarship has long been accustomed to using microfilm for access to rare texts. But reference works like concordances are still expected to be published in bound format. In 1974 appeared the first concordance published on microfiche, to Joseph Conrad's *Heart of Darkness*;[17] its format was not received with acclaim by the

---

[15] Wisbey's volumes are the first three in a series called *COMPENDIA*, published by W. S. Maney and Son Ltd., Leeds. The concordance to the Vorau and Strassburg "Alexander" (1968) was followed by a word index to the prose "Speculum Ecclesiae" (Early Middle High German and Latin, 1968) and a concordance to the "Rolandslied" (1969). Later volumes in the series cover works in other modern languages.

[16] Philip H. Smith, Jr., "Programmer's Preface," *A Concordance to "Beowulf"* (Ithaca: Cornell University Press, 1969), p. xxvi.

[17] Sibyl C. Jacobson, Robert J. Dilligan, and Todd K. Bender, eds., *Concordance to Joseph Conrad's "Heart of Darkness"* (Carbondale: Southern Illinois University Press, 1973), 2 microfiche.

scholarly world. Computer-related microform technology has expanded very rapidly in the past several years. Odd character sets are becoming available, and costs have declined as speed of production has increased. With publishing costs skyrocketing and the computer production of concordances and other reference volumes proliferating in all the ancient and modern languages, a scholar should now become aware of microfilm possibilities for his output. Economic realities may soon slow the publication of multivolume concordances in traditional hard cover, since production costs will make them too expensive to sell. No one prefers microfilm or fiche to the convenience of a portable, bound volume; yet he can buy a microfilm concordance for a fraction of the cost of a printed version.

As a rule of thumb, literary scholars might consider the following principle for publishing long, computer-produced reference materials: works on classical authors like Shakespeare and Homer that will be frequently consulted should continue to be printed in hard cover but works on writers of a more specialized or limited audience should probably be published in microform. Although less convenient to use, microform publication may be the only way to assure their publication and distribution to the scholarly community. Early Modern English materials collected in the 1920s and 1930s at the University of Michigan but never disseminated to scholars furnish a case in point. Since 1970 the Michigan Early Modern English Materials (MEMEM) project has been editing these handwritten citations with a computer and distributing them on microfiche. Because compilation of a dictionary is financially impossible at this time, Professors Richard W. Bailey and Jay L. Robinson chose to provide scholars with some of these voluminous materials for current lexicographic research in an inexpensive, workable form. Otherwise, the MEMEM files would continue to gather dust in an inaccessible archive.[18]

Because no piece of equipment has the character set needed for a particular literary project does not preclude its being done. Just as coding conventions are required for input of the characters, plotting devices that draw patterns of lines and curves on CRT screens can be adapted to produce them for output. The GROATS system (Graphical Output Package for Atlas) developed at the Atlas Computer Laboratory near Oxford, England, has had great success with unusual literary alphabets.

[18]The following articles by Bailey and Robinson contain more information about the project: "Computer-Produced Microfilm in Lexicography: Toward a Dictionary of Early Modern English," in *The Computer and Literary Studies*, ed. A. J. Aitken, R. W. Bailey, and N. Hamilton-Smith (Edinburgh: University of Edinburgh Press, 1973), pp. 3–14, and "MEMEM: A New Approach to Lexicography," *Source*, 4 (1974), 2–6. *The Computer and Literary Studies* will henceforth be denoted only by Aitken in references.

Computer scientists at Atlas have devised a procedure whereby their computers generate a magnetic tape of instructions for plotting nonstandard characters on a CRT terminal. Once drawn, they are then photographed by a microfilm recorder (originally a Stromberg-Carlson SC4020; since 1975 an Information International FR 80) for either microfilm or printed copy. Scholars there have produced remarkable output in Arabic, Russian, Greek, Armenian, and Hebrew alphabets, with 256 possible characters per font. Because a particular configuration of hardware is required, the system is presently implemented only at the Atlas Laboratory; but these successful experiments suggest the efficacy of adapting other computers and plotter devices—commonly used for graphs, architectural drafting, and computer-generated art—to print out character sets of other than roman alphabets.[19]

The most elegant form of computer-generated output has to be photocomposition, the composition of book pages directly from magnetic tape. The principle resembles that for microfilm: a computer program displays text stored on magnetic tape on a lens device similar to a CRT terminal. If the tape is coded to indicate them, boldface letters, italics, and several optional type styles are added as page proofs are produced automatically on the screen. Lines are justified on left and right, words hyphenated when necessary, and pages numbered. The resulting page is recorded photographically from the lens and reproduced by offset printing. Two concordances published in 1968 pioneered this printing technique for literary application: the Cornell volume for the plays of Jean Racine (edited by Bryant C. Freeman) and the four volumes for the prose of the Roman historian Livy (edited by David W. Packard and published by Harvard University Press). Since then, a number of large, finely executed projects have utilized this remarkable output procedure, including the complete set of Oxford old-spelling Shakespeare concordances edited by T. H. Howard-Hill and *The Index Thomisticus*, Father Roberto Busa's monumental lifetime work indexing the entire corpus of St. Thomas Aquinas. Figure 12 shows a finished page from the Oxford

[19] Susan M. Hockey's "Input and Output of Non-Standard Character Sets" (*ALLC Bulletin*, 1, No. 2 [1973], 32–37) gives the most recent published description of the GROATS system along with a sample of Greek output of Aeschylus' *Agamemnon*. Her earlier article—"A Concordance to the Poems of Hafiz with Output in Persian Characters," in Aitken, pp. 291–306—contains illustrations of Arabic output produced by the SC4020. Current inquiries about GROATS should be addressed to Mrs. Kate M. Crennell, User Services Group, Atlas Computer Laboratory, Chilton, Didcot, Oxfordshire, England.

BEDDES = 1

Vpon faint Primrose beddes, were wont to lye,   228

BEDS = 1

Already to their wormy beds are gone: 1425

BED-ROOME = 1

Then, by your side, no bed-roome me deny: 703

BED-TIME = *1

*Or after supper, & bed-time? Where is our vsuall manager   1829

BEE /252 330 368 380 797 1139 1218 1267 1586 2080 = 10, *1

*weapons in your hand, and kill me a red hipt Humble Bee,   1521

BEEFE = *1

*well. That same cowardly, gyantlike, Ox-beefe hath de-|luourd   1011

BEENE see also bin 1765 *2142 = 1*1

BEES = 1

The hony bagges steale from the humble Bees,   986

BEETLES = 1

Beetles blacke approach not neere: 672

BEFALL = 3

The worst that may befall mee in this case,   72

And those things do best please mee, | That befall prepost'rously.   1144

Wall. In this same enterlude it doth befall,   1956

BEFORE = 7*3

Be it so, she will not here, before your Grace, | Consent to marry   47

with Demetrius,

Before the time I did Lisander see,   217

*thought fit, through al Athens, to play in our Enterlude, be-|fore   273

Before, milke white; now purple, with loues wound,   544

action, as wee will doe it before the Duke.   818

Lys. He goes before me, and still dares me on: 1457

Thou runst before mee, shifting euery place,   1468

*I will sing it in the latter end of a Play, before the Duke.   1743

*Dut. How chance Moone-shine is gone before? Thisby   2105

I am sent, with broome, before,   2172

BEG = 2

I beg the auncient priuiledge of Athens: 49

Ile to my Queene and beg her Indian boy: 1416

BEGD = 1

And she, in milde tearmes, begd my patience,   1573

BEGGE = 4

I doe but begge a little Changeling boy, | To be my Henchman.   495

What worser place can I begge, in your loue   587

When thou wak'st, if she be by, | Begge of her, for remedy.   1131

I begge the law, the law, vpon his head: 1680

BEGGERY = 1

Of learning, late deceast, in beggery?   1850

BEGIN = 2

Made senselesse things begin to doe them wrong.   1050

Begin these wood birds but to couple, now?   1664

BEGINNE = 1*1

*beginne: when you haue spoken your speech, enter into   885

Her dotage now I doe beginne to pittie.   1562

BEGINNING = 1

That is the true beginning of our end.   1909

BEGON see gone

BEGUILD = 2

Because, in choyce, he is so oft beguil'd.   253

This palpable grosse Play hath well beguil'd   2149

17

FIGURE 12. A photocomposed page of a computer-produced concordance to Shakespeare's *A Midsummer Night's Dream*. The book pages were prepared directly from machine-readable files without traditional typesetting. *(Reproduced courtesy of Oxford University Press)*

volume to *A Midsummer Night's Dream* that is visually indistinguish-able from letter press printing and cheaper to produce.[20]

With photocomposition, the literary scholar can publish his machine-readable texts in any format or type style that he desires. More costly than common methods of computer output, this kind of printing is usu-ally not available at university computer centers. As with optical scan-ning, the facilities of a service bureau will probably have to be sought. Their personnel, expert in setting up page formats and type fonts, must be shown the characteristics of the machine-readable text file to be printed, such as coding conventions used for special purposes. They may have to edit at a terminal to insert shift codes for changes in type font or paragraph indicators. A scholar embarking on a literary comput-ing project that he expects to print by photocomposition will do well to get advice before preparing his data for input. He can familiarize himself with standards expected in machine-readable tapes prior to printing and thus encode the appropriate information in the input process.

In closing, one moral bears repeating for all computer applications: plan ahead. Unexpected headaches that might come up later may be avoided by careful early planning. The frequently arcane input/output devices owned by the local university computer center probably are not the most suitable for literary data processing. If there is no other choice, how best can they be adapted to fit particular needs of a contemplated project? Maybe outside technological advice needs to be sought. All kinds of information that will ultimately be required for processing or output must be considered in designing an input data structure. In short, important decisions affecting the whole throughput process must be made before investing considerable time and money in data preparation of large bodies of literary text. In computing circles, Murphy's Law is often quoted in a semihumorous vein: "If anything can go wrong, it will." Without careful planning amid the complex input/output options of literary computing, it may not be so funny.

[20] Howard-Hill's individual volumes for each Shakespeare play have been published by the Clarendon Press of Oxford University since 1969, whereas the *Index Thomisticus* in twenty-three volumes began to appear from Frommann-Holzboog, Stuttgart, in 1974. The illustration is from *A Midsummer Night's Dream: A Concordance to the Text of the First Quarto of 1600* (1970), p. 17.

FOR FURTHER READING

Galloway, Patricia. "Hardware Review: The Kurzweil Data Entry Machine." *CHum*, 15 (1981), 183–85.

    The most accessible discussion of the Kurzweil optical scanner—how it works and what it can do to read literary texts without keying.

Introduction to Computers in the Humanities. White Plains, N.Y.: IBM Corporation, 1971. Publication GE20-0382-0.

    General discussion of input/output devices with fine pictorial illustrations.

Last, R. W. "Publishing Computer Output of Processed Natural Language Texts—I." *ALLC Bulletin*, 1, No. 3 (1973), 5–7.

————. "Publishing Computer Output of Processed Natural Language Texts—II." *ALLC Bulletin*, 2, No. 2 (1974), 38–41.

    Survey articles on various output methods suitable for literary projects, with comparisons and bibliography.

Lesk, Mike. "Cheap Typesetters." *SIGLASH Newsletter*, 6, No. 4 (October 1973), 14–16.

    Short informative articles on kinds of typesetting with computers. Lesk discusses factors affecting costs and lists prices for several manufacturers.

McWilliams, Peter A. *The Personal Computer Book*. Los Angeles: Prelude Press, 1982.

    Clever, witty personal tour of one user's views on home computer fundamentals, jargon, and applications, along with comparisons of namebrand equipment.

Ott, Wilhelm. "The Emancipated Input/Output." *The Computer in Literary and Linguistic Studies*. Ed. Alan Jones and R. F. Churchhouse. Cardiff: University of Wales Press, 1976. Pp. 27–37.

    Careful, detailed analysis of pros and cons for various input/output methods. Description of a working system at the University of Tübingen for photocomposing scholarly texts directly from magnetic tape with varied typestyles and footnotes on each page.

Packard, David W. "Can Scholars Publish Their Own Books?" *Scholarly Publishing*, 5 (1973), 65–74.

Excellent account of Packard's personal experience developing a system for preparing manuscripts with unusual alphabets and footnotes for book publication by photocomposition. Discussion includes costs and feasibility of using computers to aid literary publication.

Porch, Ann. "An Overview of Devices for Preparing Large Natural Language Data Bases." *CSHVB*, 4 (1973), 81–89.

Detailed comparison of eight input devices in terms of their features, costs, and correction facilities for encoding a million words of language text. Equipment runs the gamut from keypunch machines and several kinds of terminals to optical scanners.

Schneider, Ben R., Jr. *Travels in Computerland; or Incompatibilities and Interfaces*. Reading, Mass.: Addison-Wesley Publishing Company, 1974.

Leisurely, humorous account patterned after *Gulliver's Travels* of Schneider's myriad problems with data structures and input methods for the *London Stage Information Bank*. Required reading for any novice contemplating extensive literary computing.

Wisbey, Roy A. "The Computer and Literary Studies." *Symposium on Printing*. Leeds, England: Leeds Philosophical Society, 1971. Pp. 9–26.

General article debunking early inflated claims about literary computing. Useful discussion of encoding textual data, favoring paper tape and pre-editing of essential information before preparation.

CHAPTER 3

Flowcharting and Programming for Literary Analysis

COMPUTER PROCESSING AND CONTROL take place inside the central processing unit (CPU) of the machine, which also includes the central memory. One step at a time, the computer reads material into memory, then moves it into the accumulator for processing. The results produced are put back into memory and routed to output if desired. At all times the control mechanism knows where each file of information is being held and orders it to be moved or operated on according to a prearranged set of instructions, the computer program.

The nature of computer processing is best understood in terms of the concept of an *algorithm*. An algorithm is any set of well-defined rules for problem solving by a series of logical steps. Outside of mathematics, where the notion of algorithms is fundamental, people may not be aware that many everyday processes incorporate the basic principles of algorithms. For example, following a sheet of instructions to assemble a new bicycle, toy, or appliance involves algorithmic logic. Typically we go step by step through a series of operations in order gradually to assemble the piece of equipment. Taking them in order is supposed to expedite completion of the task with a minimum of trouble in a small number of easy steps. Rearranging the order of the instructions may accomplish the same objective but by a longer or more inconvenient process. Perhaps the job cannot be done successfully unless the proper order is followed. A recipe, an algorithm for cooking, often shares an important similarity with a set of installation instructions; ingredients are added or mixed in a regular, prescribed order, one after another in linear order.

The rules of a card game like bridge or a board game like Monopoly are, on the surface, also linearly algorithmic. In bridge, cards are shuffled, dealt, bid, then played. Yet within these last two steps, as bridge players know, there are myriad options for bidding and playing the hand, since the number of possible card combinations is so large. The strategy of playing out the hand may need modifying in the midst of play because of unexpected, unusual card distribution. Linear play breaks

41

down into a series of if-then options; the algorithm is adaptable to changing conditions.

In most cases, movement around the Monopoly board is also straightforward, the number of steps calculated by a throw of two dice. At least two events disrupt the normal order of linear movement: landing on the "Go to Jail" square or being instructed to move to an unexpected location by either a "Chance" or "Community Chest" card. When a player lands on the spot ordering removal to jail, he must immediately interrupt his planned itinerary around the board and deposit his token in the jail. Similarly he has to follow the directions of a special card, which may overrule his normal clockwise movement around the board.

To chart the possible movements of a Monopoly token, schematically, we must allow for these options, which we can present in diagram form in Figure 13. Although a complete chart of Monopoly moves is

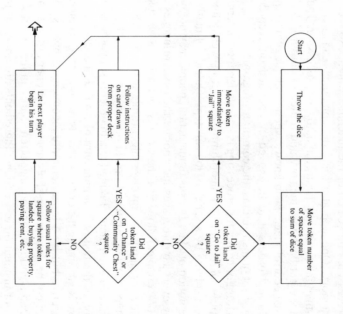

FIGURE 13. A flowchart of one player's possible moves in a Monopoly game.

42

much more complicated, this simplified diagram serves to illustrate a concept common to computer algorithms, the *flowchart* or *flow diagram*. One ordinary operation (presented in a rectangular box) follows another in normal linear order until a *decision box* mandating alternative moves (represented by a diamond-shaped block) is reached. At this point, the path of movement that is followed depends on the answer to the question in the decision box; in computer terminology, the decision box introduces a *branch* into the flow of operations. The branch is equivalent to the logical statement: if something is true, go one way; otherwise, go the other way. Normally the choice is binary, exemplified by the yes-no exits attached to each decision. The circle, another flowchart symbol pictured here, is used to denote beginning or ending an algorithm. Because we have not completely diagrammed the moves of Monopoly, there is no circle signifying the end of the game.

The example from Monopoly shows the possibilities of schematically representing an algorithm in diagram form for both linear operation and branching. Can the problem of alliteration in Hopkins' sonnet, "Hurrahing in Harvest," presented in Chapter 1, also be discussed in terms of a flowchart and an algorithm for solution? Let us look at an algorithm in the form of a full flowchart suitable for computerization. Given the poem in a machine-readable form, Figure 14 presents a diagrammatic way for a computer to check an alliterative tendency in it. The flowchart may seem unnecessarily detailed to the scholar, but the computer is a literal-minded machine that must have everything spelled out in well-defined steps. In addition to the arrows to indicate the order of processing, two new symbols occur in the flowchart: a box shaped like a punchcard to indicate input of text—in this case, one line at a time—and a print box, drawn to resemble printer paper ripped at the bottom as it is removed from the machine. The flowchart is broken down into four main sections, labeled with roman numerals. Each segment of tasks fulfills one part of the analysis and then is recycled to start the process over again. This routing of arrows back to earlier boxes of a flowchart is called *looping*, which is interrupted when conditions change in the decision box controlling the loop.

To examine the flowchart further, consider the largest loop (Section II), which represents the complete analysis of one line of Hopkins' sonnet for alliteration. Notice that Section I has read the line and removed all of its punctuation before passing into this section. To the computer one type of character is like any other, a series of binary codes. Getting rid of punctuation avoids its confusion with words or parts of words. If there is an unanalyzed word in the line, its first letter is stripped off to

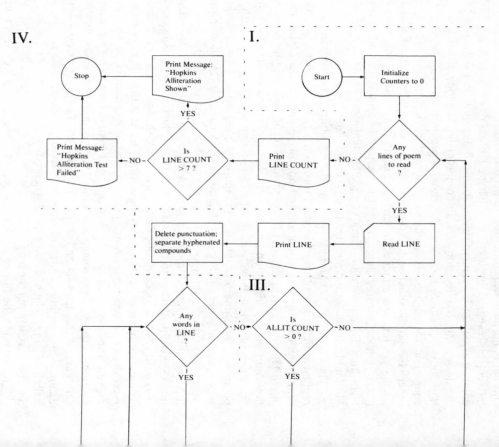

IV.

Print Message: "Hopkins Alliteration Shown"

Stop

YES

Print Message: "Hopkins Alliteration Test Failed"

NO — Is LINE COUNT > 7 ?

Print LINE COUNT

NO -

I.

Start

Initialize Counters to 0

Any lines of poem to read ?

YES

Delete punctuation; separate hyphenated compounds

Print LINE

Read LINE

III.

Any words in LINE ?

NO — Is ALLIT COUNT > 0 ?

NO

YES

YES

Flowcharting and Programming for Literary Analysis

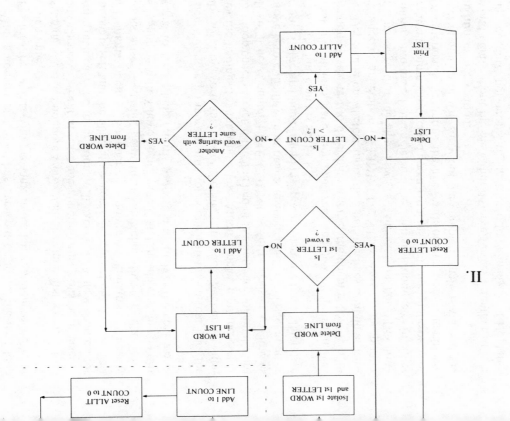

FIGURE 14. A flowchart to check for alliteration in a Hopkins sonnet.

45

see if it is a vowel. If not, a count for the consonant found (called LETTER COUNT) is incremented before analysis proceeds; if the word begins with a vowel, the flow of operations is sent back to pick up the next word. After a consonant word has been put on a list, the next loop searches for other words with the same initial letter, adding to the letter count each time.

Assuming there are no more words with the same first letter, a decision box checks to see if at least one alliterative pair has been discovered, in which case the letter count will exceed 1. A new counter, for alliteration, is set; and the alliterative words are printed out. For the first line of Hopkins' poem—"Summer ends now; now, barbarous in beauty the stocks arise,"—at this point in the flowchart the two alliterative words beginning with S have been printed, and the alliteration count is now equal to 1. The loop returns to the top to analyze the next word, *ends.*

When there are no more words to examine in the current line, the loop for word-by-word analysis of the line is finished. Section III summarizes the findings for the whole line. Much simpler than the earlier one, this loop checks to see if the line had at least one consonantal word pair. If so, a new counter LINE COUNT is set to register the line as alliterative before the flowchart begins again to read and dissect another poetic line. In the first line of Hopkins' poem, there are three alliterative pairs; thus the line count is set to 1.

Eventually all lines have been analyzed, and flow of control moves into Section IV, the test to determine whether the poem is heavily alliterative. Depending on whether more than half the lines contain at least one instance of alliteration (if LINE COUNT exceeds 7), the printer writes a message that the alliterative test succeeds or fails. The flowchart moves into the STOP circle, and the analysis is complete. In either event, the algorithm has decided about Hopkins' practice on the basis of its own criterion, by counting the lines with one or more alliterations. Once set in motion, it will carry out the complete analysis without the need of human intervention.

Several points about the algorithm deserve further attention. It is a general procedure, not necessarily restricted to an analysis of Hopkins' poetry. Any poem that has been prepared on punchcards for reading a line at a time will work with this flowchart. After the last line has been dissected, the decision box at the beginning will disrupt the inner loops and move into the section that contains the stopping procedure. Only the condition requiring the number of alliterative lines to be more than 7 (half of the number of lines in a sonnet) keeps the flowchart from applying to all alliterative poetry. Modifying that decision box to ask if the line count exceeds half the total lines in the poem would give the algorithm more general application. Of course, the flowchart would have to include a procedure to count the number of lines as they are read. The numerical criterion for proving strong alliteration remains the scholar's critical judgment, to be added to the decision box in Section IV after he has decided. Similarly, the final messages could be adjusted to leave off Hopkins' name. Another nice feature of the procedure is the listing of all alliterative word groups by letter and line in Section II. Whatever the final determination about the poem as a whole, we have the lists of alliterative words in front of us for inspection and further analysis, if desired.

The flowchart for the algorithm embodies the computer functions of processing and control, including coordination of input, output, and storage. It sets up three counters—for words by consonant and line, for alliterative groups by line, and for lines defined as alliterative—that are used to control loops and activate branching to other parts of the diagram. As these branching criteria change, the algorithm monitors itself and modifies its own activities; once it has been set in motion, it adapts without external interference to changing conditions. When necessary, counters are incremented or reset to zero to begin processing another line. This feature of internal adaptation makes the algorithm an autonomous working model for testing alliteration, suitable for computer implementation. In fact, any computer that can simulate the flowchart will be able to do the analysis for the scholar automatically.

Getting the computer to carry out the operations included in the Hopkins algorithm is the job of a computer *program*. It must have instructions to accomplish the separate tasks present in the flowchart. It will be written by a programmer and prepared for feeding to the machine by some input process, such as punchcards, terminal, or magnetic tape. Once it is read into the machine, like all materials submitted from an external source, it will be stored in the internal memory unit of the CPU.

This principle, known as the *stored program concept*, was devised by Professor John von Neumann in the 1940s at Princeton University and served as a great boost to the development of computers. Prior to that time, making computer circuits perform the operations (mainly arithmetic) they were designed for was a mechanical process, analogous to punching buttons on a modern calculator to do addition and subtraction. Von Neumann proposed that instructions for operating computer circuitry be themselves coded in binary symbols, stored in memory sequentially, and decoded one at a time to control the computer's essential operations. In terms of the five elements of a computer system, the control function is carried out as program instructions are decoded and executed. These then activate and monitor the actual processing being done in the accumulator or registers, where electrical circuits perform the basic operations of the machine. All the while, the controlling program is stored in the memory, having been read as input. The concept greatly extends the flexibility and speed of the machine for complex processing. Any program with instructions to control the elementary operations of the machine can be stored in internal memory for fast retrieval and execution. Externally produced programs are called computer *software*, a term devised to distinguish them from actual machinery, or *hardware*. Today advances in software are appearing at least as rapidly as computer hardware.

Using a computer to carry out a task involves, therefore, a partnership between program and machinery, between software and hardware. When the instructions of the program are taken from the memory and decoded, they are being treated as data; in fact, they are being processed. Yet they may call for other kinds of data to be read, processed, and printed out. A computer program for the alliteration algorithm will very early cause a line of poetry coded on a punchcard to be read and will eventually print lists of alliterative words. This textual data will also be kept in memory prior to processing or output. Thus, both the program and the data are encoded on some form of input, read into the computer, and stored in the central memory of the machine. In a typical case, the program is encoded on punchcards, with the data to be analyzed, such as the lines of the Hopkins sonnet, stacked behind it on other cards. Of course, both program and data can be read into the machine in any input form. After the program has been read and begins execution, the lines of poetry are input into memory one at a time as the algorithm requires them for processing.

Before looking at some computer programs to solve the Hopkins alliteration problem, we must say a word or two about kinds of programming languages and their suitability for processing literary materials. Without discussing programming principles in great detail, I hope to give the reader some idea about languages he may find at his computer center that can be adapted to his work. In 1972, the leading historian of programming languages, Jean E. Sammet, reported that there were more than 170 computer languages being used in the United States alone, and no doubt the last several years have seen an increase in that number.[1]

[1] Jean E. Sammet, "Programming Languages: History and Future," *Communications of the ACM*, 15 (1972), 601.

Yet most of these are designed for particular machines or specialized applications. Some cannot be used except where they are developed, and most will not apply to literary processing.

Computer programming languages fall into two general types, high- and low-level languages. Not surprisingly the internal *machine language* of any computer, the lowest level of language, is a series of binary codes that activate the circuits for processing or movement of materials from input to memory to output. Because programming in binary codes is extremely tedious and susceptible to error, *assembly languages*, the next level up from binary machine code, were developed. Instead of writing everything in strings of 0's and 1's, the programmer uses a series of mnemonic abbreviations for the machine operations, automatically converted by an *assembler* program to binary codes inside the machine. Even at the assembler level, programming is slow and complex. Normally only computer professionals do assembly language programming.

Most programs for computer applications, whether scientific, business, or humanistic, are written in high-level languages, several steps removed from machine code. These languages, usually called *compilers*, have instructions that are easy for the user to learn and write; different high-level languages are suitable for different kinds of tasks. After a program in a compiler language is submitted to the computer, it is converted by a translation process, the compiling stage, ultimately into binary machine coding. Only then does processing of the job begin, for computers do everything in binary notation. Some high-level languages, called *interpreters*, are a step removed from compilers. Their instructions are interpreted by the computer one at a time and run like machine code. Not surprisingly, the sophisticated translation algorithms to convert programs written in compiler or interpreter languages into binary machine language are written by highly trained computer specialists and stored inside the machine for general usage.

Probably all the computer languages with which literary scholars may be acquainted are the high-level type. In America the best known ones are FORTRAN and COBOL, with ALGOL60 also very familiar in Europe. The literary scholar need not concern himself with machine or assembly languages; he needs to find a high-level programming language suited for his application and available for his use. Because each computer manufacturer has its own particular binary coding scheme for machine language, translation programs for high-level languages are normally machine-dependent. This situation often causes problems for literary computing because a scholar may find that his computer center cannot implement a particular language. Programming languages especially suited for textual analysis are not as readily available as some others. The scholar may have to use a language not very convenient for his task or go elsewhere to get his program run on another machine.

The question of suitable languages for literary data processing involves more than availability. Compared to other languages, compilers for text processing often run more slowly and take up large amounts of central storage. If they are costly of computer time and space, a small computer center may not be able to provide these languages. As a result of all these factors, there is no general agreement about the best languages for literary computing.

Before considering the merits of specific languages, let us consider the kinds of computer operations needed for literary or textual processing. As a starting point, what language features does the alliteration algorithm require of a programming language? Prominent among these are ways to begin and end processing, as well as branching instructions to permit the execution of loops. We need input and output capabilities, in order to read the poem and print alliteration words and the final message. In fact, all computer languages must have these control functions regardless of the application. Virtually all algorithms include input, output, and branching.

The problem also requires processing operations for both words and numbers. We have to isolate words one at a time and check their first letters. We shall do some counting of letters, words, and lines. Generally speaking, the need of specialized operations of these kinds has led to the proliferation of programming languages. All early languages like FOR-TRAN and ALGOL60 and most modern ones have arithmetic instructions; but rules for dissecting lines (or strings) of text into words and letters, called *string processing* or *character handling*, are more recently developed computer capabilities. A few languages like COMIT II and SNOBOL4 were devised especially to do string processing with a minimum of trouble. Newer multipurpose languages, suited for a variety of scientific, business, and textual applications, provide string operations among their repertoire of diverse features; PL/I (or PL/1 or PL/1)[2] and ALGOL68 fall into this category. Modern additions to older languages—FOR-TRAN and BASIC, for example—have extended their abilities to include character handling instructions along with their earlier numerical ones.

There is no easy answer about which programming language is best for literary computing. Questions of suitable text processing instructions

50

_____

[2] There seems to be no definite standard about whether the character after the slash is a roman or arabic numeral one. One finds both in references to the language.

and availability on particular machines necessarily complicate the choice. A number of scholars have argued in favor of FORTRAN because it is the most widely used computer language in the world. All manufacturers include some version of it among their optional compilers. FORTRAN programs written for one machine will usually run on others with slight modifications. Yet FORTRAN, whose acronym stands for Formula Translation, remains primarily a language for scientific and mathematical application. Its features for character handling have never been convenient and vary among the several FORTRAN compilers in common use today.[3] In his book, entitled *FORTRAN Techniques*, Colin Day, who has long been interested in literary computing, consciously aimed to present textual aspects of FORTRAN programming, including alphabetic sorting, making lists, and identifying characters and words.[4] Day stretches the capabilities of the language to fit these applications. To understand what he is doing, however, a scholar must already be an accomplished hand with the language.

An early extension of FORTRAN called SLIP to incorporate some string functions failed to generate literary enthusiasm, but a new language called SNAP with instructions that look like English-language sentences has been somewhat successful.[5] Although it looks nothing like it, SNAP is interpreted internally in the machine as FORTRAN IV instructions. Computer centers that have FORTRAN IV compilers can thus add SNAP to their program libraries with little difficulty. Nevertheless, experiments with SNAP for literary computing at the University of East Anglia have found it somewhat verbose, inefficient, and restricted in arithmetic processing. When they had learned basic computer concepts with SNAP, users normally turned to more efficient, general programming languages.[6] If FORTRAN is his only choice, the literary scholar might consider using SNAP if his problem is not too large or complicated.

---

[3] For a fine discussion of FORTRAN differences and possibilities, see Robert J. Dilligan, "Introductory FORTRAN Textbooks: An Overview for Humanists," *CHum*, 7 (1973), 399–406.

[4] A. Colin Day, *FORTRAN Techniques with Special Reference to Non-Numerical Applications* (Cambridge: Cambridge University Press, 1972). More recently R. H. Rasche has suggested refinements of Day's FORTRAN designs for text processing in "FORTRAN as a Medium for Language Analysis," in Mitchell, pp. 250–57.

[5] For SLIP, see J. Weizenbaum, "Symmetric List Processor," *Communications of the ACM*, 6 (1963), 524–44. The definitive work on SNAP, originally available on IBM 360 and RCA Spectra computers, is Michael P. Barnett's *Computer Programming in English* (New York: Harcourt, Brace and World, Inc., 1969).

[6] The experience with SNAP at East Anglia is documented by Richard J. W. Housden, "Further Thoughts on SNAP," *CHum*, 7 (1973), 407–12. Housden discusses local adaptations that allow the language to be used on a time-sharing basis from a terminal.

The most commonly implemented language for input at a terminal and running under time sharing is called BASIC, developed at Dartmouth for teaching students FORTRAN-like concepts in a simplified form.[7] In BASIC the programmer types in his instructions one at a time; the computer checks to see if they are valid. This helpful interactive communication between programmer and machine in a time-sharing environment is called computing in a "conversational mode." The user revises any instruction that is incorrectly formed without bothering the others. When all corrections are complete, the system takes over execution of the full program. Like FORTRAN, BASIC is widely available but more suited to numerical than literary applications. Recent adaptations, culminating in Extended BASIC, do permit character handling and string processing, but not all computer systems implement this enhanced version of the language.

To improve on the poor text-processing abilities of BASIC, Peter J. Brown at the University of Kent devised SCAN. Meanwhile, he insisted on keeping the helpful features of BASIC—conversational mode, built-in correction facilities, etc.[8] Instead of numbers, SCAN focuses on analysis of "sentences," defined as groups of characters terminated by a full stop, such as a period. Any string of characters followed by a stop symbol qualifies as a SCAN "sentence," analogous to a sentence in natural language but not limited to that interpretation. SCAN is simpler but considerably less powerful than a general text-processing language like SNOBOL4, but it can be run on a computer with small central storage, whereas the SNOBOL4 language requires a large internal memory. Currently implemented on ICL 4130 and PDP-11 small computers, SCAN has not been tested as extensively as SNAP. No significant literary applications have been reported to date based on SCAN programs. Designed for portability among different machines, it seems most promising for introducing the scholar to limited literary processing in an easy-to-understand, conversational mode of operation.

Today SNOBOL4 is the most common programming language specifically designed for textual processing. In the early 1960s, its predecessor, COMIT II, paved the way in development of string operations but

---

[7] For a description, see J. G. Kemeny and T. E. Kurtz, *BASIC Programming*, 2nd ed. (New York: John Wiley and Sons, 1971).

[8] Brown describes the characteristics of the language, including its virtues and limitations, in "SCAN: A Simple Conversational Programming Language for Text Analysis," *CHum*, 6 (1972), 223–27.

lacked adequate arithmetic facilities.[9] The creators of SNOBOL4 consciously combined the best features of COMIT for character analysis with the numerical facilities of FORTRAN. Although good COMIT compilers are still in use, SNOBOL4 has been more generally accepted and made available on modern machinery.[10] Various versions of SNOBOL4 exist for ordinary serial processing of one job after another submitted on cards, tape, etc. (*batch processing*) and for the interactive mode of time sharing at a terminal.

Pattern matching represents the backbone of character handling in SNOBOL4. Consider, for example, a line of Hopkins' sonnet, "Hurrahing in Harvest," to be a string of characters called LINE—letters, punctuation marks, and spaces between words. Essential to the alliteration algorithm is the process of isolating the first letter of the first word left in the line. SNOBOL4 rules accomplish this task by initially setting up a pattern to find the word in the string LINE and then putting it into a new string called WORD. Next the first letter is separated out and called LETTER, a new string. The rules to accomplish these tasks follow:

LINE '' BREAK('') . WORD '' = ' '

WORD LEN(1) . LETTER

In the first rule, the space character ('') and the operator BREAK appear in the second, or pattern matching, field. This instruction causes the computer to move through the characters in LINE (the string being processed, named in the first field) collecting everything following the first space up to but not including the second space into a new string named WORD. That is, everything between two spaces is a WORD. Because the rule has only a space ('') on the right of the equal sign, the rest of the pattern on the left, initial space and WORD, is deleted from LINE, as required in the flowchart (see Figure 14). The second rule sets up a pattern search for a character of length 1 in WORD moving from left to right; thus, the first letter of WORD is assigned to a string called

[9] See Victor Yngve, *Computer Programming with COMIT II* (Cambridge, Mass.: MIT Press, 1972). Yngve mentions COMIT II compilers for two IBM computer series: the 7000 models and System 360.

[10] The standard programming manual for SNOBOL4 (R. E. Griswold, J. F. Poage, and I. P. Polonsky, *The SNOBOL4 Programming Language*, 2nd ed. [Englewood Cliffs, N.J.: Prentice-Hall, Inc., 1971] lists the following machines which can run it: IBM 360/370 systems, UNIVAC 1108, GE 635, CDC 3600, CDC 6000 series, PDP-10, Sigma 5/6/7, Atlas 2, and RCA Spectra 70 series. More recently a version of SNOBOL4 for the ICL 1900 series of British machines has been completed at the University of Leeds Computer Science Department.

```
*A SNOBOL4 PROGRAM TO SEE IF A HOPKINS SONNET IS ALLITERATIVE IN MORE THAN
*HALF THE LINES
*
*SET A CONTROL TO TRIM TRAILING BLANKS FROM INPUT CARDS
       &TRIM = 1
*PATTERN CONTAINING VOWELS IN ENGLISH
       VOWEL = 'A' | 'E' | 'I' | 'O' | 'U'
*INITIALIZE COUNTS OF LETTERS, ALLITERATIONS, AND LINES TO ZERO
       LETCT = 0
       ALLITCT = 0
       LINECT = 0
*
*READ A LINE OF POETRY, IF ANY; OTHERWISE, GO TO RULE OUT
READ   LINE = ' ' INPUT ' '                   :F(OUT)
*PRINT THE LINE
       OUTPUT = LINE
*DELETE ALL PUNCTUATION; SEPARATE HYPHENATED COMPOUNDS
DELPUNC LINE ANY('.,:;?!_') =                 :S(DELPUNC)
HYPHEN LINE '-' = ' '                         :S(HYPHEN)
*
*ISOLATE FIRST WORD AND ITS FIRST LETTER; DELETE WORD FROM LINE
START  LINE ' ' BREAK(' ') . WORD ' ' =       :F(TEST)
*IF NO WORDS LEFT, GO TO RULE TEST
       WORD LEN(1) . LETTER
*IS FIRST LETTER A VOWEL, NOT A CONSONANT?
*IF NOT A VOWEL, PROCEED; IF SO, RETURN TO RULE START
       LETTER VOWEL                           :S(START)
*PUT WORD ON LIST; ADD TO LETTER COUNT
AGAIN  LIST = LIST ' ' WORD
       LETCT = LETCT + 1
*
*SEARCH FOR ANOTHER WORD WITH SAME FIRST LETTER
*IF FOUND, DELETE AND RETURN TO RULE AGAIN
       LINE ' ' (LETTER BREAK(' ')) . WORD ' ' =  :S(AGAIN)
*IF NOT, SEE IF LETCT GREATER THAN 1
*IF SO, ALLITERATION FOUND; INCREMENT ALLITCT AND PRINT LIST OF WORDS
       ALLITCT = GT(LETCT,1) ALLITCT + 1      :F(BYPASS)
       OUTPUT = LIST
*DELETE LIST OF WORDS; SET LETCT TO ZERO; RETURN TO RULE START
BYPASS LIST =
       LETCT = 0                              :(START)
*
*DOES LINE CONTAIN ALLITERATION? IF SO, INCREMENT LINECT
*IF NOT, READ ANOTHER LINE
TEST   OUTPUT =
       LINECT = GT(ALLITCT,0) LINECT + 1      :F(READ)
*RESET ALLITCT TO ZERO; READ ANOTHER LINE
       ALLITCT = 0                            :(READ)
*ARE MORE THAN HALF THE LINES ALLITERATIVE? PRINT APPROPRIATE MESSAGES AND STOP
OUT    OUTPUT = 'NUMBER OF ALLITERATIVE LINES = ' LINECT
       OUTPUT = GT(LINECT,7)  'HOPKINS ALLITERATION SHOWN'  :S(END)
       OUTPUT = 'HOPKINS ALLITERATION TEST FAILED'
END
```

FIGURE 15. A SNOBOL4 program to examine alliteration in a Hopkins sonnet.

LETTER. With rules like these, SNOBOL4 can search for complex character combinations, described in the pattern-matching field (second in the rule). By finding patterns, the rules have created new strings, WORD and LETTER, containing the first word and its initial letter, respectively. Patterns found in strings can be replaced, deleted, rearranged, or duplicated in the right side of an instruction; here deletion is in order. Its features for pattern matching make SNOBOL4 a very powerful language for character handling, an especially suitable choice for text processing.

After this cursory glance at pattern matching, let us examine a computer program written in SNOBOL4 (Figure 15) to work out the complete alliteration flowchart. Comments appear in statements introduced by an asterisk to explain what is going on in various rules. Easily noticed in several rules (READ and DELPUNC, for example) are ways that branching is controlled; after a colon, control is transferred to other named rules, often on condition of success (S) or failure (F) in the rule itself. Rule DELPUNC is, in fact, a one-rule loop to delete repeatedly one punctuation mark at a time until there are no more. SNOBOL4 operators called INPUT, OUTPUT, and END incorporate these necessary functions; and addition is handled with the plus sign (+). Making lists of words by stringing one behind another, called concatenation, represents another feature important for text processing, exemplified in rule AGAIN. Even without complete explanation of the nuances of every rule, we can see how a computer programming language works out a flowchart within its own specific framework of instructions. In the case of SNOBOL4, these are usually not too difficult to follow.

PL/I and ALGOL68 are probably the nearest rivals of SNOBOL4 today for literary computing. They differ from it in being multipurpose programming languages, intended to serve a broad range of problems, not just text processing. Their body of instructions can be adapted for business analysis, scientific computation, and character handling. Computer scientists at IBM invented PL/I specifically for their well-known 360/370 series of machines; its name, Programming Language/One, stresses its general-purpose design for wide applicability and usage. With popular acceptance of these machines and the language, a number of other American computer companies (General Electric, Honeywell, and Burroughs among others) have made versions of PL/I available on some of their models. A newer language than PL/I, ALGOL68 and its predecessors in the ALGOL family have always been more favored in Europe than America. Early implemented on ICL 1900 computers, versions of ALGOL68 are reported to be now available on the IBM 370 series and some models of Control Data, Digital Equipment, and Burroughs machinery.[11]

[11] There are many textbooks for learning PL/I but no standard reference manual, except perhaps *IBM System/360 Operating System: PL/I (F) Language Reference Manual*, No. GC 28—8201—4 (Yorktown Heights, N.Y.: IBM Corporation, 1972). The standard technical reference for ALGOL68 is Charles H. Lindsey and S. G. van de Meulen, *Informal Introduction to ALGOL68* (Amsterdam and London: North-Holland Publishing Co., 1971), which is very difficult for the beginner to follow. In his much more readable discussion of the language, Andrew S. Tanenbaum ("A Tutorial on ALGOL68," *Computing Surveys*, 8 [1976], 155–90) mentions the availability of the language on IBM 370, CDC Cyber, Burroughs B6700, and a subset of it on the Digital Equipment PDP-11.

Among its repertoire of instructions, PL/I does pattern matching by combining two functions called INDEX and SUBSTR (Substring). To pick out and delete the first word and then isolate its first letter takes several more steps than in SNOBOL4:

N = INDEX (LINE, ' ');

WORD = SUBSTR (LINE, 1, N − 1);

LINE = SUBSTR (LINE, N);

LETTER = SUBSTR (WORD, 1, 1);

Instead of searching for complex patterns directly, PL/I gets a numerical position for particular characters. In the first rule, the function INDEX moves through LINE, counting the positions until it gets to the first space. In the first line of Hopkins' sonnet, the first word "Summer" has six letters; thus the first space comes in position 7, assigned as the value of N. Knowing the numerical value of N permits two new strings, WORD and LETTER, to be created. To paraphrase the second rule, WORD is a substring of LINE starting at position 1 of length 6 (N−1 characters), consequently, the word "Summer." Likewise, LETTER is defined to be a substring of WORD one character long beginning at position 1. The middle rule of the three redefines LINE to begin at the seventh character (N), behind the first word—in effect, deleting the word from the line as required by the alliteration flowchart.

Add to these functions the concatenation operator (||), and it is possible to duplicate the operations in the SNOBOL4 alliteration program. Although more complex and verbose than SNOBOL4, a PL/I solution to the Hopkins algorithm appears in Figure 16, with comments inserted in rules enclosed by the paired symbols /*...*/. For easy comparison, string names and instruction labels, where possible, are the same as in the earlier program. PL/I has more complicated input and output (GET EDIT, PUT EDIT), but its branches dependent on conditions are readily understood by their IF . . . THEN form. Repetitive loops fall between DO and END statements; the largest of these, labeled LINELOOP, incorporates all parts of the flowchart concerned with the analysis of one poetic line (Section II). The declaration of variable names, beginning at rule DECLARE at the top of the program, is a common practice in some programming languages, PL/I and ALGOL68 among them; SNOBOL4 avoids declaration by defining everything to be a string unless assigned a numerical value. The greatest difference, however, between the two languages for text processing remains the numerical nature of pattern matching implicit in the index and substring operations of PL/I.

In some ways an ALGOL68 program to carry out the alliterative test on Hopkins' sonnet (Figure 17) is more brute force than the PL/I version, although in most respects its algorithmic approach is similar.[12] Whereas PL/I provides built-in functions INDEX, SUBSTR, and VERIFY needed to isolate words, ALGOL68 requires the user to develop many of his own functions, called procedures, to carry out the necessary operations. The language has fewer basic functional components than either of the other two, but the programmer has great flexibility in combining them into whatever procedures he desires.

Before ALGOL68 can begin picking out words and checking their initial letters, three procedures are written to approximate the INDEX function of PL/I, to delete punctuation, and to regularize each line with a single space between each word. The user cannot call for INDEX directly until he has written a procedure to carry out its function. Like the other procedures, DELETE and DELPUNC, this set of rules precedes the main program and is called when needed later by referencing the name. In computer terms, the main program activates the subprograms by calling for the procedures by name within its own rules. It is worth noting that even the two procedures, DELETE and DELPUNC, have to call the INDEX routine to carry out their own jobs.

Both PL/I and SNOBOL4 include special operators to do concatenation of characters. For this operation, ALGOL68 uses either the plus sign (+) or the word PLUS, both of which also serve for addition of numbers. Although the two statements

LISTL: = LISTL + " " + WORD

and

P: = I + 1

look alike, the computer knows that the first puts a new word on LISTL and the second adds the integer 1 to the value of I and assigns it to the variable P. It is not confused by the use of the same operation symbol because early rules in the program declare LISTL to be a string variable and P and I to be integer numbers; concatenation is appropriate to strings of characters and addition to numbers. Declaring of variable types near the start of a program clears up any confusion about the meaning of operators like PLUS when used with variables in later rules.

[12] I wish to express my sincere thanks to Michael Farringdon and Peter Smith of University College, Swansea, for assistance in designing and running the ALGOL68 program on the ICL 1904S computer with the ALGOL68R compiler.

FUNDAMENTALS OF LITERARY COMPUTING

```pli
/*A PL/I PROGRAM TO SEE IF A HOPKINS SONNET IS ALLITERATIVE IN MORE THAN*/
/*HALF THE LINES */

/*SET UP PROBLEM CONTROL AND DEFINE VARIABLE TYPES */
PROB: PROCEDURE OPTIONS(MAIN);
DECLARE   LINE CHAR(81) VARYING,
          LIST CHAR(80) VARYING INITIAL(''),
          LETTER CHAR(1),
          WORD CHAR(80) VARYING,
          REST CHAR(80) VARYING,
          (LETCT, ALLTCT, LINECT) FIXED INITIAL(0),
          (I, J, K, L, M, N) FIXED;

/*WHEN NO MORE LINES TO READ, GO TO RULE OUT */
ON ENDFILE (SYSIN) GO TO CUT;
/*READ A LINE OF POETRY, UP TO 80 COLUMNS PER CARD */
READ: GET EDIT (LINE) (A(80));
/*PRINT THE LINE AFTER DOUBLE SPACING */
      PUT EDIT (LINE) (SKIP(2),A);

LINE=LINE || ' ';

/*LOOP TO DELETE ALL PUNCTUATION */
DELPUNC: L=VERIFY(LINE,'ABCDEFGHIJKLMNOPQRSTUVWXYZ -''');
         IF L=0
         THEN DO;  LINE=SUBSTR(LINE,1,L-1) || SUBSTR(LINE,L+1);
                   GO TO DELPUNC;
                   END;

HYPHEN:  M=INDEX(LINE,'-');
         IF M=0
         THEN DO;  LINE=SUBSTR(LINE,1,M-1) || ' ' || SUBSTR(LINE,M+1);
                   GO TO HYPHEN;
                   END;
LINE=LINE || ' ';

/*LOOP TO ANALYZE ONE FULL LINE FOR ALLITERATION */
/*ISOLATE FIRST WORD AND ITS FIRST LETTER; DELETE WORD FROM LINE */
START:   I=INDEX(LINE,' ');
         IF I=0
         THEN LINELOOP: DO;  IF I=1
                   THEN LINE=SUBSTR(LINE,I+1);
                   N=INDEX(LINE,' ');
                   WORD=SUBSTR(LINE,1,N-1);
                   LINE=SUBSTR(LINE,N);
                   LETTER=SUBSTR(WORD,1,1);

/*IS FIRST LETTER A VOWEL, NOT A CONSONANT? */
/*IF A VOWEL, RETURN TO RULE START; IF A CONSONANT, PROCEED */
                   IF (LETTER='A') | (LETTER='E') |
                      (LETTER='O') | (LETTER='I') |
                      (LETTER='U')
                   THEN GO TO START;

/*PUT WORD ON LIST; ADD TO LETCT */
                   AGAIN: LIST=LIST || ' ' || WORD;
                          LETCT=LETCT+1;

/*IF WORD FOUND, DELETE FROM LINE AND RETURN TO RULE AGAIN */
/*LOOP TO FIND OTHER WORDS WITH SAME FIRST LETTER */
                   J=INDEX(LINE,' ' || LETTER);
                   IF J=0
                   THEN DO; REST=SUBSTR(LINE,J+1);
                            K=VERIFY(REST,
                            'ABCDEFGHIJKLMNOPQRSTUVWXYZ''');
                            WORD=SUBSTR(REST,1,K-1);
                            LINE=SUBSTR(LINE,1,J-1) ||
                            SUBSTR(REST,K);
                            GO TO AGAIN;
                            END;
```

58

```
/*IF NOT, SEE IF LETCT GREATER THAN 1 */
/*IF SO, ALLITERATION FOUND; LOOP TO INCREMENT ALLITCT AND PRINT LIST OF WORDS*/
        IF LETCT>1
           THEN DO: ALLITCT=ALLITCT+1;
                PUT EDIT (LIST) (SKIP,A);
                END;

/*DELETE LIST OF WORDS; SET LETCT TO ZERO; RETURN TO RULE START */
           LIST='';
           LETCT=0;
           GO TO START;
           END LINELOOP;

/*DOES LINE CONTAIN ALLITERATION? IF SO, INCREMENT LINECT */
        IF ALLITCT>0
           THEN LINECT=LINECT+1;
/*RESET ALLIT TO ZERO; READ ANOTHER LINE */
           ALLITCT=0;
           GO TO READ;

/*ARE MORE THAN HALF THE LINES ALLITERATIVE? */
/*PRINT APPROPRIATE MESSAGES AND STOP */
OUT: PUT EDIT ('NUMBER OF ALLITERATIVE LINES = ',LINECT)  (SKIP (2),A,F(2));
        IF LINECT>7
        THEN PUT EDIT ('HOPKINS ALLITERATION SHOWN') (SKIP,A);
        ELSE PUT EDIT ('HOPKINS ALLITERATION TEST FAILED') (SKIP,A);
        END PROB;
```

FIGURE 16. A PL/I program for the Hopkins alliteration problem.

Given the INDEX procedure, pattern matching in ALGOL68 resembles in principle the PL/I process. The equivalent rules are as follows:

$$I: = \text{INDEX (LINE, " ")};$$

$$\text{'IF' } I \neq 1 \text{ 'THEN' WORD}: = \text{LINE } [1:I - 1];$$

$$\text{LINE}: = \text{LINE } [I + 1: \text{'UPB' LINE}];$$

$$\text{LETTER}: = \text{WORD } [1];$$

As in PL/I, the first rule determines the numerical character position of the first space encountered in scanning a line of poetry from front to back, normally behind the first word. If there is a word in LINE, the value of INDEX will not be 1 (in ALGOL68, 'IF' $I \neq 1$); and the word and its first letter can then be isolated. If I is equal to 1, the space is the first character found in LINE; and no word can be determined. The newly defined string WORD contains all characters from the first through position $I - 1$, the numeric position of the last letter in the word (immediately preceding the space). To delete the word from the line, the string called LINE is reconstituted in the third rule, beginning with the character behind the space (the $I + 1$ position) and running to the end of LINE, denoted by the ALGOL68 expression 'UPB'—the upper bound (or end) of the string. The next rule finds the first letter of WORD and puts it in a string called LETTER.

59

The next rule in the ALGOL68 program (Figure 17, line 77) checks to see if the word begins with a vowel and is, therefore, not a candidate for alliteration. Assuming the computer has found a word with an initial consonant, later rules look for other words starting with the same letter and add to appropriate counters. Although the ALGOL68 terminology and expressions differ from their PL/I equivalents, the overall design of this particular solution is identical in both languages. Rules to read cards and write them on the printer include the GET and PRINT instructions; the term NEWLINE appearing twice in the output rule OUT produces a blank line each time it appears—in effect, skips two lines here before printing a line. Comments are noted in ALGOL68 programs in rules begun with the special symbol, 'C.' In most cases, rule and variable names in this solution are identical to their equivalents in the SNOBOL4 and PL/I programs.

Solutions to the Hopkins alliteration problem in all three languages produce the same output (Figure 18). Below each line of Hopkins' sonnet, the computer lists the words in the line starting with the same consonant. The algorithm calls for treating elements of hyphenated compounds, a common stylistic feature in Hopkins, as separate words. Consequently, the programs pick out the extensive repetition of the "w" sound in lines 2 and 3, including the two hyphenated forms, "wind-walks" and "wilful-wavier."

The machine also identifies several dubious alliterative pairs, such as "two" and "they" in the twelfth line. Because the algorithm only requires inspection of the first letter of each word, it recognizes no difference between the sounds of "t" and "th." Since every candidate for alliteration is printed for the scholar's critical inspection, however, he can cull out such erroneous findings and adjust the final count of alliterative lines as appropriate. As it happens, line 12 is also alliterative with the "w" sound, so that the final count remains correct; all lines contain at least one repetitive consonantal sound. The computer ends each program by printing this count and the message denoting heavy alliteration in the Hopkins poem. The scholar has all the information discovered by the machine summarily presented for him in a clear, readable form.

I have no intention of teaching computer programming in this book. Solutions to the Hopkins alliteration problem in three programming languages have been presented to show how an algorithm in flowchart form becomes a computer program. They suggest the various ways that these particular text-processing languages can solve a literary problem. As noted earlier, the decision about the best programming language for literary computing is a complicated one. Two main factors will determine

```
ALLITERATION
'WITH' EXTRAOPS,STRINGPLUS 'FROM' :LIB.EXTLIB
'BEGIN'
'C' AN ALGOL68R PROGRAM TO SEE IF A HOPKINS SONNET IS
   ALLITERATIVE IN MORE THAN HALF THE LINES

        DEFINE VARIABLE TYPES     'C'

'CHARPUT' INCHANNEL;
[1:81] 'CHAR' CARD;
'STRING' LINE,LIST:="",WORD,REST;
'CHAR' LETTER;
'INT' I,J,K,LETCT:=0,ALLITCT:=0,LINECT:=0;


'PROC' INDEX = ('STRING' S,P) 'INT';
'C' THIS PROCEDURE FINDS THE FIRST OCCURRENCE OF THE STRING
   P IN THE STRING S. IT LEAVES AS RESULT THE CHARACTER POSITION
   OF THE FIRST CHARACTER OF P. IF THERE IS NO OCCURRENCE THEN
   IT RETURNS 0 'C'
('INT' IND:=0;
   'FOR' I 'TO' ('UPB' S-'UPB' P + 1) 'DO'
      'FOR' J 'TO' 'UPB' P 'WHILE' S[I+J-1]=P[J] 'DO'
         'IF' J='UPB' P 'THEN' IND:=I;'GOTO' FOUND 'FI';

FOUND:IND );


'PROC' DELETE = ('STRING' S,A) 'STRING';
'C' THIS PROCEDURE DELETES ALL PUNCTUATION AND TREATS
   HYPHENATED COMPOUNDS AS TWO WORDS  'C'
('INT' P:=1;'STRING' NEW;
   'FOR' I 'TO' 'UPB' S 'DO'
      ('IF' INDEX(A,S[I])=0 'THEN'
         NEW 'PLUS' S[P:I-1],P:=I+1 'FI');
NEW 'PLUS' S[P:'UPB' S]);


'PROC' DELPUNC = ('STRING' S) 'STRING';
'C' THIS PROCEDURE CHECKS FOR DOUBLE SPACES BETWEEN WORDS AND
   DELETES THEM. THE RESULT LEAVES ONE SPACE BETWEEN WORDS  'C'
('STRING' ALPHA=("ABCDEFGHIJKLMNOPQRSTUVWXYZ- ");
'STRING' CLEAN,COMPACT:="";
'INT' J:=1,P:=1;
CLEAN:=DELETE(S,ALPHA);
'WHILE' INDEX(CLEAN," ")#0 'DO'
   (P:=INDEX(CLEAN," ");
      COMPACT 'PLUS' CLEAN[J:P];CLEAN[P]:=CLEAN[P+1]:="*";J:=P+2);
COMPACT:=COMPACT+CLEAN[J:'UPB' CLEAN]+" ");


OPEN(INCHANNEL,FILE READER,1);

READ('CLEAR' CARD;
'C' READ A LINE OF POETRY, UP TO 80 COLUMNS PER CARD 'C'
GET(INCHANNEL,(NEWLINE,CARD[1:80]));
'C' WHEN LINE CONTAINS "****" IN COLUMNS 1 TO 4, GO TO
   RULE OUT 'C'
'IF' CARD[1:4]="****" 'THEN' 'GOTO' OUT 'FI';
PRINT((NEWLINE,NEWLINE,CARD[1:80]));
'C' USING PROCEDURE DELPUNC, DELETE ALL PUNCTUATION 'C'
LINE:=DELPUNC(CARD);
```

FIGURE 17. An ALGOL68 version of the Hopkins alliteration program (continued p. 62).

61

```
'C' LOOP TO ANALYZE ONE FULL LINE FOR ALLITERATION 'C'
START:I:=INDEX(LINE," ");
   'C' ISOLATE FIRST WORD AND ITS FIRST LETTER; DELETE WORD
      FROM LINE 'C'.
   'IF' I#1 'THEN' WORD:=LINE[1:I-1];
                   LINE:=LINE[I+1:'UPB' LINE];
                   LETTER:=WORD[1];
   'C' IS FIRST LETTER A VOWEL, NOT A CONSONANT ?
      IF A VOWEL, RETURN TO RULE START; IF A CONSONANT, PROCEED. 'C'
      'IF' LETTER="A" 'OR' LETTER="I"
           'OR' LETTER="E" 'OR' LETTER="O" 'OR' LETTER="U"
      'THEN' 'GOTO' START 'FI';
   'C' PUT WORD ON LIST; ADD TO LETCT 'C'
   AGAIN:LISTL:=LISTL+" "+WORD;
         LETCT 'PLUS' 1;
   'C' LOOP TO FIND OTHER WORDS WITH SAME FIRST LETTER
      IF WORD FOUND, DELETE FROM LINE AND RETURN TO RULE AGAIN 'C'
      J:='IF' LINE[1]=LETTER 'THEN' -1 'ELSE' INDEX(LINE," "+LETTER) 'FI';
      'IF' J<0 'THEN' J:=0 'FI';
      'IF' J#0 'THEN' REST:=LINE[J+1:'UPB' LINE];
              K:=INDEX(REST," ");
              WORD:=REST[1:K-1];
         'IF' J=0 'THEN' LINE:=REST[K+1:'UPB' REST]
              'ELSE' LINE:=LINE[1:J-1+REST[K:'UPB' REST]
         'FI';
         'GOTO' AGAIN
      'FI';
   'C' IF NOT, SEE IF LETCT GREATER THAN 1
      IF SO, ALLITERATION FOUND. INCREMENT ALLTCT AND PRINT
      LIST OF WORDS 'C'
      'IF' LETCT>1 'THEN' ALLTCT 'PLUS' 1;
                          PRINT((NEWLINE,LISTL))
      'FI';
   'C' DELETE LIST OF WORDS; SET LETCT TO ZERO; RETURN
      TO RULE START 'C'
      LISTL:="";LETCT:=0;
      'GOTO' START
   'FI';
   'C' DOES LINE CONTAIN ALLITERATION ? IF SO, INCREMENT LINECT.
      RESET ALLTCT TO ZERO; READ ANOTHER LINE 'C'
      'IF' ALLTCT>0 'THEN' LINECT 'PLUS' 1 'FI';
      ALLTCT:=0;
      'GOTO' READ;
   'C' ARE MORE THAN HALF THE LINES ALLITERATIVE ?
      PRINT APPROPRIATE MESSAGES AND STOP 'C'
OUT:PRINT((NEWLINE,NEWLINE,"NUMBER OF ALLITERATIVE LINES = ",LINECT));
      'IF' LINECT>7 'THEN' PRINT((NEWLINE," HOPKINS ALLITERATION SHOWN"))
           'ELSE' PRINT((NEWLINE," HOPKINS ALLITERATION TEST FAILED"))
      'FI'
'END'
'FINISH'
```

FIGURE 17 (*continued*).

a scholar's particular choice: the compiler languages implemented on the computer available for his use and their capabilities for string processing. If he only wants statistical analysis and has no text to process, a numerical language will suit his needs well. But most literary problems require some character handling, and choosing among alternatives usually depends on local conditions.

The scholar should consider his options with the advice of consultants at his computer center. Maybe he will want to learn to program for himself in one of the languages discussed. Or perhaps, like the Literary and Linguistic Computing Centre at Cambridge, the center will offer this service for its customers. The scholar may have to compromise about software (the programming language for processing his data) as he is

```
SUMMER ENDS NOW; NOW, BARBAROUS IN BEAUTY, THE STOCKS ARISE
SUMMER STOCKS
NOW NOW
BARBAROUS BEAUTY

AROUND; UP ABOVE, WHAT WIND-WALKS! WHAT LOVELY BEHAVIOUR
WHAT WIND WALKS WHAT

OF SILK-SACK CLOUDS! HAS WILDER, WILFUL-WAVIER
SILK SACK
WILDER WILFUL WAVIER

MEAL-DRIFT MOULDED EVER AND MELTED ACROSS SKIES?
MEAL MOULDED MELTED

I WALK, I LIFT UP, I LIFT UP HEART, EYES,
LIFT LIFT

DOWN ALL THAT GLORY IN THE HEAVENS TO GLEAN OUR SAVIOUR;
THAT THE TO
GLORY GLEAN

AND, EYES, HEART, WHAT LOOKS, WHAT LIPS YET GAVE YOU A
WHAT WHAT
LOOKS LIPS
YET YOU

RAPTUROUS LOVE'S GREETING OF REALER, OF ROUNDER REPLIES?
RAPTUROUS REALER ROUNDER REPLIES

AND THE AZUROUS HUNG HILLS ARE HIS WORLD-WIELDING SHOULDER
HUNG HILLS HIS
WORLD WIELDING

MAJESTIC_AS A STALLION STALWART, VERY-VIOLET-SWEET!_
STALLION STALWART SWEET
VERY VIOLET

THESE THINGS, THESE THINGS WERE HERE AND BUT THE BEHOLDER
THESE THINGS THESE THINGS THE
BUT BEHOLDER

WANTING; WHICH TWO WHEN THEY ONCE MEET,
WANTING WHICH WHEN
TWO THEY

THE HEART REARS WINGS BOLD AND BOLDER
BOLD BOLDER

AND HURLS FOR HIM, O HALF HURLS EARTH FOR HIM OFF UNDER HIS FEET.
HURLS HIM HALF HURLS HIM HIS
FOR FOR FEET

NUMBER OF ALLITERATIVE LINES = 14
HOPKINS ALLITERATION SHOWN
```

FIGURE 18. A sample printout from one of the Hopkins alliteration programs.

likely to have to do about hardware, especially regarding the input problems with literary materials. Even so, in recent years programming for literary analysis has been greatly improved. In most cases, processing the text with a computer program will be less troublesome than getting it into the machine easily with all its characteristics intact.

More important for our purposes than details of specific programming languages is the algorithmic approach to problem solving. For literary data processing, the scholar must become accustomed to analyzing what he wants to do into a series of logical steps. No matter who does the programming, a flowchart for a solution must take into account the structure of the materials when they are put into machine-readable form. For instance, the Hopkins program would not work in its present form if the poem were submitted one word per card; the algorithm depends on reading and processing a line at a time. Given this data structure, the processing operations, including loops and branches, are set down in the form of a flowchart. Analyzing the problem in this way minimizes the chances of trouble in programming. All that remains is writing the program to translate the flowchart into the specific instructions of a particular computer language.

The algorithmic approach to computer processing precedes programming and is normally independent of it. As we now turn to detailed discussion of different ways the computer has been applied to literary tasks, we shall think in terms of algorithms and look at flowcharts for various applications. If the scholar can learn to define his literary problem in this logical way, he will be thinking in terms applicable to computer solution. He can make the computer into a powerful tool for assisting him. Given materials in a form it understands and instructions about what to do with them, this accurate and speedy electronic machine awaits a chance to be of service to literary research.

FOR FURTHER READING

Boillot, Michel, and Lister W. Horn. *BASIC*. St. Paul, Minn.: West Publishing Co., 1976.

A new programming guide to the BASIC language designed for self-instruction. Included are features for character handling and analysis of errors a user is likely to make in learning the language.

Farringdon, Michael. "Natural Language Data Processing with AL-GOL68." *The Computer in Literary and Linguistic Studies*. Ed. Alan Jones and R. F. Churchhouse. Cardiff: University of Wales Press, 1976. Pp. 1–7.

The easiest-to-follow discussion in print of the features of ALGOL68 appropriate for text processing, illustrated by several small examples. Farringdon is a computer scientist with the rare ability to appreciate problems in the humanities and apply computing concepts to them that humanists can understand.

Gimpel, J. F. *Algorithms in SNOBOL4*. New York: John Wiley and Sons, 1976.

Hefty handbook of information and useful algorithms in SNOBOL4 for all kinds of applications. Included are routines for character conversion from uppercase to lowercase, formating of paragraphs, and hyphenation of English text.

Griswold, R. E., and M. T. Griswold. *A SNOBOL4 Primer*. Englewood Cliffs, N.J.: Prentice-Hall, Inc., 1973.

A SNOBOL4 programming text written for the novice. Unfortunately it omits some features of the language such as methods of alphabetizing words often needed in humanities problems.

Griswold, R. E., J. T. Poage, and I. P. Polonsky. *The SNOBOL4 Programming Language*. 2nd ed. Englewood Cliffs, N.J.: Prentice-Hall, Inc., 1971.

Complete programmer's reference guide, including useful techniques for word processing like alphabetization and word counting but hard for the beginner to follow.

Learner, A., and A. J. Powell. *An Introduction to ALGOL68 Through Problems*. London: Macmillan Press, 1974.

The best programming guide available for ALGOL68 but still very difficult for the new programmer not accustomed to thinking in mathematical terms.

McCammon, Mary. *Understanding FORTRAN*. New York: Thomas Y. Crowell Co., 1968.

One of innumerable introductions to FORTRAN IV emphasizing numerical calculation. Its distinguishing feature is a detailed comparison of FORTRAN dialects available on a variety of American computers.

Shortt, Joseph, and Thomas C. Wilson. *Problem Solving and the Computer: A Structured Concept with PL/I (PL/C)*. Reading, Mass.: Addison-Wesley Publishing Co., 1976.

A recent PL/I programming textbook distinguished from a host of others by its approach to problem solving with procedures and a long chapter devoted to character handling with well-chosen examples.

Tanenbaum, Andrew S. "A Tutorial on ALGOL68." *Computing Surveys*, 8 (1976), 155–90.

Intended as a readable introduction to the complete features of the language. Recommended for the beginner after Farringdon's article for fuller understanding before tackling the Learner and Powell programming text.

Wexelblat, Richard L., ed. *History of Programming Languages*. New York: Academic Press, 1981.

The edited papers with transcripts of question-and-answer sessions of an Association for Computing Machinery SIGPLAN conference on the history of major programming languages, including FORTRAN, BASIC, PL/I, SNOBOL, and the ALGOL dialects. Although much is technical, pioneer developers of each language discuss its special features, weaknesses, and contributions to the evolving family of programming languages, which many beginning programmers will find enlightening.

Wyatt, James L. "SNOBOL4 Applications in Natural Language Research." *SIGLASH Newsletter*, 8, Nos. 2–3 (April-June 1975), 12–21.

Similar to Farringdon's article for ALGOL68, presentation of some features of SNOBOL4 appropriate for literary and linguistic processing illustrated with the results from thirteen diverse projects, most of them programmed by students with only a few weeks of instruction in the language.

PART II

Computers in Literary Research

CHAPTER 4

Concordances

IT SEEMS APPROPRIATE to begin discussion of specific types of literary data processing with concordances, the oldest and most common applications of the computer in the humanities. Compared to other projects, computerized concordances are today neither innovative nor experimental. Since the late 1950s, the number of authors whose works have been digested and dissected by machines has now passed a hundred; works in most of the modern and ancient Western languages have been concorded. From the appearance in 1959 of the Cornell concordance to the poetry of Matthew Arnold produced photographically from computer printout,[1] refinements have been marked in the actual printed appearance of these works; and the kinds of analyses carried out on the texts have become increasingly elaborate and detailed. Scholars experimented with computer techniques for literary texts in making the first concordances; and through the years the best examples have made an art of the process. In the 1970s scholars have no excuse for producing an inaccurate or inconvenient concordance to clutter up library shelves for years to come.

Because concordance making involves several basic elements of data processing, it is not surprising that this literary application was the first to receive computer assistance. Designers of programs to do concordancing simply analyzed the operations inherent in the process of hand concordancing since the days of Cruden's work with the Bible and substituted equivalent computer routines. In the time-honored method, the established text is divided into individual words, which are usually filed one per index card. To each word is appended its location in the text by title and line or page. After the complete text has been indexed, the scholar arranges the file of cards in alphabetical order. In the concordance itself the alphabetized words are printed along with the location and line of context in which they occur.

[1] Stephen M. Parrish, ed., *A Concordance to the Poems of Matthew Arnold* (Ithaca: Cornell University Press, 1959).

The equivalent data-processing operations include storage of the master text, preparation and alphabetization of the word index with locations appended to each word, retrieval of the contextual passages for each appearance of a word, and printing of the completed concordance by some computer output device. Of course, the process embodies all five elements of a general computer system. Methods for input and output have already been discussed in Chapter 2 for the general case of any literary text. Besides these, there remain three operations essential to a concordance algorithm: breaking up the text into words with appended locations, alphabetizing the word list, and merging it with the passages of context from a master text. Even the merging can be eliminated if the line of context itself—not just a locational abbreviation—is attached to every word as the text is dissected. Although this process seems intuitively more sensible than separating master text from word index, it is usually not preferred because it requires more storage space in the computer memory. Without merging, a line of poetry containing five words must be stored five times (that is, with each word) in the making of the word index. With merging, there is only one stored copy of the line, in the master text file. The decision about which procedure to use will probably depend on the amount of text involved and the availability of large computer-storage capacity. In any case, the computer algorithm parallels very closely the tasks of creating a hand-produced concordance.

While the algorithm to generate a concordance is very straightforward, editorial decisions made before any text is prepared for input will ultimately determine the success of the project. The scholar must choose a suitable structure to represent his text and must decide how the machine will treat variants, homographs, and other tricky problems. Initially he should not begin a concordance without having an authoritative edition on which to base it. Concordances are often large works that represent a sizable library investment; for instance, the one to Shaw's plays and prefaces fills ten volumes.[2] Unlike critical interpretations or biographical studies based on new evidence, they will not soon be redone but will take their places as standard reference works on library shelves for decades to come. If a concordance cannot be based on an accepted text, it is probably better left unpublished.

Having a reliable text, the scholar must decide what kind of context is finally to be printed for each location of a word. One possibility, adopted by Leslie Hancock for James Joyce's *A Portrait of the Artist as*

[2] E. Dean Bevan, ed. *A Concordance to the Plays and Prefaces of Bernard Shaw*, 10 vols. (Detroit: Gale Research Co., 1971).

a Young Man, is a simple *index verborum*, a word index with appended locations and no printed context.[3] Strictly speaking, such an index is not a true concordance, which usually shows some context for each entry. With it, the user must refer back to the source text to check the usage of a word in the novel.

Related to the *index verborum* is the so-called keyword-out-of-context (KWOC) format of the more recent concordance to Joseph Conrad's *Heart of Darkness*, printed out from machine storage on two microfiche cards. One fiche contains a copy of the novel which includes variants between the two authoritative editions. Lines of this text are numbered serially from beginning to end by fiche line. The other fiche comprises an index to all the words on the first fiche identified by reference to the numbered lines of the text. Having picked out the words of interest to him from the index, the scholar refers back to the master text on the first fiche to see them in context. This KWOC concordance is essentially an *index verborum* to a copy of the text which comes with it. The designers of this concordance argue that their format is the most suitable for prose texts; the user decides on his own contextual frame of reference.[4]

Concordances have traditionally been done for poetry, where a suitable immediate environment for each word has been the poetic line in which it appears. Most of the poetic concordances, from Matthew Arnold (1959) to Stephen Crane (1975),[5] have been produced on this principle. Another popular alternative, the keyword-in-context (KWIC) format, has been widely adopted for prose writers and occasionally used for poetry. Instead of showing the entire context of a sentence, which may run several lines, the computer centers the word under consideration in the middle of the page. The printed context consists of enough characters before and after the word to fill out the printed line. For instance, Figure 19 reproduces a page of the concordance to Scott Fitzger-

[3] Leslie Hancock, ed., *Word Index to James Joyce's "Portrait of the Artist"* (Carbondale: Southern Illinois University Press, 1967).

[4] See Sibyl C. Jacobson, Robert J. Dilligan, and Todd K. Bender, eds., *A Concordance to Conrad's "Heart of Darkness"* (Carbondale: Southern Illinois University Press, 1973). A complete discussion of the rationale for KWOC concordances appears in "Report on the Project in Literary Applications of Computer Technology at the University of Wisconsin–Madison" by Jacobson, Dilligan, Bender, and James G. Parins (*SIGLASH Newsletter*, 7, No. 3 [June 1974], 12–14).

[5] Andrew T. Crosland, ed., *A Concordance to the Complete Poetry of Stephen Crane* (Detroit: Gale Research Co., 1975). Incidentally, this Crane concordance is the first one to be based on an American text prepared under the accepted editorial guidelines of the Center for Editions of American Authors—in this case, volume 10 of the University of Virginia Edition of Crane (Charlottesville: The University Press of Virginia, 1975).

RULES

ROSY-COLORED (2)
We walked through a high hallway into a bright / rosy-colored space, fragilely bound into the house by French   9,23
hips, the two young women preceded us out onto a / rosy-colored porch, open toward the sunset, where four candles   14,11

ROT-GUT (1)
the prowler came there, and Ed Legros and James B. / ("Rot-Gut") Ferret and the De Jongs and Ernest Lilly—they   75,1

ROT-GUT (1)
the prowler came there, and Ed Legros and James B. / ("Rot-Gut") Ferret and the De Jongs and Ernest Lilly—they case   75,1

ROTOGRAVURE (1)
expression had looked out at me from many / rotogravure pictures of the sporting life at Asheville and Hot   22,27

ROTTEN (2)
reducing. clicked a button on one man's coat. / "rotten drive," I protested. "Either you ought to be more   71,21
I remembered something odd turned around. / "rotten crowd," I shouted across the lawn. "You're worth the   167,1

ROUGED (1)
shadow, an inordinate procession of shadows, who / rouged and powdered in an invisible glass. "Who is this   110,10

ROUGH-NECK (1)
it vanished—and I was looking at an elegant young / rough-neck, a year or two over thirty, whose elaborate   59,1

ROUGHLY (1)
at the car. "Let's have some gas!" cried Tom / roughly. "What do you think we stopped for—to admire the   147,6

ROUND (1)
had moved her ball from a bad lie in the semi-final / round. The thing approached the proportions of a   70,27

ROUNDED (1)
that most limited of all specialists, the "well- / rounded man." This isn't just an epigram—life is such more   5,16 / 107,13

ROUNDS (1)
of Castile. The bar is in full swing, and floating / rounds of cocktails permeate the garden outside, until the   46,23

ROWBOAT (1)
pants, but it was already Jay Gatsby who borrowed a / rowboat, pulled out to the Tuolomee and informed Cody that a   48,9

ROUT (1)
At first I thought it was another party, a wild / rout that had resolved itself into "hide-and-go-seek" or   96,9

ROVED (1)
to eat with ferocious delicacy. His eyes, meanwhile, / roved very slowly all around the room—he completed the arc   85,24

ROW (6)
gray, scrawny Italian child was setting torpedoes in a / row along the railroad track. "Terrible place, isn't it,"   31,10
Daisy, and it began to pass again. "So," I said into a / row that nearly reached the newspapers—a suggestion that   70,25
window," I began to pass again. "So," I said into a / row looking at the corrugated surface of the road. "If I   112,19
"Go on," Gatsby said politely. "What kind of a / row are you trying to find out in my house anyhow?" "If I   155,22
at last and Gatsby was content. "We isn't causing a / row." Daisy looked desperately from one to the other. "They were   155,29
desperately from one to the other. "You're causing a / row." Daisy looked desperately from one to the other.   155,27

ROWDY (1)
sitting at a table with a man of about my age and a / rowdy little girl, who gave way upon the slightest   118,9

ROWS (1)
I could answer, Daisy came out of the house and two / rows of brass buttons on her dress gleamed in the sunlight.   57,9

ROYCE (1)
over cataracts of foam. On week-ends his Rolls- / Royce became an omnibus, bearing parties to and from the city   109,19

RUB (1)
Sometimes in the course of gay parties women used to / rub champagne into his hair for himself he forced the habit   47,10

RUBBER (1)
on the lawns because I had on shoes from England with / rubber nobs on the soles that bit into the soft ground. I   121,17

RUBBING (1)
sit on the same sand with his head in her lap by the hour, / running her fingers over his eyes and looking at his with   40,2 / 91,12

RENDEZVOUS (1)
Venice, Rome—collecting jewels, chiefly / rubies, hunting big game, painting a little, things for   79,3

RUBIES (1)
on the grand Canal; I saw him opening a chest of / rubies to ease, with their crimson-lighted depths, the   80,2b

RUBBED (1)
by side standing in it. I was going to ask to see how / rubbed when the phone rang; and Gatsby took up the receiver.   115,26

RUDE (1)
I broke out impatiently. "Not only that, but you're / rude. Daisy's sitting in there all alone." He raised his   106,14

RUDELY (1)
Tell him Mr. Carraway came over." "Who?" he demanded / rudely. "Carraway." "Carraway. All right, I'll tell him."   135,17

RUG (1)
on the ceiling, and then rippled over the wine-colored / rug, making a shadow on it as wind does on the sea. The   10,2

RUGS (1)
side died out about the room, and the curtains and the / rugs and the two young women ballooned slowly to the floor.   10,15

RUIN (1)
oak, and probably transported complete from some / ruin overseas. A stout, middle-aged man, with enormous   54,28

RULE (2)
the sister, Catherine. She must have broken her / rule against drinking that night, for when she arrived she   187,17 / 207,11

RULES (2)
after he is dead," he suggested. "After that my own / rule of behavior associated with amusement parks. Sometimes   56,1 / 72,8
her. but I am slow-thinking and full of interior / rules that act as brakes on my desires, and I knew that first

FIGURE 19. A page from the computer concordance to *The Great Gatsby*, produced by an uppercase and lowercase line printer in the keyword-in-context (KWIC) format. (*Photo courtesy of Bruccoli Clark Books*)

ald's *The Great Gatsby*,[6] in which the indexed words appear in the middle of the line, which may contain a maximum of 120 printed characters. Besides the locational information, about 50 characters of context, including spaces and complete words, are printed on both sides of the keyword, the exact number of characters depending on the length of the keyword. Not only is the keyword set off by additional spaces for easy reading, but the rest of the context is usually justified on left and right to fill out the line of print.

E. Dean Bevan, the editor of the Bernard Shaw concordance, argues that the choice of the KWIC concordance is more appropriate for prose than for poetry, which has a natural "organic-line format."[7] The KWIC method presents the word in an artificial unit comprising only one printed line, yet still illustrates enough context to show the word in its environment. Any concordance will be much longer than the text on which it is based. The one-line limitation with KWIC on length of context reduces this bulk much more than printing a complete sentence in prose. J. Russell Reaver should probably have chosen the KWIC format for his concordance to the plays of Eugene O'Neill.[8] His boundaries of context seem to be determined by phrasal punctuation (he does not explain), and often entries take up two lines of print. Considering the enormous size of the O'Neill concordance, restricting each entry to one printed line would have eliminated some of the length (three volumes and more than 1800 pages) and reduced the cost ($87.50 in 1978).

If a string of several words occurs together, as in poetic formulas in Old English verse, a KWIC concordance reveals these recurring sequences clearly lumped together under each indexed word. In fact, J. B. Bessinger, Jr., and Philip H. Smith, Jr., prepared a partial KWIC concordance to *Beowulf*, along with a traditional one bound by poetic line, so that formulaic patterns could be easily discerned.[9] A fine general-purpose concordance program called COCOA, developed at the Atlas Computer Laboratory in England, allows alphabetization of the context

[6] Andrew T. Crosland, ed., *A Concordance to F. Scott Fitzgerald's "The Great Gatsby"* (Detroit: Gale Research Co., 1975), p. 13.

[7] Bevan, p. xi.

[8] J. Russell Reaver, ed., *An O'Neill Concordance*, 3 vols. (Detroit: Gale Research Co., 1969). This concordance is one of the most ill-conceived computer projects yet produced. In many ways, it represents the classic case of poor results to be expected when there is little critical thought given to the project before computerization.

[9] J. B. Bessinger, Jr., ed., *A Concordance to "Beowulf"* (Ithaca: Cornell University Press, 1969).

on the word either to the left or the right of the keyword.[10] This program would also arrange poetic formulas of *Beowulf* alphabetically one after another under the keyword entry for instant recognition.

Linda D. Misek is another of the few poetic concordancers to use the KWIC format for context. Not only does her concordance to John Milton's *Paradise Lost* disrupt the natural line units of verse (for a word coming at the end of a line, the context spans parts of two lines), but she includes more contextual information than just the line location. Her concordance lists the numerical position of the word in the line, the scene in which the word occurs, its speaker, and the character addressed. By including this extra material, Misek intended to "expand the concept of concording to include content analysis of structurally thematic import."[11] Without referring back to the text, the scholar can see which keywords are more frequently associated with one character than with another.

Whether to show context and in what form are decisions dependent on the text to be concorded. J. E. G. Dixon, editor of a concordance to Rabelais, is more of a purist about matters of context than most scholars. In an important article in 1975, Dixon argued that the poetic "organic-line format," the KWIC index for prose or poetry, or a KWIC-like line delimited by punctuation marks are all often unsatisfactory for presenting context.[12] Illustrating inadequate context segments for particular keywords with all three methods in several, well-chosen examples, Dixon concluded that the editor must pre-edit his text into "complete and distinct thought units, regardless of their length."[13] especially for prose texts. By means of editorial tags, Dixon shows how to mark off thought segments before the text is prepared in machine-readable form, even allowing for overlapping of some words in different contexts within

[10] COCOA, an acronym for Count and Concordance generation on Atlas, is one of the most flexible and efficient KWIC concordance programs available today. It is written in the USASI version of FORTRAN and can be run on a number of modern computer systems: IBM 360/370, CDC 6600 and 7600, ICL System 4 and 1900 series, Honeywell 635, PDP-10, UNIVAC 1110. For a description of COCOA's many features, see Godelieve L. M. Berry-Rogghe and T. D. Crawford, "Developing a Machine-Independent Concordance Program for a Variety of Languages," in Aitken, pp. 309-16. Inquiries about obtaining COCOA for local implementation should be addressed to Mrs. Susan M. Hockey, Oxford University Computing Service, 13 Banbury Road, Oxford OX2 6NN, England. It is already being used successfully in many parts of the world.

[11] Linda D. Misek, *Context Concordance to John Milton's "Paradise Lost"* (Cleveland: Andrew R. Jennings Computing Center, Case Western Reserve University, 1971), p. vii.

[12] J. E. G. Dixon, "A Prose Concordance: Rabelais," *ALLC Bulletin*, 2, No. 3 (1974), 47-54.

[13] Dixon, p. 51.

complicated syntactic constructions. In essence, the editor reads his complete text and chooses all the units of context before he encodes anything—certainly a laborious chore. More recently John L. Dawson has explained how to program the machine to sift out complicated, embedded contexts from the tags Dixon has inserted in the machine records of the text.[14]

According to Dixon, the citation of the word in context constitutes the primary *raison d'être* for a concordance. I would argue that finding the location of a keyword in a text is more important than having the actual context printed out; if a scholar is not satisfied with the printed context, he can always retrieve the complete passage because the location of the keyword is available. In most cases, the line of verse usually will serve for poetic texts; and the keyword-in-context seems an appropriate compromise for prose. It shows the keyword inside its immediate environment within the limits of one printed line. Of course, the KWOC principle with an index keyed to an associated text allows the user to choose his own context. Yet it is inconvenient for checking collocations of several terms for thematic associations or poetic formulas. This task needs context to reveal parallel wordings at a glance. The COCOA program even allows the user to specify searches for the co-occurrence of two specific words within a set number of words. Instead of a full concordance, only passages containing these words falling within the numerical range chosen by the user will be printed. In general, the right format for context for a particular literary text should be the one that will best insure the published concordance to be the most convenient and useful reference tool for scholars.

The typical hand-produced concordance usually includes only the index words with context and location abbreviation because the indexing job alone normally takes several man-years to complete. But the computer can produce this kind of index very rapidly. Whereas the Arnold concordance in 1959 required about thirty-eight hours of machine time, less than a decade later the Cornell concordance to Blake's complete writings (ed. David V. Erdman, 1967), involving more than twice as much text, was run with an updated version of the same program on modern equipment in less than three hours. In 1975 the prose concordance to *The Great Gatsby* was generated by an IBM 360/65 computer system in six minutes. Even with several months of editorial preparations and programming, the time to prepare a concordance of moderate

[14] John L. Dawson, "Textual Bracketing," *ALLC Bulletin*, 5 (1977), 148–57.

size today should total little more than a year.[15] By comparison, Ione Dodson Young labored twenty-five years to complete the concordance to Byron by hand in 1965; no doubt, she was correct when she called her work "the last of the handmade concordances."[16]

While the texts are stored in memory, the computer can produce a number of helpful auxiliary indexes and tables that earlier concordances have lacked. For instance, good computer concordances include in an appendix a list of the writer's words displayed in descending order of numerical frequency, and a few print separate frequency lists arranged both numerically and alphabetically. Such lists offer a quick rough estimate of the preoccupations of a writer. Yet frequency lists in descending order are not perfect, since two forms of the same word (for example, singular and plural forms of a noun) normally appear in different places with separate counts. In these cases, the alphabetical list with the words printed near each other serves a handy purpose.[17]

A cursory glance at the frequency list for Emily Dickinson's poetry reveals not surprisingly her heavy reliance on personal pronouns, especially "I" (1682), "my" (755), and "me" (616). Among most frequent nouns are common natural items, like "day" (232) and "sun" (170), and many words of religious connotation: "life" (156), "heaven" (143), "death" (141), "God" (130), "time" (130), "soul" (125), and "heart" (124).[18] The effort involved in adding frequency counts to a concordance program is minimal in comparison to their potential benefit. Indeed, computer concordances produced in the 1970s should not be without some kind of frequency tables.

Another index useful for some authors and types of text is a reverse alphabetical index. Because the computer understands words as strings of letters surrounded by blank characters, it can be programmed to reorder words alphabetically as easily from back to front as in the normal order from front to back. A reverse index makes it possible to study patterns of rhymes or word endings in inflectional languages. Because

[15] Demetrius J. Koubourlis reports that his concordance of the Russian poet Osip Mandelstam (Cornell, 1974), printed in an uppercase and lowercase Cyrillic alphabet, required a total of 2000 man-hours to complete, about a year's full-time work.

[16] Ione Dodson Young, ed., *A Concordance to the Poetry of Byron*, 4 vols. (Austin, Tex.: Pemberton Press, 1965), p. ix.

[17] It should be noted that the alphabetical frequency list repeats the same numerical information included with each word entry (see the sample from Fitzgerald, Figure 19. However, the user can thumb through it more quickly than through the entries printed with context.

[18] Information taken from the frequency list in S. P. Rosenbaum's *A Concordance to the Poems of Emily Dickinson* (Ithaca: Cornell University Press, 1964).

rhyme constitutes an important element of the heroic couplet, it might be advantageous for concordances to eighteenth-century English verse to include this feature, although none of the newly published computer concordances to the poetry of Swift, Pope, or Dr. Johnson have done so.[19] In highly inflected languages, morphological endings come together in reverse indexes; for this reason, their inclusion in Roy Wisbey's concordances to Middle High German texts readily allows the historical study of both stems and endings in the development of the German language.[20] A scholar contemplating the production of a computerized concordance will want to consider the practical and scholarly value of adding a reverse index to his program.

Besides word frequencies, the computer can also tabulate a number of numerical features about a text being concorded. Perhaps the scholar will want to include a count of punctuation marks or calculate averages for sentence or word length. COCOA and the related CONCORD program developed at Edinburgh[21] permit selective concording of words that fall within a predetermined frequency range or begin or end with particular prefixes or suffixes. For instance, this feature can limit the output to all words ending in -ly that occur at least twice in the text; such information may be especially helpful to lexicographers looking for statistical evidence of vocabulary items. Numerical measures like these, not usually expected by scholars using concordances, can be generated with little additional trouble by the computer program if they are desired.

Besides context selection and appropriate auxiliary indexes to accompany his concordance, the designer must decide how to treat different categories of words. Some words, such as articles, prepositions, conjunctions, and forms of the verb "to be," are usually omitted from

---

[19] Michael A. Shinagel, ed., *A Concordance to the Poems of Jonathan Swift* (Ithaca: Cornell University Press, 1972); Emmett G. Bedford and Robert J. Dilligan, eds., *A Concordance to the Poems of Alexander Pope*, 2 vols. (Detroit: Gale Research Co., 1974); and Helen H. Naugle, ed., *A Concordance to the Poems of Samuel Johnson* (Ithaca: Cornell University Press, 1973).

[20] For a more comprehensive discussion of the uses of reverse indexes, see Wisbey's article, "The Computer in Literary Studies," in *Symposium on Printing* (Leeds: Leeds Philosophical and Literary Society, 1971), pp. 22–23.

[21] CONCORD, which shares many features with the current version of COCOA, was written at the Edinburgh Regional Computing Centre in a local programming language called IMP. It has been tested on an IBM 360/50 system and an ICL System 4/75 and described in N. Hamilton-Smith's article, "A Versatile Concordance Program for a Textual Archive," in *The Computer in Literary and Linguistic Research*, ed. Roy A. Wisbey (Cambridge: Cambridge University Press, 1971), pp. 235–44. Further information about CONCORD can be obtained from Mr. Hamilton-Smith, Edinburgh Regional Computing Centre, Mayfield Road, Edinburgh, Scotland. *The Computer in Literary and Linguistic Research* will be denoted hereafter as Wisbey.

concordances because they convey little meaning and unduly lengthen the final index. The scholar chooses which words to put on the list of exclusions, so that the computer will not index them. The KWOC concordance requires no such decision because it prints only line references for any entry; every word can be indexed without unduly adding to the length of the final product. Linguists studying the usage of function words will find a KWOC concordance as handy as will scholars investigating content words for literary themes.

Among traditional concordances with context, Marvin Spevack decided not to exclude any words from his original "complete and systematic" concordance to Shakespeare. It runs to six volumes, costing $320, and 4000 pages, including over 320 double-column pages of entries for "and," "of," and "the." When he decided to republish the materials as the one-volume *Harvard Concordance to Shakespeare* ($45.00), Spevack chose to omit context for about forty of the most frequent English words.[22] Apparently, for the money not many scholars wanted to thumb through all those pages to compare uses of the preposition "of" in *Hamlet* and *King Lear*.

More practical is the excluding of these function words from the indexing process, provided the complete list of exclusions is appended to the volume. The O'Neill concordance, along with other concordancers, has no such list. Only by consulting the alphabetical entries does the user find that "good" and "can" have been omitted, while "bad" and "cannot" are completely indexed. Nowhere does the editor explain or justify these curious and inconsistent anomalies. Fortunately most concordance volumes do contain discussion and listing of words left out.

In 1968, the designers of the Racine concordance in the Cornell series introduced perhaps the most sensible solution for handling exclusions, which has since been adopted by several other concordancers.[23] Their computer counted the appearances of every word, no matter how insignificant, but printed only the raw numerical frequency for the six most frequent function words in French (*à, ce, de, et, le,* and *un*). Other words of high frequency often omitted appear with their count and location in Racine but without the printing of their context. In a third category are the content words printed with frequency, location, and full

[22] In Spevack's *Complete and Systematic Concordance to the Works of Shakespeare* (Hildesheim, Germany: Georg Olms, 1968–70), the first three volumes index the comedies, histories and poems, and tragedies as individual plays. The last three index the entire Shakespearean canon as one body of text and comprise the basis for the *Harvard Concordance to Shakespeare* (Cambridge: Harvard University Press, 1973).

[23] Bryant C. Freeman, ed., *Concordance du théâtre et de poésies de Jean Racine*, 2 vols. (Ithaca: Cornell University Press, 1968).

context. Except for the most common function words, an interested scholar can retrieve the occurrences of prepositions, pronouns, and conjunctions. The editors have picked a compromise solution to give as much information as possible without wasting pages printing these words with complete context.

Choosing the words to exclude can be a thorny problem in itself. For instance, forms of the verb "to be" and other auxiliary verbs are usually omitted. However, some of these forms, such as "will," "might," and "can," are homographic with content words; that is, they look just like them. The scholar preparing a hand concordance has no difficulty separating wheat from chaff, but the computer is not so clever. It "knows" words only as strings of characters and can rarely be programmed to account for nuances of meaning automatically. To circumvent this situation, two strategies are typical. Some scholars pre-edit their text in the input process, perhaps adding a number to the spelling of "can" to mark the unwanted verb. Thus, the computer will treat the unchanged form of "can" as a noun in the usual, full manner, whereas the verb "can" will be handled as an exclusion word. Before the final printout showing the verb and its frequency, the appended number can be edited out.

Combining this post-editing with multiple runs of the computer program is useful not only for separating homographs. Some editors let the machine index all the words fully as content words on its first run. They then manually remove unwanted homographs before a second computer run produces the finished concordance. In proofreading the original output, they may also discover spelling errors overlooked in checking the input text. A misspelling that shows up as a unique form the first time can be merged with other correct spellings of the word before processing again.

An editor can also use interim editing to cross-reference odd spellings and unhyphenated compounds by hand. For instance, under the entries for "eye" and "shine" in the Dickinson concordance, the reader is referred also to the entries for "e'e" and "ashine." The chance to do these kinds of medial editing to make the concordance more useful argues in favor of the need and practicality of two computer runs. With the fast computers and efficient programs of today, the cost of two computer runs (neither requiring much computer time) is usually worth the expense, inasmuch as beneficial manual editing can be done on the interim results.

An editor must also decide for his concordance how to handle textual variants, titles or dramatic speech tags, and hyphenated words. Critical editions of poetry often show several variant words to fill a slot in a poetic line or have completely different, alternative lines. For the concordance to Stephen Crane's poetry, the computer indexed and counted alternate readings as separate words. Under their entries, the complete variant line marked as unauthorized is shown as context, following the critically accepted line. The machine kept accurate frequencies by not counting repeated words in similar lines with a variant of only one or two words.

In both the Yeats and Dickinson volumes, hyphenated words like "a-dreaming" were automatically sorted to appear in two places in the index, under "a-dreaming" and "dreaming." The full citation appears under "a-dreaming" with the second word cross-referenced to it. Deciding whether to concord titles or speech tags in dramatic works is another editorial judgment that will depend on the nature of the text. Neither of the widely known computerized concordances to Shakespeare lists speakers as separate entries. A reader who wants to examine first lines of Othello's speeches can check the play as conveniently as consulting the concordance. In this regard, it is well to keep in mind that concordances are intended not as substitutes for literary texts but as aids to their understanding.

Another optional feature which some concordance programs tackle is normalization of spelling or principal parts of irregular verbs. Normally various forms of the verb "to go" ("go," "went," "gone," "goes," "going") all appear individually indexed and alphabetized. Of course, all these forms except "went" occur within a few words of each other and can be readily spotted. At least two general-purpose concordance programs of the 1960s (BIBCON designed by Richard L. Venezky at the University of Wisconsin and a concordance generator prepared by Philip H. Smith, Jr., at New York University) allowed the user to specify initially not only words to be excluded but also those to be normalized and listed together.[24] Merging together of related forms as the index is compiled replaces later manual cross-referencing. Occurrences of "went" can be printed under "go," and nonstandard spellings can be shown

[24] For details about these programs, see Richard L. Venezky, "Computer-Aided Humanities Research at the University of Wisconsin," *CHum*, 3 (1969), 128–38; and Philip H. Smith, Jr., "The State of the ICRH Concordance Generator," *ICRH Newsletter* (Institute for Computer Research in the Humanities, New York University), 4, No. 5 (January 1969), 1–4. BIBCON, which produces a concordance in KWOC format, was originally implemented on a CDC 3600 computer and later updated for a UNIVAC 1108 system. Information about its current status can be obtained from the Computer Sciences Department, University of Wisconsin in Madison. With the dissolution of the ICRH at NYU in 1969, Professor Smith moved to the University of Waterloo in Ontario, Canada. No information about the current status of his program is known at present.

with the usual forms. With the BIBCON program, for instance, Middle English spelling variants, such as "dette," "det," "dete," and "debt," can be alphabetized under their modern form, "debt." Probably procedures for automatic normalization are more important for concordances of old texts, in order to aid lexicographic study, than for modern authors. Yet they permit automatic listing under one heading of any forms of spellings that an editor chooses to group together. An ideal concordance program might include some general normalization procedures adaptable to individual textual situations.

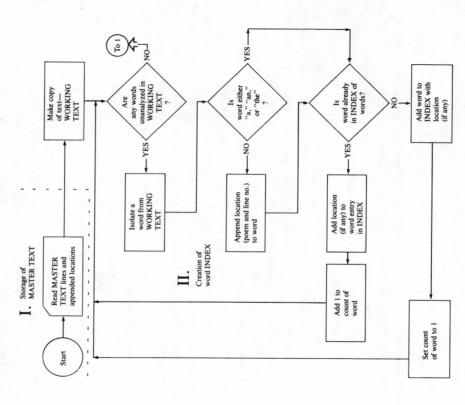

FIGURE 20. A flowchart for a computer concordance to some modern English poet (*continued p. 83*).

Having decided about auxiliary indexes, cross-referencing, variants, and other editorial problems, the maker of a computer concordance has completed the theoretical aspects of the problem. He has decided what jobs the machine must do to digest a literary text and produce a concordance, and he is ready to compose his own algorithms or adopt a general concordance system like BIBCON or COCOA. To concentrate on the algorithmic process in more detail, let us design a flowchart to concord the works of a modern English poet. We shall assume an accurate text and choose as context the line of verse in which each word occurs. Except for the most common English articles ("a," "an," and "the"), excluded words will be listed partially in the manner of the Racine concordance with frequency and location. Auxiliary indexes will be kept to a minimum: two frequency counts arranged in numerical and alphabetical order. Granted that this concordance represents only a basic skeleton with no tricky textual problems, presenting it schematically (Figure 20) will elucidate the overall concordance process, to which modification can be made for more complex cases.

Labeled with roman numerals in the flowchart are the five main computer tasks necessary for concordance making. In this case, one copy of the complete master text is stored for later retrieval of poetic lines needed for printing context (Section I). As they are added to the index (Section II), words have only locational information appended to them. Dissecting the text into words is probably best done a line at a time, since every word other than "a," "an," and "the" gets the same locational identification. James A. Painter's algorithm used to produce most of the Cornell concordances represents a modification of the present flowchart.[25] One large loop both creates the master text and indexes the words one line after another. After each line is read, it is added to a "line directory," then broken apart into words. Gradually the line directory grows to become the complete master text file. By contrast, in the current flowchart, the entire text is stored before indexing begins.

Computer scientists have developed a variety of fast, efficient programs for alphabetic sorting. For this reason, most concordancers collect their word indexes in memory or on magnetic tape, then alphabetize them with a standard utility program package available at their computer

[25] Painter's description of his highly successful program appears in the "Programmer's Preface" to *A Concordance to the Poems of W. B. Yeats*, ed. Stephen M. Parrish (Ithaca: Cornell University Press, 1963), pp. xxix–xxxvii. Recent Cornell concordances were produced by an updated version of the program written in PL/I and including modern input/output facilities with uppercase and lowercase letters. As the General Editor of the Cornell series, Professor Parrish (Department of English, Cornell University) should be able to supply current information about the program.

Concordances

center (Section III). COCOA even permits the user to define his own alphabetical order; this facility is especially helpful if the text is in a language different from English. In Spanish the letter pairs "ch" and "ll" are normally sorted after "c" and "l." The COCOA feature preserves this order, so that *llano* comes after *luz* instead of in the midst of the words beginning with a single "l." Other cases in which the order of alphabetization departs from the usual roman alphabet may trouble the scholar unexpectedly and may require modifying the normal letter sequence of the sorting procedure for his word index.

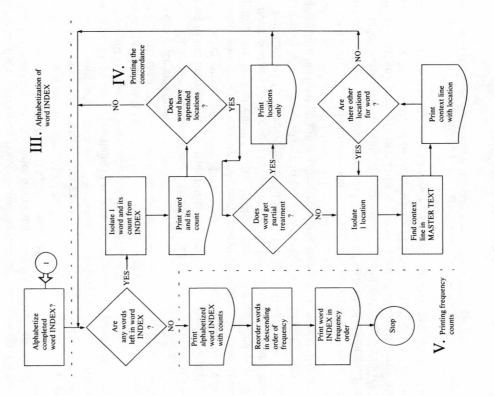

FIGURE 20 (*continued*).

83

Having merged the words in the index with their context, the program is ready to prepare the final output, including the frequency counts (Sections IV and V). We have noted previously the role that computer concordances have played through the years in the development of input/output equipment for preserving the full range of characters found in literary texts. Nevertheless, even as late as 1969, the O'Neill concordance, all in uppercase, contained punctuation deficiencies that had been eliminated in the 1964 Dickinson volume. The editor substituted characters available on the printer he was using for such expressive marks as the exclamation point (/) and the question mark ($). It is somewhat disconcerting to encounter under the entry for "dare" lines of context like "LAUGH IF YOU DARE/" and "HOW DARE YOU COME HERE$" when the situation could have been avoided with other equipment. Computerized concordances produced today will remain standard works for many years to come. The moral is obvious: there is no excuse for them not to take advantage of recent technological advances in input and output so that the finished products will have all the characters present in the original texts. As always, decisions about final output made before encoding the input text will determine the success of the whole concordance enterprise.

In the future, computer concordancing may become a standard adjunct to the preparation of an authoritative edition. Working on a text of the Roman physician Galen, Phillip de Lacy several years ago concorded a provisional text by machine, examined his results, and made appropriate textual emendations. In the process, the working concordance became obsolete and full of ghost readings rejected for the final text; in fact, de Lacy never intended to publish it.[26] However, after consulting an interim concordance to expedite the editing process, the scholar can update his final text in machine-readable form, then publish the critical edition and a concordance to it simultaneously.

Using the same machine-readable texts, it is possible to prepare ad hoc concordances to meet the special needs of individual scholars. For example, someone may want the computer to print out only those sentences containing proper names or a specified list of verbs. Dolores M. Burton's stylistic study of function words like "a," "the," and "this" in Shakespeare's *Antony and Cleopatra* and *Richard II* exemplifies the

[26] Phillip de Lacy, "Editing and Translating a Galenic Text," in *Modern Methods in the History of Medicine,* ed. Edwin Clarke (London: Athlone Press, 1971), pp. 233–37.

84

possible scholarly rewards of a grammatical concordance devoted to these normally excluded forms.[27]

When her concordance to Byron's poetry appeared after twenty-five years of work in 1965, Ione Dodson Young acknowledged the replacement of her method by computers but wistfully remarked that "much pleasure would be lost on the unthinking machine."[28] On the other hand, because of the computer, a great variety of authors who would never have been concorded by hand have now been analyzed; and the number is steadily increasing. Some scholars contend that the glut is becoming overwhelming, that rising printing costs will soon put an end to published concordances, especially of secondary literary figures. Instead, the future will see the scholarly acceptance of machine-readable text on magnetic tape as more useful than a printed version. Through CRT terminals, scholars and their computers will sort through these files to retrieve full or partial concordances or answer related textual and literary questions. As Joseph Raben, the editor of *Computers and the Humanities*, expressed it in 1969: "The very technology that has made possible more and better concordances will very soon be responsible for their death."[29]

The peculiar problems involved in adapting the computer for literary analysis were originally encountered in concordancing. Today the major theoretical and technological issues have been solved. Production of concordances themselves has become a fine art, and the experience gained in developing them has opened other new frontiers of literary data processing. The dubious scholarly pleasure of hand indexing, praised by its last practitioner, has been replaced by the ready availability of convenient new reference materials for classical authors. Only time will reveal whether extensive collections of machine-readable texts and indexes in scholarly libraries will supersede widely accepted computer-produced concordances in published form. Instead of a choice, the scholarly world would be blessed to have both.

[27] See Dolores M. Burton, "Some Uses of a Grammatical Concordance," *CHum*, 2 (1968), 145–54, for a full discussion of stylistic uses of a concordance devoted to function words, enlivened by her own Shakespearean findings.

[28] Young, p. ix.

[29] Joseph Raben, "The Death of the Handmade Concordance," *Scholarly Publishing*, 1 (1969), 69. More extensive thoughts advocating the primacy of "electronic" versions of a text are expressed by Sibyl C. Jacobson and Todd K. Bender in "Computer Assisted Editorial Work on Conrad," *Conradiana*, 5, No. 3 (Fall 1973), 37–45.

Hockey, Susan, and Ian Marriott. *Oxford Concordance Program, Version 1.0, User's Manual.* Oxford: Oxford University Computing Service, 1980.

The standard reference to OCP, the concordance program written in FORTRAN to supersede the popular COCOA program. Compared to COCOA, OCP has many more options; is far more flexible in input, indexing, and output features; and has simple commands written in English.

Howard-Hill, T. H. *Literary Concordances: A Guide to the Preparation of Manual and Computer Concordances.* Oxford: Pergamon Press, 1979.

The fullest discussion to date of the many scholarly considerations and choices faced by the maker of a concordance, written by one of the genre's leading practitioners, the editor of the Oxford old-spelling Shakespeare concordances.

Ingram, William. "Concordances in the Seventies." *CHum,* 8 (1974), 273–77.

A current assessment of the state of the art. Examples show the possible dangers of relying on frequency counts too closely.

Painter, James A. "Programmer's Preface." *A Concordance to the Poems of W. B. Yeats.* Ed. Stephen M. Parrish. Ithaca: Cornell University Press, 1963. Pp. xxix–xxxvii.

Full description of the algorithm for the first Cornell Concordances, widely adopted for later volumes in the series. Although the machinery and programming language have changed over the years, the basic principles have remained the same.

Parrish, Stephen M. "Concordance-Making by Computer: Its Past, Future, Techniques, and Applications." *Proceedings: Computer Applications to Problems in the Humanities.* Ed. Frederick M. Burelbach, Jr. Brockport, N.Y.: SUNY College at Brockport, 1970. Pp. 16–33. The General Editor of the Cornell Concordances looks back at a decade of work and suggests trends for the future, discussing helpful indexes and developments in computer hardware.

Raben, Joseph. "The Death of the Handmade Concordance." *Scholarly Publishing*, 1 (1969), 61–69.

A critical look at computerized concordances at the end of the 1960s. Early forecast of ad hoc concordancing via CRT terminals from machine-readable files of literary texts.

Smith, Philip H., Jr. "Programmer's Preface." *A Concordance to "Beowulf."* Ed. J. B. Bessinger, Jr. Ithaca: Cornell University Press, 1968. Pp. xxi–xxix.

Fine, practical account of concording an Old English text, including treatment of compounds and several methods for printing Old English characters. Description of two forms of word index, KWIC and poetic line.

Smith, Philip H., Jr. *WATCON: A Concordance-Generator Program Package.* Waterloo, Ontario: University of Waterloo Arts Computing Office, 1980.

A readable user's guide to a general-purpose, highly flexible concordance program written in PL/I and widely adopted by many North American universities and colleges. Developed by one of the pioneering innovators of concordance programs, WATCON can handle all sorts of conditions and constraints imposed by different texts and languages.

Tallentire, D. R. "Towards an Archive of Lexical Norms: A Proposal." *The Computer and Literary Studies.* Ed. A. J. Aitken, R. W. Bailey, and N. Hamilton-Smith. Edinburgh: Edinburgh University Press, 1973. Pp. 39–60.

An argument that the word, and thus the concordance, is the most reliable stylistic unit and a call for augmented concordances to include total frequencies for all words in a text and type-token ratios, so that vocabulary norms for authors, genres, and periods can be established.

CHAPTER 5

Information Retrieval: Historical Dictionaries and Scholarly Bibliographies

NEW AREAS of computer application that have grown up in recent years include computational linguistics and library automation. Subfields of these disciplines, lexicography and automated bibliography, encompass literary and philological interests as well. In this chapter, we shall limit our discussion to two kinds of applications that are of a literary nature: the construction of historical dictionaries and bibliographical data files for literary research. In both cases, massive files of material, not necessarily literary text, are encoded in computer-readable form for various kinds of processing that fall into the computer specialty of *information retrieval*.

Often the bulk of material for these projects far outstrips the works of an author being considered for a computerized concordance. To illustrate the large data files common in lexicography, consider the case of a modern medium-sized historical dictionary, the *Dictionary of the Older Scottish Tongue (DOST)* being compiled by Professor A. J. Aitken and his colleagues at the University of Edinburgh. In addition to the usual information about pronunciation and etymologies, a historical dictionary incorporates a selection of illustrative quotations and references to show the historical development of meanings and senses for each word. Normally the corpus of texts from which the editors draw their citations runs into the thousands of volumes. For *DOST*, Aitken reports a selective examination of more than 2000 volumes, at least 200 million words of text. Out of all this text, the completed dictionary will probably run to a few hundred thousand quotations.[1] By comparison, the *Oxford English Dictionary (OED)* was based on 16,000 volumes analyzed by hand over a period of five decades.

[1] A. J. Aitken, "Historical Dictionaries and the Computer," in Wisbey, pp. 3–4.

Two current national historical dictionary projects in France and Italy, both using computers extensively, involve the encoding of thousands of volumes of text into the machine.[2] French lexicographers in Nancy led by Paul Imbs have a staff of thirty-eight full-time clerks to transcribe texts on keypunch cards of nineteenth- and twentieth-century French authors. The result, the *Trésor de la Langue Française*, began to appear in 1971 and ultimately will contain 90 million entries culled from about 1500 modern French authors. The reviewer in the *Times Literary Supplement* noted that these 90 million examples were processed by machine "in as many months as the *OED* required years to compile and publish."[3] Without the machine the *Trésor* could, no doubt, not be completed within this century.

On the other hand, neither the scholars nor their institutions can afford the costs of converting all of this text into machine-readable form for computer processing. In fact, large historical dictionary projects currently in progress (French, Italian, Dutch, and Hebrew, for instance) are receiving governmental support and financial assistance. No doubt a large proportion of the budgets for such projects is consumed by input costs, usually on punchcards or magnetic tape. Practical optical scanning would ease this burden immensely. In fact, the *Dictionary of American Regional English (DARE)*, a smaller lexicographic project being compiled at the University of Wisconsin by Frederick Cassidy, has had success with scanning materials prepared at a typewriter using an ASA scanner font type ball. This typing element includes the twenty-six letters of the English alphabet, the ten numbers, and twenty-five punctuation marks and symbols, all suitable for the kinds of information in the *DARE* files. According to Richard Venezky, a CDC 915 scanner at Wisconsin reads these materials more cheaply than keypunching them.[4] Even so, the sheer bulk of a larger corpus inhibits scanning for the national dictionaries. In general, such massive scanning remains economically and practically unsuitable at present, and input costs remain

[2] For information about the French dictionary project, see the editorial introductions to the first volume (*à* to *affiner*) of *Trésor de la Langue Française: Dictionnaire de la langue du XIXe et du XXe siècles (1789–1960)*, ed. Paul Imbs (Paris: Centre National de la Recherche Scientifique, 1971). Aldo Duro and his associates at Accademia della Crusca, Florence, are working on *The Historical Dictionary of the Italian Language.* See Duro, "Les nouvelles méthodes du dictionnaire historique de la langue italienne," *Cahiers de Lexicologie*, 8 (1966), 95–111; and Antonio Zampolli, "L'Automatisation de la recherche lexicologique: état actuel et tendances nouvelles," *Meta*, 18 (1973), 103–38.

[3] "France's Word Horde," *Times Literary Supplement*, 13 October 1972, p. 1229.

[4] For more details about DARE materials—their structure and input by scanning—see Venezky's article, "Storage, Retrieval, and Editing of Information for a Dictionary," *American Documentation*, 19 (January 1968), 71–79.

an initial hurdle to be overcome for compiling large textual data banks.

Files of relevant text initially prepared in machine-readable form for other purposes may be added to the stockpile of texts to be used for lexicographic excerpting at little or no cost. Although the format and typing conventions used to encode special characters will probably not match the rest of the lexicographer's text, the chances of adapting such a file to lexicographic use should not be discounted. Richard W. Bailey and Jay L. Robinson at the University of Michigan have been collecting materials for a proposed *Early Modern English Dictionary*. In addition to the large files collected under the supervision of Charles Fries in the 1930s, Bailey and Robinson have been able to glean many citations from Renaissance texts such as Sidney's *Defense of Poetry*, originally key-punched by William Elwood at the University of Virginia for other purposes.[5] Similarly, the Italian Dictionary project represents a combined effort of a number of European scholars collecting Italian texts for machine processing.

Editors of *The American Heritage Dictionary of the English Language* had access to the most representative machine-readable sample of contemporary American English, the Brown University Standard Corpus of 500 samples of modern American prose, approximately a million words. Having been selected at random from American periodicals and books published in 1961, the Brown Corpus is made up of 500 samples, each of approximately 2000 words, and covers the entire spectrum of subject matter and prose style of modern American writing, divided into 15 genres from press reports and detective fiction to scholarly and technical writing.[6] At present, scholars at the University of Lancaster are in the process of replicating the Brown Corpus for British prose of the same period. When completed, there will be two million words of modern English prose already in machine-readable form suitable for modern dictionary making, as well as a variety of other stylistic and linguistic areas of inquiry.[7]

[5] Richard W. Bailey and Jay L. Robinson, "The Computer in Lexicography," in *Lexicography and Dialect Geography: Festgabe for Hans Kurath*, ed. Harald Scholler and John Reidy (Wiesbaden: Franz Steiner Verlag, 1973), p. 40.

[6] Henry Kučera and W. Nelson Francis present a complete description of the Brown Corpus and its properties in *Computational Analysis of Present-Day American English* (Providence: Brown University Press, 1967). Kučera discusses its usefulness for dictionary making in his preface, "Computers in Language Analysis and Lexicography," to *The American Heritage Dictionary*, ed. William Morris (Boston: Houghton Mifflin, 1969), pp. xxxviii–xl.

[7] Rosemary Leonard describes the Lancaster Corpus and makes a number of valuable suggestions about the uses of such files for grammatical, lexical and stylistic studies in "Some Possible Uses of the Computer Archive of Modern English Texts," *ALLC Bulletin*, 2, No. 2 (1974), 13–19.

When the dictionary editor has got his file of texts in machine-readable form, he can use the computer as a mechanical aid to editing. As we have noted for concordances, the machine is remarkably adept at separating the words out of a text, making lists of them, and alphabetizing the lists. A problem with this mechanical help, as Aitken has cogently remarked from experience, arises because the computer does its simple tasks all too well. It will soon glut the editor with too much lexical information, which he must sift through by hand. It can readily excerpt every word with appropriate context, but it cannot easily discriminate valuable information from masses of worthless trivia. Because the business of scholarly editing of dictionary entries remains a sensitive, selective, manual task, using the computer to assemble materials for the scholar's perusal may, in fact, slow down the final process. Inundating the editor with all the citations from a given text means work for him culling out the useful ones from masses of dross. The result: uninhibited collection of citations by the computer may impede rather than hasten the production of the dictionary.[8]

Solutions proposed to make computer citation gathering more selective include random sampling or deciding not to include words above a certain frequency, but neither seems very promising. To illustrate the problem with ignoring high-frequency words, Bailey and Robinson cite the example of the definite article *the* in Early Modern English. A historical dictionary would want to feature phrases like "from the Latin" or "in the German." Yet the machine would throw out such interesting uses of *the* with names of languages along with the myriad of other common *the*'s because of the exclusion rule for high-frequency words. In short, discriminating valuable from worthless citations remains the human editor's prerogative.[9]

Granted that the machine can only serve as a mechanical aid to the editor, it can be adapted to a number of what Richard Venezky calls "the non-creative tasks of lexicography."[10] From texts in machine-readable form, concordances can be produced to display words with context for the editor's use in gathering citations. Different dictionary projects have tackled the problem of appropriate context in different ways. One obvious solution is use of the KWIC format with the boundaries of context determined by a fixed number of characters before and after each

[8] See Aitken's remarks in Wisbey, pp. 5–10, for fuller discussion of these problems.

[9] Bailey and Robinson, p. 40.

[10] Richard L. Venezky, "Computer Applications in Lexicography," in *Lexicography in English*, ed. Raven I. McDavid, Jr., and Audrey R. Duckert, Annals of the New York Academy of Sciences, vol. 211 (New York: New York Academy of Sciences, 1973), p. 287.

word entry. Yet as Venezky has pointed out, the KWIC principle works better for context in published concordances for prose than for dictionary citation gathering. In collecting illustrative citations for a word, some syntactic or semantic unit of context is needed, not just an arbitrary number of words or characters surrounding the head word.[11]

In adapting a concordance procedure for lexicography, the length of context need not be restricted to one printed line as in a printed concordance. The computer output can be adjusted to produce index card slips for later editorial analysis—a process pioneered by Aitken for the Old Scottish dictionary. The computer produced a slip for each keyword along with three lines of context, the reference source, and other information, including rhyme words where applicable, in the form of a 4-inch-by-6-inch index card.[12] The Italian and French dictionary projects have programs to provide a similar kind of expanded context, but of many more lines—ten or eleven in Italian and eighteen in French. The French editors at Nancy have this long context for reference but actually do their work with shorter three-line concordances.[13]

Examining the context problem for dictionary excerpts, F. de Tollenaere has concluded that all of these modified KWIC procedures involving a number of lines of context surrounding the keyword are too mechanical; like Venezky, he argues for variable, more or less syntactic units of context. One possibility for texts of limited length is marking prose contexts before computer processing, a cumbersome instance of pre-editing. Even better is designing a computer algorithm to choose context automatically without pre-editing. The program can be based on formal properties of the text and language, especially types of punctuation. number of characters needed, and positions of blanks. Using end punctuation—in English, a period for a full stop (denoted by two spaces after the mark, as opposed to one for a period in an abbreviation), question mark, exclamation point, or semicolon—the computer can decide in most cases on a natural context boundary of a desired length. De Tollenaere reports successful tests of such a program yielding a flexible context six or seven lines long for words in Bernard Shaw's prose preface to *Saint Joan*. Although this length is usually more than the dictionary editor needs, de Tollenaere notes that it is always easier to abridge a context than to return to the source in order to lengthen it. The com-

11 Venezky, p. 289.

12 A. J. Aitken and Paul Bratley, "An Archive of Older Scottish Text for Scanning by Computer," *English Studies*, 48 (1967), 60–61.

13 All of these context problems are summarized cogently in F. de Tollenaere's article, "The Problem of the Context in Computer-Aided Lexicography," in Aitken, pp. 26–27.

puter-generated file will be copious, but having more than enough material is better than having too little.[14]

Often the same quotation may contain several words for which it would be a proper illustrative citation. Sir William Craigie, first editor of the *Older Scottish Dictionary*, devised a hand system many years ago to reuse the same index card several times for different citations. The editor filed the slip under the first word in alphabetical order; when editing for that word was complete, he refiled it under the next alphabetical word. Gradually the same slip was used for multiple words, and needless duplication of cards was removed. Bailey and Robinson have adapted this procedure into a computer process they call "primary" and "secondary" indexing of their Michigan Early Modern English materials (MEMEM). The computer lists words chosen to be primary along with their context in one index and makes a secondary index of all other words occurring in primary citations along with their locations for later retrieval by the editor if he wishes. High-frequency words put on an exclusion list are the only words not indexed in the secondary list; yet they can be retrieved if necessary from the machine-readable text file.

With the secondary indexing, the editors have access to hundreds of other words which appear in citations originally chosen for the primary index words. In the first MEMEM test run, the primary index covered examples and citations for only nine Early Modern English modal verbs, whereas the secondary index contained about 20,000 additional words. By monitoring new words revealed in the secondary index, Bailey and Robinson guessed that eventually the information contained in three million MEMEM slips can be essentially covered with judicious selection of 100,000 citations from the computer file. New slips will be added only if they introduce new or novel words in the primary or secondary categories. The machine's capacity to do complete indexing of materials given to it can reveal to the editor later uses for the same citation slip that he has not even considered.[15]

A computer procedure for information retrieval has been adapted by Venezky and his associates working on the American regional English dictionary (*DARE*). They have taken the 200 million characters of *DARE*

[14] de Tollenaere, pp. 27–32.

[15] See Jay L. Robinson and Richard W. Bailey, "Computer-Produced Microfilm in Lexicography: Toward a Dictionary of Early Modern English," in Aitken, pp. 9–10. The complete computer analysis of citations for the primary index of Early Modern English modal verbs and its associated secondary index has been published on microfiche with a helpful bound guide to the collection: Richard W. Bailey, James W. Downer, Jay L. Robinson, and Patricia V. Lehman, *Michigan Early Modern English Materials* (Ann Arbor: Xerox University Microfilms, 1975).

information about American colloquial speech and built a computer file of them. Associated with each term are its part of speech, pronunciation, definition, geographical location, the type of speaker who uses it, information about its currency, the source of the citation containing it (probably an interview or questionnaire), and a semantic classification assigned to it by the project. After the entry has been encoded into the file, it can later be called back for editing or updating with additional information; or it can be scanned along with hundreds of other entries during selective searches of the file. For instance, the editor might want to see all the terms from a certain state or region. A more complex search might look only for words from the area that are verbs or for words spoken there by young people under twenty years of age. The computer program allows sorting of such multiple fields simultaneously; only those terms filling all the desired specifications will be retrieved for the editor. Venezky reports that the most difficult searches involve semantic classes of words and definitions because the editor may not be able to match his search terms with the ones stored internally with each word.[16]

Information retrieval files seem particularly appropriate for dictionary projects like *DARE* that are based on raw data from the field. To classify such materials, scholars may need to try out many speculative groupings or arrangements; the computer can carry out complex sorting tasks more routinely, accurately, and efficiently than thumbing through a file of index cards. Yet any dictionary file organized in machine-readable form by term or entry with associated information appended to it is ideally suited for machine searching.

Alphabetic sorting, indexing, partial concordancing, and information retrieval are all standard computer tasks that can be applied to machine-readable dictionary materials to offer mechanical aid to editors. Once they have decided on the words to be included in the dictionary, lexicographers are less optimistic about the use of machines in the editorial process itself—separating nuances of meaning or arranging variant forms of a word under their common root. Automating the process of lemmatization, for example, has been tried by computers with only partial success. It would be helpful if the machine could sort all forms of the verb *to have* as they appear in contextual excerpts under their root or arrange all inflected spellings of an Old English noun like *stan* under its normalized, nominative form. Heretofore, this process has been done manually as the editor examines his citations. Aitken remains convinced that the

[16] Venezky, *American Documentation,* pp. 71–79.

computer can help little with this time-consuming process. He mentions one partially automated algorithmic attempt at lemmatization by Duro and his colleagues on the Italian Dictionary project. Two computer readings of the file are required. In the first, each word is numbered sequentially within the running text while it is being indexed for citations. Perusing the index, the editor selects terms to be merged under the same entry. He then informs the computer the sequential numbers of headwords and the numbered words to be reassigned to them; during a second computer run, the machine re-sorts and lemmatizes words with no difficulty.[17]

Venezky, a computer scientist and consultant to several automated dictionary projects, has examined the lemmatization problem in some detail. We have already mentioned the normalization features of Venezky's BIBCON general-purpose concordance program developed at the University of Wisconsin; the scholar can designate before the program is run as many as a hundred word forms and variant spellings that he wants to be sorted together. Because this number of words is too small for any large dictionary project, Venezky was already planning in 1970 to expand the BIBCON facility to handle about a thousand terms.[18] Even this many normalized terms chosen by the editor before the machine begins to index the text will not exhaust the possibilities for a large file of citations. As the machine finds and re-sorts the most obvious terms in its initial indexing, it will no doubt reveal other words for normalization or lemmatization.

In 1973 as computer advisor to the planned *Dictionary of Old English*, a cooperative venture headquartered at the University of Toronto, Venezky projected a more general machine procedure for normalization of inflected Old English terms as a two-part process. The computer would first break up a word into its morphological units, then look up its stem in a list of the thousand most common Old English words. Each entry in this word list would note the usual spelling of the word, show legitimate suffixes that may occur, and indicate occasions where the word with a suffix attached is homographic to (spelled exactly alike) another Old English word. After this automated process of matching morphological stems to their root words is complete, the list of keywords found in the text is printed, along with the various spellings for them. From this list, the editors can check for errors in matching, look for new

[17] Aitken, in Wisbey, p. 12.

[18] See Venezky's remarks in *Computers and Old English Concordances*, ed. Angus Cameron, Roberta Frank, and John Leyerle (Toronto: University of Toronto Press, 1970), p. 45.

homographs, and make corrections or additions to the master word list.

Venezky hopes that his program of morphological segmentation and word matching will provide proper identification of between 70 and 80 percent of the words in the concordance phase of the Old English project. The editorial staff will encode words unidentified by the machine and make other modifications to the word list based on what the computer has discovered. The result will be what Venezky calls a "headword file" of main entries, their total frequency, and a breakdown into variant spellings. Every occurrence of a word, no matter what the spellings, will be coded for source document, genre, dialect, and date of composition. This headword file will become the editor's basic tool for examining variant spellings, checking on dialectal or chronological differences, and selecting citations for inclusion in the final Old English dictionary. In 1973 Venezky was ready to write his programs for word segmentation and construction of the headword file.[19] If his computer can lemmatize at least seven of ten words correctly in an inflected language like Old English, his methods will become models for automatic lemmatization in a future that is not as pessimistic as Aitken envisioned in 1971.

The machine will not always make the correct choice in assigning words to their stem forms. The editor will have to come behind and separate homographs into their different forms and isolate shades of meaning in construction of definitions for the dictionary entries. At this point he is moving into the final stage of his work, composing the dictionary for final publication. Given his files in computer-readable form, he can use interactive computing (man-machine cooperation) to assist this last, most important editing process. At Michigan, Bailey and Robinson have experimented with interactive composition of definitions at a terminal. Calling up a citation slip for a word, they write a provisional definition which is associated with the word. Other citations of the word yield other usages and definitions, but all are associated with the headword in a family tree arrangement. Using the tree structure for storing the definitions permits the editor to arrange the definitions according to a hierarchy of word senses for the published dictionary. In fact, storage of information in a tree arrangement is very common in computer memories; retrieval or modification of the information is convenient, efficient, and easily accomplished. As is often the case, standard computer

[19] Venezky's description of the method with illustrations of the various files appears in "Computational Aids to Dictionary Compilation," in *A Plan for the Dictionary of Old English*, ed. Roberta Frank and Angus Cameron (Toronto: University of Toronto Press, 1973), pp. 307–27.

processes—interactive editing and storage in a tree diagram—have been adapted to fit one of the dictionary editor's major tasks, the construction of definitions.[20]

What about computer assistance in production of the printed dictionary? Two modern American general-purpose dictionaries furnish cases in point. When *The Random House Dictionary of the English Language* was ready for publication in 1966, computer-typesetting methods were not sufficiently sophisticated to produce the kind of printed book from the word entries stored on magnetic tapes that such a large, important project deserved. The tape records were written out on microfilm and reproduced in enlarged form for final proofreading by the editorial staff, but the book itself was printed by the usual method of manual typesetting.[21] By 1969 developments in computer typography permitted the production of *The American Heritage Dictionary of the English Language* (Houghton Mifflin) directly from machine-readable files with all the typographical complexities demanded by the dictionary. For successful microfiche production by machine of lexicographic materials, the work of Bailey and Robinson on the Michigan Early Modern English project has already been discussed (Chapter 2). By this inexpensive means of reproduction, Bailey and Robinson are able to disseminate their great quantities of word information to editorial scholars throughout the world. As emendations and citations are collected, they can be added interactively to the computer file, then rapidly and economically reproduced and sent out on new computer-produced fiches.

Given a computer file of historical dictionary materials, it would be possible to make abridgments or specialized dictionaries for scholarly use directly from the machine-readable source, ad hoc dictionaries much like ad hoc concordances discussed earlier. In short, if his materials are prepared in a computer form, the lexicographic scholar gains new possibilities for editing, retrieval, updating, and getting specialized outputs that earlier, traditional methods of lexicography lacked. The editorial processes inherent in dictionary construction seem particularly suited for man-machine cooperation through interactive computing.[22]

Literary bibliographies and indexes are other reference tools whose production can be aided by computers. These important tools can be conceived as special applications of that large specialty in computer sci-

[20] Bailey and Robinson, *Lexicography and Dialect Geography*, p. 42.

[21] For full discussion of computer aspects of the Random House project, see Laurence Urdang, "The Systems Designs and Devices Used to Process *The Random House Dictionary of the English Language*," *CHum*, 1 (1966), 31–33.

[22] For fuller discussion of the output phase of computerized dictionary work, consult Bailey and Robinson, *Lexicography and Dialect Geography*, pp. 42–43.

ence known as information retrieval, which includes bibliography, documentation, and automatic indexing. Before considering the specific kinds of problems inherent in computer experience with literary bibliography, let us examine a typical data-processing approach to the production of a bibliography. The problem can be schematically presented as shown in Figure 21. First the materials must be put into the machine by some method to create a large computer-readable data file. Assuming a suitable

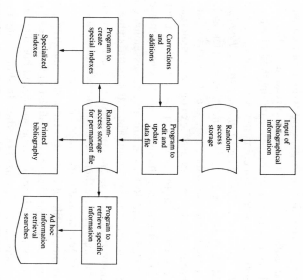

FIGURE 21. A sample flow diagram for a computerized bibliography.

method of input and a means of structuring the materials for useful retrieval have been chosen, the scholar will have his file of materials stored in computer memory for processing. Normally he will have to have a way to correct erroneous entries or to add new bibliographical references to the master file; for this purpose, he will need correction and updating procedures, perhaps by means of interactive editing of the master file at a computer terminal.

Once the file has been created, corrected, and stored in memory, three kinds of processing are typical of automated bibliography: the production of a full printed bibliography, the creation of specialized indexes to the master file, and individual searches through the file to meet the needs of a particular scholarly task. Any or all of these applications can be done by manipulating the master file with different computer programs if the relevant information has been included in the records when they were created. In other words, the same old lesson applies: be careful to design the data file before encoding the materials so that it contains all the kinds of information that will ever be needed for bibliographical searches and printout.

Given this general scheme for automated bibliography, let us examine in greater detail how it can be adapted for the kinds of problems and requirements peculiar to literary data files. Typically in literary applications, the sheer bulk of the information itself poses input problems. Ben R. Schneider's computer-readable version of *The London Stage 1660–1800* is surely the largest, most well-known literary data file in bibliographic form yet compiled. *The London Stage* comprises 11 volumes, about 8000 pages, 3 million words, or, as Schneider analyzed them for character encoding, 23 million keystrokes on an electric typewriter to prepare the text for optical character reading (in actuality, 21 million characters and 2 million shifts for capital letters).[23] Nevertheless. Schneider's achievement is small by comparison with its projected sequel, *The London Stage 1800–1900*, being undertaken by Joseph Donohue and James Ellis. They estimate that the information bank for nineteenth-century London theater will comprise about a million performances, which amounts to approximately a billion characters to be read into the machine. Without the use of the computer, they could never attempt such a gargantuan task.[24] Even moderate-sized projects deal with enormous numbers of entries when one considers having to pay for converting them into computer-readable form, whatever the input medium. For instance, in the late 1960s Burton Pollin's computerized bibliography of criticism of William Godwin and his index of names and titles in the works of Edgar Allan Poe—neither of which would seem projects of insurmountable size—had, respectively, 3379 main entries for Godwin and 5672 annotated items for Poe.[25] Even such modest projects rapidly develop large data files and argue for computer assistance in carrying them out.

[23] *Travels in Computerland*, p. 101. Schneider's roundabout experiences in deciding on an economical input device for *The London Stage* are discussed in Chapter 2.

[24] For a general discussion of the planned project, see Joseph Donohue, "*The London Stage 1800–1900*: A Data Base for a Calendar of Performances on the Nineteenth-Century London Stage," *CHum*, 9 (1975), 179–85.

[25] See Burton Pollin, *Godwin Criticism: A Synoptic Bibliography* (Toronto: University of Toronto Press, 1967) and *Dictionary of Names and Titles in Poe's Collected Works* (New York: DeCapo Press, 1968).

Having decided to use the machine, the scholar must give careful consideration to the design of a data structure suitable for his job. The experience of the Integrated Bibliography Pilot Study (IBPS) undertaken at the University of Colorado in the early 1960s provides "a cautionary tale" about data files and structures, to use the term applied by Lewis Sawin, one of the principals involved.[26] The plan was to encode a sample of all the yearly bibliographies of English studies and then to integrate them into one computerized information retrieval file. Gaining inclusiveness, however, collected many redundant entries, which were included in several listings. The computer was to bring together these identical entries, keep only one entry for each, and merge the subject categories under which they were indexed for use in retrieval. Yet each bibliography had its own format for each entry: not even the *MLA International Bibliography* and the *MHRA Annual Bibliography* use exactly the same format. The editors were faced with two courses of action: either to edit by hand every entry into the same format or to do no preediting and leave the machine to decipher each bibliographic style prior to merging common items. When it gradually became apparent how complex this decoding of different formats was, the pilot project bogged down almost before it got started, with only the completion of the programs to read the *MLA International Bibliography* and assign the subject categories to each entry. Looking back at the project in retrospect, Sawin speaks of "the notions out of which IBPS came . . . [that] continue to have value in themselves"—the ideal of an integrated bibliography.[27] To the outside observer, another lesson to come out of the work seems clear indeed: the conflicting structures of the different bibliographical styles were bound to undercut the noble enterprise before it really got going. The project never received funding after its pilot study, and no literary scholar has attempted anything so grand in the intervening decade.

Burton Pollin had more modest goals. To start with, he had no prepared bibliography to computerize. A synoptic bibliography on William Godwin had never been done, although there was more material than most scholars would suspect. To make his research available for easiest usage, Pollin did a lot of pre-editing before encoding so that the computer could prepare a variety of indexes along with the primary bibliography. He inserted symbols in front of names and titles to mark them for

[26] Lewis Sawin, "The Integrated Bibliography Pilot Study in Retrospect," *ALLC Bulletin*, 3 (1975), 207. Consult the article for a clear overview of the project from the perspective of hindsight after ten years.

[27] Sawin, p. 207.

later indexing and coded each item with a letter according to its type: books, book reviews, articles, necrologies, etc. The bibliography itself is divided into two parts, materials arranged chronologically before and after Godwin's death in 1836. The machine then compiled auxiliary indexes broken down into names, book titles, book reviews, death notices, and even statistics that graph Godwin's rising and falling reputation based on the number of entries for different periods of time. Pollin considered carefully the kinds of sortings that could be done to his materials and went to the trouble to add appropriate editing symbols before data preparation. Once the machine had the complete file, it readily reshuffled the materials into different categories to produce the multiple indexes accompanying the main bibliography.[28]

Schneider's *London Stage* Information Bank afforded many more challenges than Pollin's initial problem. Like Sawin, he started with a standard format, the calendar of performances established for the eleven volumes of *The London Stage.* With the help of an able computer programmer, Schneider soon set out to develop the "Specs," the standard specifications of fields and delimiters that made up the usually predictable structure of each entry. Because entries were more complicated than they originally seemed, Schneider and colleague eventually produced eight editions of the Specs "to make sure that the computer could identify the various classes of things it contained and which it was our mission to make automatically accessible—such classes of things as titles, actors, and roles."[29] The more fields the computer could decipher from an entry without manual pre-editing of an already prepared and formated text, the easier the job of typing the materials for input. The published volumes included several types of shorthand; for instance, if a play had the same cast on two nights, the second one would contain in the cast field, "As 18 Jan," or maybe "As 11 Dec. but King Henry—Gibson." It was left to a computer program to fill these empty cast fields automatically by reference back to the entry for the earlier date, a process dubbed "ladder updates" by Schneider's programmer. After several months of trial and error, Schneider developed a standard data form to express nearly everything that appeared in the text with a minimum of pre-marking, primarily of names and titles in extraneous material that would be treated as separate items in the final index.

Perhaps a closer examination of the design of a more typical schol-

[28] Full details of Pollin's problems and programs are included in two introductions to *Godwin Criticism* by Pollin and his programmer, George Logemann, pp. vii–xlvi.

[29] Schneider, *Travels in Computerland,* p. 53. Complete discussion of the development of specifications for each entry is included in Chapter 3, "Concerning the Specs."

arly bibliography will be helpful to clarify the decision making involved in the structuring of the data so crucial to the final outcome of a bibliography project. Several years ago, with the aid of major research and provincial libraries in Scotland, G. Ross Roy began compiling materials for the first complete scholarly bibliography of Scottish poetry.[30] He eventually decided to store all the information in a permanent computerized data file for two reasons: from this data bank he could publish his printed bibliography, and also he would have the information in a format suitable for selective information retrieval. Initially Roy plans to publish in book form a bibliography of items printed before 1900, over 12,000 in all; when twentieth-century editions are added, the total number of entries will exceed 15,000. A good literary bibliography includes a much more detailed description of each book and other ancillary material than a typical library information-retrieval system contains. In this case, there were fourteen possible, significant kinds of information for each volume of poetry, divided into two types: facts pertaining to the author or editor and an accurate description of the book itself, headed by the title. Of course, not every book required a complete analysis into all categories.

Roy decided to separate the authorial information from the book titles and description, since the authorial data will be printed only once for each poet, preceding his first book citation. The files are linked by means of an author's number attached to each title. Figure 22 shows an early working card for a volume of William Edmondstoune Aytoun's poetry from which the computer record is made. Included in the authorial information are author's epithet (item 2); author's dates, if known (item 3); and notation of appropriate biographical references for poets noteworthy enough to have any (item 3 also). For instance, the first printed entry for Aytoun in the bibliography will note his professorship at the University of Edinburgh, give the dates of his life (1813–65), and mention his inclusion in the *Dictionary of National Biography*, the standard British biographical reference. For less well-known poets, any information that can be included may be helpful in identifying a particular author. For example, between 1825 and 1834 were born four poets named James Thomson who wrote in the later nineteenth century. To identify the work of one of them, an epithet on the title page may be the only clue.

There are ten possible kinds of information that can be recorded about the book itself, most of them established from the title page. In

[30] See G. R. Roy, R. L. Oakman, and A. C. Gillon, "A Computerized Bibliography of Scottish Poetry," in Mitchell, pp. 168–74.

```
SCOTTISH POETRY                              13  GRR.

1  [AYTOUN, William Edmondstoune]

2  Professor, Edinburgh University       3   1813-1865,
                                             see DNB.

4  FIRMILIAN A "SPASMODIC" TRAGEDY, by T. Percy Jones (pseud).

                                    6

7  New York:         8  [J.S.] Redfield.

9

10  1854.         11  165 pp.

12  Blank verse; in ridicule of the "spasmodic" school of Philip
    James Bailey, Sydney Thompson Dobell and Alexander Smith.
```

FIGURE 22. A working entry card used in the early stages of the Scottish poetry bibliography project, illustrating the numbered fields of information collected for each book. (*Reproduced courtesy of G. Ross Roy*)

addition to the usual citation of title, publisher, and place and date of publication (items 4, 8, 7, and 10, respectively—the fields of the computer record do not correspond in order to the items on the working card) are added the editor's name, if appropriate (item 5); the number of pages or volumes (item 11); and the name of at least one location of the book (item 13—the initials "GRR" signify that this Aytoun volume belongs to G. Ross Roy himself). Also included is a final "catch all" category for other information (item 12) to note unique features of a particular volume, such as the format of books printed before 1800 (folio, octavo, duodecimo, etc.) or the notation that Aytoun's poem is a spoof of the "spasmodic" poets. This detailed bibliographical and scholarly material is needed in a literary bibliography which will become a standard reference work and thus must be included in the computerized record from which the book will be produced.

The need to preserve all of this information about each book in standard bibliographical form affected the choice of input devices. Most of the conventional bibliographical symbols and all uppercase and lowercase letters had to be encoded. At least two special characters, the square brackets [ ] and the degrees symbol (°) were needed, as well as the usual punctuation marks. Square brackets may enclose information about a book not shown on the title page (for instance, J[ames] Sibbald), and the degrees symbol is conventionally used in bibliographies to denote book format (i.e., 8° for an octavo volume). In the early stages of the project, the records, copied unedited off the working slips, were produced on paper tape by a Dura 1041 device, which incorporates a standard typewriter keyboard with a paper tape punch. The typewriter had all the characters required for the bibliographical entries, and the machine could be operated with ease by anyone who could use an electric typewriter. The paper tape records were converted to magnetic tape, even in uncorrected form (see Chapter 2 for discussion of error codes inserted in the paper tape by the operator when a mistake was made in punching).

More recently, a CRT terminal with uppercase and lowercase characters and all the requisite special symbols has replaced the paper-to-mag-tape procedure for input. Roy uses the terminal to call up items, whether author or title, from the master files for inspection, correction, and updating. At this time he adds any information not originally recorded in the preparation of the data, such as new biographical information discovered about an author. After updating a particular entry at the terminal, Roy then enters it in the permanent master file of magnetic disk storage that contains all the final edited information. Roy's decision to use two interrelated files, for author and title, rather than one for all the information about each book was made to handle a particular situation—that the author information would be printed only once no matter how many books he wrote. Similarly Pollin coded all his articles by type in order for the computer to index them by categories.

Other projects have also developed special data structures to fit particular needs and circumstances which may have practical application for other work. For instance, a large British bibliographical experiment, called Project LOC, set out in 1968 to investigate the means of compiling a machine-readable union catalog of books published before 1801 in the libraries of Oxford, Cambridge, and the British Museum, now the British Library. The pilot project restricted itself to works whose authors' last names began with the letter "O." Of course, somewhat like the Integrated Bibliography Pilot Study, there were copies of the same book in different libraries differently cataloged; comparing full entries would not match the same book, due to different citations or possible input keying errors. Several schemes were tried to establish a unique "fingerprint" for each book; the one finally chosen bore no resemblance to the usual kinds of author, title, and publication information expected in bibliography. The "fingerprint" needed to be short to save computer storage and speed up the matching process. After some experiment, it was decided that the fingerprint would consist of eighteen characters, "the last two characters on three specified lines close to the bottom of three specified pages of each book."[31] Combining this code with the date of the volume proved to match the same books and eliminated different editions, except for exact reprints with the same date. Accustomed as traditional bibliographers are to examining collations and title pages of old books, they will be surprised that a simple eighteen-character code and a date readily stored and matched by the computer does as well at matching up two copies of the same work. Vinton Dearing, reviewing the LOC Project, comments humorously that "with the rarest of exceptions a Library of Congress card [for modern books] and now, we discover, even a fingerprint [for old ones],

Does as much as Bowers can
To categorize books for man.[32]

According to the project report, the fingerprint, evolved out of a need to have a compact, unique formula for each book that could be easily recognized by the machine, "may well be the most widely significant result of Project LOC."[33] The machine forced its users to think consistently, economically, and unambiguously about identifying their material before its encoding.

When the data file in structured records has been stored in the memory of the machine, it is at last ready for machine manipulation: sorting, merging, indexing, searching, and printing. These tasks represent the basic computer operations of information retrieval. The Scottish poetry bibliography project is typical of the kinds of machine processes that apply to large bibliographical files. Roy's massive bank of data will become the basis for the published bibliography of Scottish poetry printed before 1900. First the computer must merge the author file with the file of book information, each item of which is coded with an author number. In the newly created master file, the record on each

[31] *Computers and Early Books* (London: Mansell, 1974), p. 8.
[32] Vinton Dearing, rev. of *Computers and Early Books*, *CHum*, 10 (1976), 59.
[33] *Computers and Early Books*, p. 7.

author will be followed by his books. In order to set up this data file for final printing, the machine will alphabetize the list of poets and sort the titles of books for each poet in chronological order of publication. For Robert Burns the task will be formidable, since there have been more than 1200 volumes of verse by Scotland's national poet. Additional editing procedures will allow insertion of cross-references for variant spellings of authors' names or pseudonyms; these additions can be inserted into the output data file via the CRT terminal before final printout. Roy's primary objective is publication of a printed bibliography. At present it has not been decided whether to use photocomposition or photo-offset printing of computer printout with the uppercase and lowercase character set. In either case, the full repertory of bibliographical symbols will be necessary.

Alphabetization and sorting by date do not exhaust the computer jobs that may be required in manipulating a data file. In fact, a well-known package of reliable computer programs called FAMULUS, programmed mostly in FORTRAN and implemented for IBM 360/370, CDC 6600, ICL System 4 and 1900 series computers, was written especially for bibliographical applications with a modest number of entries.[34] Originally designed by a librarian to replace manual handling of filing slips on index cards, the FAMULUS system includes thirteen separate programs to create and update files; then alphabetize, sort, search, and merge them; and produce a variety of indexes, such as word lists and a vocabulary of keywords shown in context (a KWIC index). A sample program within the series, called MULTIPLY, expands a compound field of information into multiple fields, all sharing the same remaining information. For instance, a book with two authors has a compound author field; MULTIPLY would make two records out of one, so that both authors could be indexed separately.

FAMULUS records are restricted to ten fields of information, not enough to handle the complex set of bibliographical categories needed for the Scottish poetry bibliography but easily adaptable to a wide variety of less complicated bibliographical tasks. It has even been used to index Hebrew periodical materials with some fields in English and others in Hebrew into the different alphabetic orders of both languages.[35] For a relatively small file of bibliographical material (about 3000 entries) re-

[34] K. M. Crenell critiques the FAMULUS system in detail in *CHum*, 10 (1976), 233–34, and tells where to get information about its implementation on specific computer systems.

[35] See Susan Hockey, Alan Jones, and George Mandel, "Indexing Hebrew Periodicals with the Aid of the FAMULUS Documentation System," in Jones and Churchhouse, pp. 38–46.

quiring the usual sorts of analysis, the FAMULUS system looks especially promising because of its implementation in FORTRAN on widely used computers and its repertoire of standard information retrieval functions.

Perhaps the most common application associated with computer processing of information organized into categories is selective information retrieval. The Scottish poetry bibliography and both *London Stage* projects are planned to be permanent repositories of information from which scholars can request specialized bibliographical or dramatic searches and printout. The computer can carry out complicated searchings and orderings on machine-readable files that are cumbersome to do with a box of index cards, awkward with the eleven volumes of the *London Stage 1660–1800*, and virtually impossible with the bulk of its proposed nineteenth-century descendant.

With the Scottish poetry project, up to eleven different fields can be queried; the complete list of possibilities breaks down as follows:

(1) Author
(2) Title of book
(3) Publisher
(4) Place of publication
(5) Printer
(6) Place of printing
(7) Editor
(8) Epithet
(9) Comment
(10) Library that has the book
(11) Date of publication

To retrieve a particular kind of information, a "search specification" punchcard is prepared and run with the sorting program to query the entire data file. The card defines the fields and the specific information within the fields that are to be compared in passing through the file. For example, only one request card is needed to ask for a complete listing of the poetical works of Robert Burns; after the sorting, over 1200 entries would be printed out in bibliographical format on the uppercase and lowercase printer. Three search fields—epithet, comment, and dates—need further explanation. In general, epithets are either occupations or place names associated with the authors. A search for "minister" in this field would find all authors whose epithets identified them as clergymen, whereas requesting the town of Dumfries in this field would retrieve books by authors whose epithets included the name of the town. The comment field can be used for names of persons other than author, editor, publisher, or printer. A person searching for a preface by a specific person might look for his name in this "catch all" field of information, where authors of prefaces would be added. The date field permits searching for single or inclusive dates. A scholar can request the program to extract all the books published in one year, or if he wants all entries of Scottish poetry published in the 1820s, he can query the date field for all books published from 1820 through 1829.

In addition to such detailed queries involving only one data field, a search specification can combine several categories to delimit, or specify more closely, the books desired. The sorting program could find all editions of Burns' poetry printed in London between 1800 and 1835. This complicated request requires multiple sorting in three data fields as follows: Robert Burns as author, London as place of printing, and the inclusive years 1800–1835 as the date. Only those books meeting all three of these criteria would be matched.

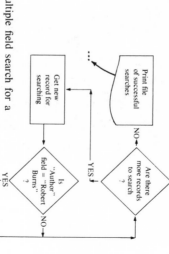

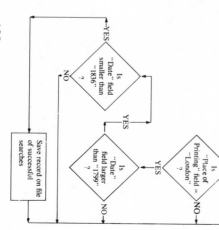

FIGURE 23. A flowchart for a multiple field search for a Robert Burns bibliographical entry printed in London between 1800 and 1835.

Multiple searches of this type are central to information retrieval and can be schematically presented in flowchart form for the analysis of one book entry (Figure 23). Note that such a search involves a series of tests of different fields of data which can only be answered with a "Yes" or a "No," a binary choice appropriate to a binary device like the computer. Whenever the answer to any question is "No," the whole bibliographical record cannot fulfill the search specifications, and another record is tried. To find a date within the inclusive range 1800–1835, two criteria must be tested separately: is the date both greater than 1799 and also less than 1836? If so, it is within the proper span of years; otherwise, it is not wanted. In general, the criteria for a search of this kind can be worded using the English expressions *and*, *or*, and *not*, familiar in logic as *Boolean* operations. The Burns query can be stated as a series of *and's* as follows: if an entry has Burns as author *and* London as place of printing *and* a date within the years 1800–1835, then it meets the demands of the search. Any request which can be put in such a form can be searched by a competent information-retrieval program.

For another illustration with Scottish poetry, bibliographical entries containing the same name in different fields can be recorded together. In order to do a complete search for the works of William Edmondstoune Aytoun, the requester would specify that the program pick up Aytoun's name in any of the author, editor, publisher, or comment fields. In Boolean terms, if any author *or* editor *or* publisher *or* comment entry contains Aytoun's name, the search has been successful. It is also possible to list multiple entries within one category, such as looking for books published by both T. Cadell in Edinburgh and T. Cox in London (in Boolean language, the publisher field must contain T. Cadell *and* T. Cox with proper addresses). Indeed, the computer's ability to do sophisticated sortings of multiple categories represents one of its great powers for selective information retrieval. A well-designed retrieval procedure should permit a maximum of flexibility and complexity in the kinds of searches it can perform.

At present, in literary studies the significant bibliographical projects have adapted the usual machine abilities to sort, search, and alphabetize to their specialized text files. It is perhaps fitting to mention in closing some of the more complicated kinds of programs that have been discussed by Gerard Salton, a recognized leader in information retrieval, that may have application in literary work. Salton has been primarily concerned with automatic text analysis and document retrieval of scientific materials. His well-known package of programs, called the SMART system, works with unedited English abstracts of scientific articles and descriptive search requests and attempts by combining a series of programs to retrieve relevant bibliography items for specific topics.[36] Included in his repertory of complex automatic procedures are stored dictionaries and thesauri to reduce texts to word stem forms and to assign them to content categories. There are programs to do syntactic analysis of phrases and statistical association methods to test co-occurrence patterns of important words in a document. Articles in the bibliographical data file are correlated with important concepts in the search request and ranked in order of most probable fit. At an intermediate stage, the user also has an opportunity to look at some of the preliminary documents found by SMART and to mark them as more or less useful. This interim feedback allows the program to focus in more closely on document areas which seem most relevant to the user.

Test comparisons with other kinds of automatic document finding suggest that the SMART system with its several programming approaches works better than other schemes using manual pre-editing of content keywords.[37] In sum, the variety of practical programs—linguistic, statistical, and interactive—being researched by scholars of information retrieval like Salton seem to offer hope of fully automated bibliographical searches in the future. A lot of strategies are being tried and compared to see which are more useful than others.[38] At present most of this work is concentrated on scientific literature. Let us hope that the most fruitful results can be adapted to literary bibliography before it becomes too enormous and unmanageable for scholarly research.

[36] Salton uses the first chapter of his book, *Automatic Information Organization and Retrieval* (New York: McGraw-Hill, 1968), to present the SMART approach in summary form before covering each aspect in greater detail in subsequent chapters. For several years, this book has been a standard text for courses in information retrieval. More information is included in a collection of papers edited by Salton: *The SMART Retrieval System: Experiments in Automatic Document Processing* (Englewood Cliffs, N.J.: Prentice-Hall, Inc., 1971).

[37] See Gerard Salton, "Recent Studies in Automatic Text Analysis and Document Retrieval," *Journal of the ACM*, 20 (1973), 258–78.

[38] Karen Sparck Jones and Martin Kay provide a helpful overview of much research linking linguistics and information retrieval in their joint book, *Linguistics and Information Science* (New York: Academic Press, 1973).

FOR FURTHER READING

Aitken, A. J. "Historical Dictionaries and the Computer." *The Computer in Literary and Linguistic Research*. Ed. Roy A. Wisbey. Cambridge: Cambridge University Press, 1971. Pp. 3–17.

Reasonable, practical assessment of the computer's role in the production of historical dictionaries from the vantage point of an editor (*Dictionary of the Older Scottish Tongue*).

Bailey, Richard W., and Jay L. Robinson. "The Computer in Lexicography." *Lexicography and Dialect Geography: Festgabe for Hans Kurath*. Ed. Harald Scholler and John Reidy. Wiesbaden: Franz Steiner Verlag, 1973. Pp. 37–45.

Overview of ways computers can and cannot aid dictionary making. The authors emphasize three positive aspects of the process: collection of a usage file, editorial assistance, and production of the finished product.

Bratley, Paul, and Serge Lusignan. "Information Processing in Dictionary Making: Some Technical Guidelines." *CHum*, 10 (1976), 133–43.

Advisors to the *Dictionary of Old English* suggest computer assistance for various stages of the dictionary-making process. They propose a total system design using a minicomputer, a CRT terminal with editing capability, and photocomposition equipment and discuss pros and cons of machines selected for the *DOE*.

de Tollenaere, F. "La table ronde des dictionnaires historiques (Florence 3–5 mai 1971)." *Cahiers de Lexicologie*, 19 (1971), 116–28.

Report of a meeting of editors of twelve important European historical dictionaries to discuss mutual problems and concerns, of interest for the comments on automation being used by several of the projects.

Donohue, Joseph. "*The London Stage 1800–1900*: A Data Base for a Calendar of Performances on the Nineteenth-Century London Stage." *CHum*, 9 (1975), 179–85.

Clear, well-thought-out design of a massive data base, its structure, and input/output considerations—including a new type of bar-code optical scanning and computer output microfiche.

Raben, Joseph, and Gregory Marks, eds. *Data Bases in the Humanities and Social Sciences*. New York: North-Holland, 1980.

More than fifty papers from a 1979 conference at Dartmouth bringing together scholars with large archival or textual computer files. Lacking any overall theme, the conference included reports from recognized leaders—Schneider on the *London Stage,* Kučera on the Brown Corpus, Cassidy on *DARE*—and some promising new applications—Jeffrey Huntsman on lexicography in Plantagenet England, L. D. Burnard on the Codasyl data base management system, and Randolph Hock on the Lockheed DIALOG information retrieval system.

Salton, Gerard. "Automatic Text Analysis." *Science*, 168 (April 17, 1970), 335–43.

Survey for the general reader of research on automated indexing with comparisons of success among different approaches, including Salton's own SMART system.

Schneider, Ben R., Jr. *Travels in Computerland: Or, Incompatibilities and Interfaces*. Reading, Mass.: Addison-Wesley, 1974.

The unsuspecting humanist meets the bewildering world of computers in developing the *London Stage* Information Bank—full, frustrating, and often amusing details about data structures, input methods, and computer programs to set up and retrieve information from the eleven-volume *London Stage*.

Venezky, Richard L. "Computer Applications in Lexicography." *Lexicography in English*. Ed. Raven I. McDavid, Jr., and Audrey R. Duckert. Annals of the New York Academy of Sciences, Vol. 211. New York, 1973. Pp. 287–92.

A computer scientist who has consulted on several dictionary projects critiques mundane applications and suggests promising frontiers for development—routines for semantic analysis and more interaction between scholar and machine.

CHAPTER 6

Textual Editing with a Computer

THE SCHOLARLY PURSUITS of textual criticism and editing, intent on reconstructing accurate texts of classical works, have a long and distinguished history. Yet scholars still work to refine their editing tools to gain scientific rigor, generality, and practicality. In recent years, not surprisingly, there have been a number of attempts to enlist the aid of the computer in the tedious, exacting, and time-consuming processes of editing. Involving large amounts of data to be analyzed, editing is an appropriate humanistic task to utilize two of the computer's main advantages: incredible speed and accuracy of operation.

Most phases of the editing process can use computer assistance. At least three textual scholars with computer experience have broken editing up into six separate steps:

1. Collection of the texts to be compared
2. Collation of the texts to discover variants
3. Establishment of the genealogical relationships between the texts
4. Emendation of the copy text to incorporate authoritative corrections
5. Compilation of the critical apparatus, the table of variants
6. Printing of the text and the critical apparatus.[1]

For each of these generally accepted subtasks, they have suggested possible kinds of computer assistance for the scholar. Some have already been tried; others have been proposed for the future.

At present computers have been little used in the location and collection of texts. There already exists a lot of hand-accumulated biblio-

[1] Harold Love, "The Computer and Literary Editing," in Wisbey, pp. 47–56; T. H. Howard-Hill, "A Practical Scheme for Editing Critical Texts with the Aid of a Computer," *Proof*, 3 (1973), 335–56; and Wilhelm Ott, "Computer Applications in Textual Criticism," in Aitken, pp. 199–223.

graphical information about the location of manuscripts and early printed books. Harold Love notes that computers can be used to expedite the creation of a machine-readable world union catalog, suitable for automatic bibliographical searches. Recent work on computerization of the national catalogs at the Library of Congress and the British Library suggests that Love's idea may someday be feasible.[2] Meanwhile the scholar will continue to find the locations of materials he needs in standard bibliographical reference works.

Among the several phases of editing, textual collation has received the largest share of experimentation by computer. Up to the present, there have been at least eight independent attempts to do computer collation of texts, as well as a number of published criticisms and suggested refinements of the process. The bulk of this chapter will attempt to sort out salient features of the collation problem, to analyze how various solutions work, to assess their relative strengths, and to see how their results may be used in automating other aspects of the editing job.

Theoretically there is no reason why the computer should not replace the scholar at collation. No matter what method is used, collation involves careful character-by-character comparison of two or more related texts. Normally working with two texts at a time, the scholar searches for variations between them and notes these for later reconstruction of an accurate copy text. A computer program can perform similar tasks. Given material to analyze, it can recognize whether one set of symbols—words, letters, punctuation marks, etc.—is identical to or different from another set, store the differences, and retrieve them for final output. Making the computer capable of performing collation, then, involves the processes basic to all computer applications: devising a data structure for machine storage of the material, writing a set of instructions to find differences between texts (the collation algorithm itself), and arranging for output of the text and variants in a suitable form. The user must think through the collation problem in computer terms, so that each of its parts can be subsumed into the specific devices and logical procedures of the machine. The computer ought to be able to collate perfectly, something people have a lot of trouble doing.

---

[2] Love, pp. 48–49. For an early general discussion of the MARC Project (Machine Readable Cataloging) at the Library of Congress, see Paul R. Reimers and Henriette D. Avram, "Automation and the Library of Congress: 1970," *Datamation*, 16 (June 1970), 138–43. Eveline Wilson has described a pilot project to use a computer to decode entries in the British Museum Catalogue of Printed Books automatically into explicit bibliographical fields: "The Use of a Formally Defined Structure for the Input of Data from the British Museum Catalogue of Printed Books," in Wisbey, pp. 209–20. See also discussion of the LOC Project in Chapter 5.

Before collation by computer, the editor must convert the literary texts from the printed page or manuscript into a form which the computer can read and store. As we have noted before, this process is often the most challenging, difficult, and frustrating task of literary computing. Preparation of a large amount of language text in machine-readable form is tedious, costly, and often, at best, a compromise, because many input devices do not have the full repertory of symbols present in the scholar's text. As noted earlier, George Petty, Jr., and William Gibson tried three different devices for their collation work to overcome the problems of input and "found them all depressing":[3] the keypunch machine with special conventions; the Flexowriter, which produces punched paper tape from a typewriter keyboard; and the Mohawk Data Sciences 1181 machine, which produces machine-readable magnetic tape directly from a typewriter keyboard. Both of the machines with typewriter keyboards offered more characters occurring in literary texts than the keypunch machine. Petty and Gibson finally decided that the Mohawk machine was their least unsatisfactory method because it permitted skipping one stage required by the other two: the conversion of cards or paper tape into magnetic tape for permanent storage.

With all three methods, the problem of correcting mistakes made in typing remained troublesome. For collation the computer needs a clean copy in machine-readable form of the various printings or manuscripts. The act of human transcription introduces an error factor that is equivalent to compositional or typographical error in printing; yet it is another step removed from the author's original manuscript. Petty and Gibson finally decided to run their collation program twice rather than to try correcting errors in data preparation. The first run showed that about 40 percent of the variations between the texts resulted from input errors. After correcting these on the magnetic tape, they ran the program again to do the actual collation of accurate texts.[4]

In all of the applications examined earlier, concordances, dictionary citations, and large bibliographical files, the computer works with only one copy of the text. All of the experimental collation projects, however, do text-by-text comparison within the machine; thus the burden of input is compounded, since *all* the texts under consideration must be in machine-readable form. At present, Ruth L. Widmann's Shakespearean collation project has the largest data file: twenty-five editions of *A Mid-*

[3] George R. Petty, Jr., and William M. Gibson, *Project OCCULT: The Ordered Computer Collation of Unprepared Literary Text* (New York: New York University Press, 1970), p. 34.

[4] Petty and Gibson, pp. 34–38.

summer Night's Dream prepared on punchcards with a set of typing conventions and special symbols to indicate capital letters and italicized materials in the original texts.[5] Even this quantity of data does not approach the magnitude of the editing job for classic American novelists, many of whom are being edited under the auspices of the Center for Scholarly Editions. Collations of six printings of a three-hundred-page book are not uncommon. For such cases, the massive problems of input currently argue against computerized collation. It does not seem likely that such major projects will become automated until an accurate and inexpensive form of optical scanning becomes available.[6]

Having decided on editing by computer, the editor must consider the best format for storage of his materials. As usual, choosing a workable data structure may determine the effectiveness of the whole project. Typically the scholar breaks up his text into blocks of data and then tags them with some identification of text, chapter, page, etc. If the machine cannot resolve some major rewriting between two texts, the scholar has the location information associated with the troublesome passages. He can go back to the originals and examine the difficulties.

Poetic material is usually structured into machine records by line. Each complete verse line is coded with poem name and line number. Vinton A. Dearing's early collation project with Dryden encoded one line of verse per punchcard for each of his texts. He then presorted the cards by machine so that all the cards containing corresponding lines in different texts were together; the collation program itself compared all versions of line 1, line 2, and so forth. How the sorter handled situations where a line in text 2 had been inserted between two lines in text 1—readjusting the poetic line numbers in text 2—is unexplained.[7] Ruth Widmann adopted the Through Line Numbering System from Charlton Hinman's First Folio facsimile for all of her versions of *A Midsummer Night's Dream*. Lines which appeared in quarto texts but were omitted from the Folio were noted as additions to the Through Line Number of the Folio (for example, line "1384 + 1" would be a quarto line which was omitted in the Folio between lines 1384 and 1385).[8]

---

[5] Ruth L. Widmann, "Computer Collation," *CSHVB*, 4 (1973), 45–47.

[6] In late 1976, I heard that Peter and Miriam Shillingsburg of Mississippi State University were planning a new edition of Thackeray's novels which would use optical scanning of typed copy prior to computer collation. So far, I have seen nothing in print about this work.

[7] See "Methods of Textual Editing," in *Bibliography and Textual Criticism: English and American Literature 1700 to the Present*, ed. O. M. Brack, Jr., and Warner Barnes (Chicago: University of Chicago Press, 1969), pp. 87–88.

[8] Widmann, p. 46.

Unlike poetry, running prose does not fall into natural groupings. One general guideline seems to have been agreed upon by three of the collation projects in prose: use of the physical line from the source text as the basic unit for input. Working with medieval manuscripts, Penny Gilbert numbered each line and coded it at a computer terminal in eighty-character blocks, as if she were using punchcard format (ten columns for identification number, one for continuation, and sixty-nine for text). Manuscript lines longer than sixty-nine characters were continued on the successive cards with the identifiers repeated at the beginning. She then corrected her file with an interactive text-editing program of the IBM 370 editing system at the University of Manitoba.[9] Margaret S. Cabaniss, also collating manuscript materials, decided on lines of text as her units and coded them on punchcards with identifiers in the last eleven columns.[10]

Petty and Gibson chose one line of the book page to form one machine record for novels of Henry James and Herman Melville. But they eliminated line boundaries from the incoming data inside the machine before actual text comparison began. Otherwise, the sequence "Winterbourne-line ending" in text 1 of *Daisy Miller* would not correspond to the sequence "Winterbourne-space" in text 2. Such a difference, a product of separate typesettings of the work, is not usually considered significant in collation. Internally their comparison procedures were carried out on sets of twelve consecutive words of text.[11] For modern prose Petty and Gibson's solution seems practical and acceptable: copying data on input devices from lines of the page but eliminating line boundaries internally so that collation can be carried out on continuous segments of running text.

With the texts in machine-readable form, the process of comparing them to discover substantive or typographical differences between them is carried out by a computer collation program. As noted, a number of scholars have developed algorithms to carry out character-by-character comparison of texts. Some can handle only two texts at a time, while others are designed for comparing a large number simultaneously. Most of the simpler procedures are geared to line-by-line checking of poetry; the more difficult problem of running prose has required more complicated programs.

[9]Penny Gilbert, "Using the Computer to Collate Medieval Latin Manuscripts," in Jones and Churchhouse, p. 106. See also Gilbert's earlier article: "Automatic Collation: A Technique for Medieval Texts," *CHum*, 7 (1973), 139–47.

[10]Margaret S. Cabaniss, "Using a Computer for Text Collation," *CSHVB*, 3 (1970), 2–3.

[11]Petty and Gibson, pp. 16–17.

In computer terms, the collation problem can be divided into three parts analogous to manual collation: comparing two or more versions of a text by matching character for character, identifying variants between the texts, and resolving the variation so that the original matching scheme can be continued. Unquestionably the last of these tasks is the most difficult to carry out automatically. Suppose an author has made a large addition to the second edition of a novel. A person can scan the text for several pages and immediately recognize a return to the original narrative. But the computer must be supplied with an explicit, quantifiable definition of what it is to do. It must have built into it numerical answers to two basic questions: (1) What constitutes a variation between texts? (2) How must it search in each text for an end to the variation?

Dom Jacques Froger and Vinton Dearing are the acknowledged pioneers in computer collation. They faced the tough questions first, although their solutions did not handle some of the particularly vexing questions that later scholars have attacked. When he began his work with Molière's *Le Malade imaginaire* in 1960, Froger was looking only for verbal differences between texts.[12] He did not attempt to encode punctuation, accents, or other special symbols, because the Gamma Tambour ET Bull computer he was using had no way to express them. Most modern textual critics are interested in all variants and would have to add special characters to Froger's practice. Given two lines read on punchcards from different texts, Froger's comparison process moves word by word until a mismatch occurs. The computer then compares pairs of words, looking for an end to the difference.

As an illustration consider the following lines:

I saw my friend in Chicago.

I saw a friend yesterday in Chicago.

The first word of the pair in text 1 ("my friend") is compared to each word of the pair in text 2 ("a friend"). Since "my" does not match either word, the second word in pair 1 is tried; and the matched words "friend" resolve the variation. The computer aligns the texts again and notes whether text 2 added or omitted a word relative to text 1. In this case, we have a substitution, treated by Froger's algorithm as a simultaneous omission of "my" from text 2 and the addition of "a" to text 2. Similarly a transposition of words is considered to be a word addition to text 2 followed after an interval by an omission of that word. There-

---

[12] See Froger's section entitled "La Collation des manuscrits par ordinateur," in *La Critique des textes et son automatisation* (Paris: Dunod, 1967), pp. 130–44.

fore, the computer will also mark "yesterday" as an addition to text 2.

Sometimes variations are so extensive that comparing pairs of words will not do. The computer then picks up larger blocks of text for analysis—five words in a group, then twenty-five words—until it finds a proper alignment of texts. At all stages of the process, all the words of text 1 are compared successively and in order with all the words in text 2. Because resolution requires only a one-word match in both texts, the computer will sometimes find false matches of function words in cases of long additions or omissions. Dearing pointed out this troublesome aspect of Froger's comparison procedure and suggested requiring several consecutive words to be identical before the variation was considered ended.[13]

Froger compares two texts at a time and prints out variants and their locations, noting whether they are additions or omissions. A later phase of the system, which can handle up to forty-four texts of 3500 words each, combines all two-text collations together for printing and punches cards summarizing variants for all texts. The collator must then go through the cards, cull out insignificant variants, and consolidate all that are part of long reworked passages. Compared to later collation algorithms, the practice of classing every change as either an omission or addition of single words is liable to error and necessitates considerable editing of results. In fact, Froger contributed more to computerized collation by being one of the first to show that computers could collate than by devising his own particular method.

Dearing's project in Dryden collation (first announced in 1962) is more straightforward in operation than Froger's and yields more readable output. In its most recent version, it is written in FORTRAN for implementation on the IBM 360 computer system—a combination that could enjoy wide distribution and usage.[14] It compares versions of the same poetic line in different editions (it can handle as many as ninety-nine texts of any length) after the cards have been presorted to arrange corresponding lines together. The program checks beginnings and endings of lines for identity, then works in toward the middle looking for differences. Even if there are intervening identical words in both texts, the entire segment of the line between the outermost differences is held

---

[13] Vinton A. Dearing, rev. of *La Critique des textes et son automatisation*, by Dom Jacques Froger, *CHum*, 4 (1969), 151.

[14] See Vinton A. Dearing, "Computer Aids to Editing the Text of Dryden," in *Art and Error: Modern Textual Editing*, ed. Ronald Gottesman and Scott B. Bennett (Bloomington: Indiana University Press, 1970), pp. 256–66.

for printout. For the sentences quoted above, Dearing's program considers the three-word sequence "a friend yesterday" in text 2 as a rewritten version of "my friend" in the first sentence. In cases of omitted, misplaced, or added lines, the computer looks ten lines forward and backward in text 2 for a match. If no match has yet been effected, it then looks forward ten lines in text 1; there is no need to look back in text 1 over lines already processed. A line that is interchanged or displaced by more than ten lines is treated as an omission in one location and an addition in the other.

Output from the collation resembles the widely accepted method of showing variants developed by John M. Manly and Edith Rickert for their edition of *The Canterbury Tales* (Chicago: University of Chicago Press, 1940). A line from the base text is printed in full; below it are printed only those portions of the line which vary in other texts. Dearing's program is not a completely accurate collation, since identical segments of lines occurring between differences (the word "friend" in the example) are repeated. The editor must check the printout to eliminate such redundancies. Dearing defended this "trade off" of cutting down computer programming and operating time at the cost of requiring manual editing of the results.[15] Perhaps a more serious drawback of Dearing's work is its practical limitation to collation of poetry because it depends on the line format of dramatic or poetic texts. He suggests that it would work on prose units of simple sentences and independent clauses but reports only experimental results.

Another collation project for lined texts deserves mention here: Widmann's work with Shakespeare, involving eventual collation of about 120 editions of *A Midsummer Night's Dream*. Over the years Widmann's basic procedures for comparison have gone through much revision and testing: a trial run on six texts programmed by Joel Cohen in 1969, adoption of Gerald Berns' text-handling program called FORMAT available on the IBM 360/75 system, and a new PL/I version incorporating the features of FORMAT. Widmann chose FORMAT because of its capacity to handle uppercase and lowercase characters and its flexible options for output, such as left and right justification and page numbering.[16]

Initially all editions of the play, arranged in order of composition, are printed separately, from line 1 through line 2223. The computer then au-

[15] Dearing, *Art and Error*, p. 260.

[16] In addition to Widmann's article already mentioned (note 5), see her "The Computer in Historical Collation: Use of the IBM 360/75 in Collating Multiple Editions of *A Midsummer Night's Dream*," in Wisbey, pp. 57–63.

```
5      Draws on apase : fower happy daies bring in
q2     Drawes      apace   foure
f1                 apace: foure happy daies bring in>w
f2     Drawes      apace: foure happy daies bring in>w
f3     Drawes      apace   four        dayes
f4                 apace   four        dayes
6      An other Moone:/ but oh, me thinks, how slow
q2     Another Moone :        me-thinks, how slow>w
f1     Another Moon: but oh, me thinkes, how slow>w
f2     Another Moon: but oh, me thinks, how slow>w
f3     Another Moon :
f4     Another Moon :
7      This old Moone waues! She lingers my desires,
q2     This        wanes : She lingers my desires
f1     This    Moon wanes;              desires
f2     This    Moon wanes ? She lingers my de-sires
f3     This    Moon wanes?              desires
f4     This    Moon wanes ? She lingers my desires
8      Like to a Stepdame, or a dowager,
q2             Step-dam,      Dowager,
f1             Step-dame,     Dowager,
f2             Step-dame,     Dowager,
f3             Step-dame      Dowager,
f4             step-dame      Dowager,
9      Long withering out a yong mans reuenewe./
q2                           young      reuenew.
f1                                      reuennew.
f2                                      revennew.
f3                           young      revenue.
f4                           young      re-venue.
10     H )U ip )U . Fower daies will quickly steepe themselues in night:
q2     )U Hip )U . Foure daies will quickly steepe themselues in nights>w
f1     )U Hip )U . Foure daies will quickly steep themselues in nights>w
f2     )U Hip )U . Foure daies will quickly steep themselves in nights,>w
f3     )U Hip )U . Four dayes will quickly steep themselves in nights,>w
f4     )U Hip )U . Four dayes will quickly steep themselves in nights,>w
11     Fower nights will quickly dreame away the time:
q2     Foure daies                            time:
f1     Foure       wil
f2     Foure
f3     Four                    dream          time :
f4     Four                    dream          time :
12     And then the Moone, like to a siluer bowe,
q2                                          bow,
f1                                          bow,
f2                             silver bow,
f3             Moon,           silver bow,
f4             Moon,           silver bow,
```

FIGURE 24. A computer printout of Widmann's machine collation of lines 5 through 12 from six editions of *A Midsummer Night's Dream*: the Quarto of 1600 (labeled with the Through Line Numbers), a later quarto, and four later folios. (*Reproduced courtesy of R. L. Widmann*)

tomatically merges identical lines together, by sorting on the Hinman Through Line Number for each line of the play. Since all editions have been assigned standard Through Line Numbering, the computer has no problem with losing its place. An edition which is missing a line (say 100) would not have that Through Line Number; its next line would have the proper next number assigned to it (number 101). Before printout, each line in the copy text (the Quarto of 1600) is compared character-by-character with the corresponding line in all later editions. Below the copy-text line are printed only those portions of the other lines that are variants, arranged in chronological order (Figure 24). Even a difference in line length is noted. Widmann remarked that analyzing this output format, much like that of Dearing, is less tiresome and troublesome than deciphering the typical historical collation formula in a scholarly edition. Her printout (Figure 24), when completed with all editions, "will show the history of an entire line at a sweep of the eye down the page."[17] In summary, Widmann's collation procedure seems very similar to Dearing's. They both do simultaneous, multiple comparison of more than two texts of lineated material and present results in a similar printed form. Its chief advance is automatic sorting of identical lines before comparison, eliminating the necessity of presorting the texts.

Georgette Silva and Harold Love also learned from Dearing in preparing their more completely automatic poetic collation routine.[18] Their programs were designed for editing the Restoration dramas of Thomas Southerne but have been tested on Book II of Wordsworth's *Prelude*, more challenging textually because of extensive authorial revisions between the first and second versions of the text. They are implemented in FORTRAN on the CDC 3000 series of machines to analyze two texts at a time. Without needing to presort cards before input, this project employs input on magnetic tape and "makes its own decisions as to which lines correspond."[19] Operationally several levels of comparison can be carried out on two texts. Initially the program looks at every fifth line of texts 1 and 2; if they match, it assumes an overall correspondence for the blocks of five lines. In order to keep the computer from losing its place on revised versions of the same line, Silva and Love do not require complete character matches to consider two lines in the same lineation. In comparing lines, the machine first ignores capitalization, punctuation, blanks, and the letters *e* and *s* (which are troublesome in word pairs like *lived* and *liv'd* and *lives* and *live*). Then only the first and last seven characters of the lines are checked. If either set of characters is the same, the lines are assumed to correspond. A later procedure which prints out corresponding lines in pairs examines them character-by-character and displays the exact variants between them in the output.

When the five-line check breaks down, the computer must set about finding another place in the text where the lines are again similar. It switches to line-by-line comparison starting at the first noncorresponding pair of lines. One of the following situations must account for this noncorrespondence:

1. The line in text 2 may be a variant of the line in text 1.
2. The line in text 2 may be an addition to text 1.

[17] Ruth L. Widmann, "Shakespeare and the Computer," *ALLC Bulletin*, 1, No. 3 (1973), 23.

[18] Georgette Silva and Harold Love, "The Identification of Text Variants by Computer," *Information Storage and Retrieval*, 5 (1969), 89–108.

[19] Love, in Wisbey, p. 50.

3. Text 2 may not contain the line in text 1.
4. Both lines, in texts 1 and 2, may have been displaced elsewhere.
5. Another line in text 2 may have been displaced here, so that the line in text 2 corresponding to the line in text 1 has been moved ahead.

The several machine searching procedures are intended to handle all of these circumstances. Initially the computer searches text 2 for forty lines on either side of the current, noncorresponding line. If a line matching text 1 is discovered, the intervening lines in text 2 are noted as a possible addition; and the five-line check is begun at the new point of identity. When it finds no match in forty lines of text 2, the program examines forty lines of text 1—twenty before and twenty after the point of dissimilarity. If a correspondence is found, the original line in text 1 is marked as a probable omission in text 2. After verifying that it is back in sequence, the computer again begins comparing every fifth line. In case neither of the troublesome lines in texts 1 or 2 is discovered in the other, they are assumed to be greatly revised variants of the same line (since the earlier seven-character matching did not work). Fifth-line checking starts again as soon as the other lines in the five-line block are verified as similar.

Silva and Love designed their scanning method to find only the grossest differences between texts. As a consequence, short interchanged passages (one or two lines) that fall within a five-line block are missed. They considered adding a rule that no line in text 2 be passed over until its status has been investigated. However, this would defeat the efficiency of the five-line rhythm, which "proved most valuable in aligning lines which comprised a true positional match without corresponding verbally."[20]

Nevertheless, the line or two that are interchanged, as well as spelling, punctuation, and word variants between two versions of the same line, are not overlooked. As soon as the computer certifies that either two five-line blocks or two lines correspond in both texts, these are sent to output. They are printed in pairs with text 1 given in full and variants only shown for text 2. The result resembles Dearing's output, both being similar to the Manly-Rickert format for listing variants. In tests the procedure made a few mistakes; yet the editors could easily spot errors by inspection. Compared to the collation schemes already surveyed, this one is the most automatic and complex procedure for handling difficult

[20] Silva and Love, p. 97.

lined poetry. With planned modification, it will be able to collate several editions of the same text by progressive conflation of comparisons carried out between the base text and one of the derived texts. By its method of ordered levels of searching, the method of Silva and Love finds complicated poetic correspondences with a high degree of accuracy and presents the results in a form easily analyzed by the scholar.

Margaret S. Cabaniss has also developed an automatic algorithm, implemented in PL/I on an IBM 360/75 system at the University of California at Los Angeles, which finds its place in two revised versions of a text.[21] But her texts were in prose: two medieval French manuscripts, translations of a Latin encyclopedia, *De Proprietatibus Rerum*, written by Bartholomaeus Anglicus about 1230. She had to specify levels of deviation in running text, not in lined material. The computer had to be provided with a quantifiable definition of what constituted a variation between texts and how it must search in each text to end variation. Cabaniss broke down these two problems into five component queries, in order to establish levels of textual deviance that could be represented numerically:

1. What is a variant? Normally any deviation between texts.
2. Once a variant is found, how many words must match in succession before the texts are again considered equal? Normally two consecutive identical words are sufficient—"words" being taken to include punctuation marks as well as combinations of letters.
3. How long a word-by-word search should be made in looking for a difference of "medium size"? Normally twenty-word units are set aside, and each word in the master-text is compared with each word in the slave-text.
4. How long a word-by-word search should be made in looking for a difference of "large size"? Normally fifty lines at a time are scanned coarsely.
5. What degree of coarse scanning is to be used in searching for a match in texts with a difference of "large size"? Normally every tenth word is taken from the master-text and compared with the entire sample of fifty lines of slave-text until there is a match.

A researcher unwilling to accept the Cabaniss model of "small," "medium," and "large" textual variation can set his own numerical val-

[21] Cabaniss, pp. 1–33 (see note 10).

124

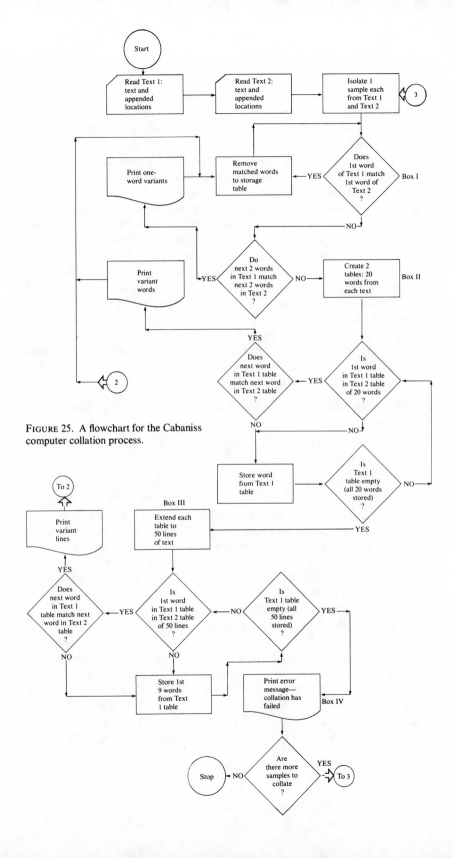

FIGURE 25. A flowchart for the Cabaniss
computer collation process.

ues for each. He can, for example, require that up to five consecutive words, instead of two, be identical before textual variance is terminated. Or he may redefine coarse scanning by substituting any number of words to be skipped, from one to twenty, for Cabaniss' choice of ten. Naturally the less coarse the scan the greater the possibility of finding a match, but also the greater the computer time and cost.

Because the Cabaniss idea of having levels of scanning for resolving variations is typical of automated collation schemes for prose, let us look more closely at her method in flowchart form (Figure 25). Given two texts in computer memory and the hierarchy of operations established by the standard numerical values, the computer begins to compare text 1 against text 2 word by word (Box I). When a difference is encountered, the automatic procedure for analyzing variation takes over. A difference of only one word is printed out, and the program returns to its normal checking routine. Otherwise, the program constructs tables of twenty consecutive words from each text (Box II). The computer compares words from text 1 against the twenty words from text 2 in its hunt for two consecutive matching words. For example, consider two versions of the same sentence:

> This man, the one from London, acted as if he had seen me before. . . .

> This man, the one whom I had met in London, acted as if he had seen me before. . . .

The Cabaniss program would establish two tables of twenty words beginning after the last two matched words—"the one." The word "from" in text 1 begins the variation, because there is no match for it in the Text 2 table. Yet the second word in the Text 1 table ("London") is found and recorded as the first of the two necessary matches required to terminate a difference. The computer discovers its second match in the following comma, which it perceives as a "word." It sends the variant words to output and proceeds anew with normal comparison in Box I.

Coarse scanning begins when variation is not resolved within the twenty-word tables. They are extended to fifty lines each (Box III). The first word in the first table, and thereafter every tenth word (the standard option for coarse scanning—Question 5), is looked for in the entire fifty lines of text 2. Should there be a match, lines between the first and last unmatched words are printed out. If there is still no match after all fifty lines of both texts have been coarsely scanned, all of Cabaniss' comparison routines have failed to resolve variation. The computer prints a message to this effect (Box IV), then goes to a new starting point for the matching procedure to continue, such as the next chapter of the texts. Collation of the skipped passages is left to the scholar.

This "fail-safe" procedure, a distinctive features of Cabaniss' work, calls for manual collation in worst cases; the computer proceeds to collate later passages it can handle. In test runs on the French manuscripts with only minor differences between them, the program found all the textual changes. Like Silva and Love, Cabaniss used a group of ordered strategies to resolve small, then large, variations; but her tables of words were not dependent on the text's being in lines. This feature makes her work more generally applicable than earlier projects and well suited to prose.

Developed by George Petty, Jr., and William Gibson, Project OC-CULT (Ordered Computer Collation of Unprepared Literary Texts) is perhaps the best known collation program because of its association with the Center for Editions of American Authors.[22] Petty and Gibson tried to design a completely automatic procedure to collate two prose texts uninterrupted from beginning to end. For the sake of searching efficiency, the editor chooses the shorter of his texts as the master text. Hence, the computer does not spend time fruitlessly searching through a short comparison text for a passage that occurs only in a longer master text.

Operationally the program attempts to match a test set of twelve words of comparison text (sample sizes are optional and may be changed). Whereas the Cabaniss procedure does not consider variation concluded until two consecutive words are alike, Project OCCULT uses a statistical procedure to define matching in terms of similar word sequences. Although unlike either the five-line check of Silva and Love or the coarse scanning of Cabaniss, the statistical test has a similar purpose: to take into account the possibility of rewritten passages, only roughly identical because of simultaneous deletion and addition. After considerable experiment, Petty and Gibson decided that if, in comparing two sets of twelve words each, the sum of the number of words in the longest continuous sequence plus the total number of matching sequences is six or more, the sets are to be considered matched.

To see how this rule applies, consider the following twelve-word sequence:

This program uses the standard operations found in most common computer languages. . . .

---

[22] See Petty and Gibson, *Project OCCULT, passim.*

> This program employs the fundamental string operations found
> in common computer languages. . . .

There are three matching consecutive sequences—"This program," "operations found in," and "common computer languages"—of which two have three identical words. By the statistical formula, the number of words in the longest sequence (three) plus the number of sequences (three) equals a total of six. Hence, the computer defines these test blocks as matched, that is, as two versions of the same sentence. Experiments indicate that the computer can identify more than 90 percent of matching twelve-word sequences with this rule.

Initially the computer looks for the first two words from the master test set of twelve words in the larger block of three hundred words of comparison text. If there is no match, the second and third words are tried. When a two-word match is found, the program extends the sequence as far as it will go. If the texts become unmatched again before either block of text is exhausted, control is transferred back to the original routine to look for another two-word match; counters keep track of the number of matched sequences and their lengths. After all twelve words in the master set have been checked against the comparison block, the computer applies the statistical test for similarity. If no statistical match is found for the test set, it is printed out as a deletion from the comparison text. When a number of twelve-word master test sets fail to match any of the comparison text, the latter is labeled an addition and printed out. In either case, the matching procedure starts again on newly generated blocks of text.

Whereas the Cabaniss program resorts to coarse scanning only when short samples of text do not match, the OCCULT algorithm always tests a small set of twelve words against a larger block of comparison text. If one test set does not work, another is tried. Presumably the 10 percent error in matching occurred because two master test sets were out of synchronization in such a way that neither met the statistical criterion for similarity with the comparison text. With other boundaries for the twelve-word sets, matches would have been found. Because the OCCULT program continues automatically until both texts have been collated, mismatches of this type do not disrupt the procedure and are not denoted on the printout. The Cabaniss program warns the editor about the worst cases, but Project OCCULT requires its users to inspect their output for errors and then to do recollation by eye. Gaining efficiency by automatic operation on complete texts requires increased vigilance in checking results for mistakes.

128

All the collation projects under review have relied on serial input of text on cards or paper tape, later converted to magnetic tape. However, Penny Gilbert has developed an innovative modular procedure in PL/I, called COLLATE, which feeds information to the computer through a typewriter or CRT terminal.[23] With text editing, Gilbert encodes lines of her texts (medieval manuscript versions of Buridanus' *Quaestiones super libros Metaphysicae*) with punctuation, capitalization, and locational information, then corrects her errors directly at the terminal. The information is stored on magnetic tape prior to analysis by a series of modular programs designed to keep core storage requirements reasonably small.

Following the typical strategy, the most recent version of Gilbert's comparison procedure includes four levels of automatic searching, the ordered comparison of larger and larger groups of words in order to resolve mismatches. Initially pairs of words in text 1 are compared with ten words in text 2. If these five pairs fail to correspond, this level of search is abandoned. The decision to stop searching text 2 after ten words is determined by the high frequency of certain two-word expressions in medieval Latin texts, e.g., *id est, sed est, non potest*, which would probably be found farther on in the text and lead to false matches. Gilbert admits that she made this decision because of the nature of her texts;[24] in fact, almost all of the collation projects are designed for particular kinds of texts rather than for the general case.

Higher levels of searching are modifications of the first-level procedure. Four-word groups extracted from fifty-word samples of text 1 are tested against fifty words of text 2; then nine-word groups taken from one hundred words in text 1 are searched for in a hundred words of text 2. If all these searches find no matched text, the program looks for corresponding paragraphs. It compares the first four words of the next ten paragraphs until it finds two with a common beginning. If the computer still has not found its place, it prints a message indicating the location of the last match. The scholar must intervene to provide a new starting point in both texts.

Gilbert's programs collate two texts at a time. Textual differences are collected on a variant file. After the master text has been compared to all others, the separate variant files are merged into one. The printed collation contains the base text at the top of the page with the variants in the other manuscripts printed below. Gilbert is working on a final module to produce camera-ready output of base text, variants, and foot-

---

[23] For references, see note 9.
[24] Gilbert, *CHum*, p. 144.

notes.[25] Presumably she will prepare the footnotes at a terminal after analyzing the results of the automatic collation.

The most recent experimenter with collation for prose has drawn together some theoretical results of research in computer science to propose an improved, "optimal" scheme. A theoretical computer scientist with an interest in applications in the humanities, Robert L. Cannon, Jr., approached the problem from the mathematical perspective of a computer professional, unlike the literary background of others who have done computer collation. He noted that the number of word comparisons between one text and another is "the dominant factor affecting the efficiency of a collation algorithm."[26] His algorithm, called OPCOL, is designed to optimize efficiency of this process basic to all collations. Recent research into the "longest common subsequence" (*lcs*) problem—finding the longest common sequence between two texts of length M and N—has shown that both the maximum and minimum number of comparisons is M times N.

Applying the longest common subsequence principle to collation of two texts means finding the largest common set of words between them, not necessarily in sequence; what is left will be the shortest collection of textual variants. For instance, given the two sentences:

This is the man of whom I spoke.

This is the person about whom I was speaking.

The *lcs* is the sequence of words "this is the whom I" with the variants "man of / person about" and "spoke / was speaking."[27] Cannon develops the principle of numerical "distance" between texts, the "cost" of transforming one text into the other. For example, an insertion or deletion from one text to another costs the computer 1 unit; a textual change costs 2 units, since it amounts to a simultaneous deletion and insertion. Like other procedures, OPCOL matches words between the two texts until they are no longer identical. It then builds a table of numerical "distances" between the master and comparison texts as new words in sequence are added to both from the point of mismatch. Without going into the mathematical details, it happens that the "distance" between texts increases as long as they lack identity and begins to decrease when a word in common is finally encountered. The computer continues to check distances every time it adds and looks at another word in either

[25] Gilbert, in Jones and Churchhouse, pp. 112–13.
[26] Robert L. Cannon, Jr., "OPCOL: An Optimal Text Collation Algorithm," *CHum*, 10 (1976), 33.
[27] Cannon example, p. 36.

text. When the distance stops decreasing again, the maximum common sequence has been found, the variants can be printed, and normal checking resumes.[28]

Cannon's approach is intended to minimize comparisons and the amount of computer storage required for large collations; the mathematical elegance of his approach argues for the further application of theoretical results in computer science to complicated, real problems like literary collation. Rarely do theoretical breakthroughs in computer science ever reach the needs of literary scholars; Cannon deserves commendation for his commitment to concrete applications of theoretical principles. His algorithm, only tested experimentally, also deserves a test with a significant literary textual problem and modification to present the variants in a form easily analyzable by the scholar.

Having examined a variety of experiments with computers for collation, how can we assess the efficiency, effectiveness, and economy of these projects? Let us assume that the scholar has decided to prepare his texts in machine-readable form, knowing all of the attendant problems which the input process involves. Which collation procedure is best for his purposes, is most accurate, uses the computer most efficiently?

For poetry, the methods of either Dearing or Widmann will work well as long as the texts are similar and aligned, so that the computer does not have to find its place in heavily revised passages. Given more complicated poetic revision, certainly the Silva and Love routine is the best choice, even though it collates only two texts at a time. Compared to the other procedures, this program incorporates levels of searching as differences between texts become more marked. Silva and Love report that incorrect matches made by the computer are easy to spot by inspection of the output.

With prose the scholar has a more difficult choice to make among the routines of Cabaniss, Petty and Gibson, Gilbert, and Cannon. For some of these projects, test runs with actual texts offer one measure of comparison. In terms of textual difficulties, Cabaniss' French manuscripts presented few challenges: short omissions, additions, and spelling variations. The computer did not have to initiate coarse scanning and found all of the variants accurately in a short time. Cabaniss has suggested that her method can collate about 300 lines per minute.[29] With a more difficult

---

[28] See Cannon's full description illustrated with an example and "distance" tables, pp. 37–39.
[29] Cabaniss, p. 10.

textual situation, all of her search procedures would be necessary; and no doubt this rate of collation would be reduced.

Petty and Gibson set themselves a tough test for their method—collation of two versions of Herman Melville's *Bartleby the Scrivener* and two editions of Henry James' *Daisy Miller*. The 1879 first English edition and the greatly rewritten 1909 New York edition of *Daisy Miller* are essentially two different versions of the same work. Because Project OCCULT is a totally automatic method, completely processing two texts before it stops, the scholar must examine the final output carefully for a few troublesome inaccuracies. One such annoyance is incorrect association of the correct page and line numbers with the section of text being collated. Each set of twelve test words is tagged with a line location number, which is transferred to the output along with textual differences discovered by the computer. In most cases, however, the set of words is longer than the identifying line of text; often a variant occurs in a line or two farther down the page than the line where the first, numerically identified word is located. Line numbering is sufficiently close for the editor to locate the variants easily but not accurate enough to be printed directly as textual notes for an edition.[30]

Project OCCULT also has some difficulty handling punctuation marks at the end of a printed line, especially in cases where a word is hyphenated in one text and not in the other. Also troublesome is a period at the end of a line, which may be either terminal sentence punctuation or the last character of an abbreviation. Normally an abbreviation is followed by one space character and the end of a sentence by two spaces, but this input rule does not apply when the period occurs last in a line.[31] Since many of the important differences between versions of a modern work are changes in punctuation, an editor using the OCCULT program for complete character-by-character collation needs to inspect the machine-produced collation for punctuation errors.

Gilbert reports no problem in the handling of errors with the COL-LATE program. When the machine gets lost, it signals the operator at the terminal to give it another starting point in the two texts. Visual collation is necessary for these worst cases. Gilbert ran several text comparisons between her procedure and those of Cabaniss and Petty and Gibson. Her modular system with smaller core storage requirements processed Cabaniss' materials in half the time and used only half as much computer memory. Compared to Petty and Gibson, she had simi-

[30] Petty and Gibson, pp. 30–31.
[31] Petty and Gibson, p. 29.

lar success in greatly increased speed. Collating 3000 lines of text on an IBM 360/65 system, Gilbert's PL/I routine took only 13 minutes, whereas Petty and Gibson's SNOBOL4 program ran for 146 minutes.[32]

It would seem that Gilbert's COLLATE programs are the natural choice for prose collation if the scholar has interactive terminal facilities. Cannon, however, looked at these same prose collation projects later in terms of the dominant factor in all of them—the number of actual word comparisons carried out between the two texts—and came out with entirely different conclusions.[33] All of them compare progressively more and more words in order to resolve a major variation between two texts. Cannon proposed a worst-case analysis to discuss their relative efficiency: how many total word comparisons are required between two texts of one hundred words each with each method, assuming that the variation cannot be resolved within the hundred-word samples. In this case, the principle of the longest common subsequence embodied in Cannon's OPCOL method demands 10,000 comparisons (number of words in text M times number of words in text N).

Given Gilbert's earlier computer runs, the results are quite surprising. Her method requires by far the most comparisons (83,527) because some words are repeatedly and redundantly compared in each level of searching. Petty and Gibson do much better with the hundred-word samples. Without considering the statistical criterion for matching inherent in its work, Project OCCULT does 17,424 comparisons, almost twice as many as the minimal number demanded by the mathematics of longest common subsequence. The explanation is simple: Petty and Gibson require each pair of words to be compared at least twice, although it fails the identity test the first time. The coarse-scanning level of the Cabaniss method wins the prize, only 1699 comparisons between the two hundred-word texts! Because coarse scanning looks at only every tenth word, it is bound to beat even the OPCOL program, which is mathematically minimal for a worst-case comparison of *every* word in both texts. Cannon's conclusions are worth considering: "the Cabaniss algorithm announces with insufficient information to support its decision [looking at only every tenth word] that normal matching cannot be resumed, whereas the Gilbert algorithm announces a correct decision only after it has done eight times the amount of work necessary [84,000 comparisons to 10,000 for OPCOL] to obtain the information for making its decision."[34]

[32] Gilbert, *CHum*, p. 147.
[33] Cannon, pp. 34–37.
[34] Cannon, p. 37.

The scholar setting out to do prose collation has conflicting reports to consider. Compared to Gilbert's test runs of different programs on the same machine, Cannon's analysis of total word comparisons is perhaps more basic and suggestive, since it examines a fundamental process of collation independent of any computer hardware. In general, OPCOL uses the absolute minimal number of comparisons of every word, but it has not been tested on any large-scale collation project. The methods of Petty and Gibson and Gilbert have performed well in tough textual situations but are inefficient comparison techniques if economy is a factor. The Cabaniss routine embodies efficiency and works well with her texts having few textual difficulties; whether coarse scanning can handle complex problems like *Daisy Miller* attacked by Petty and Gibson remains unresolved. Both the Cabaniss and Cannon approaches seem especially appropriate at this time for large-scale testing with texts offering considerable variations. Meanwhile, the scholar is left to consider his own particular textual problem and take his choice.

Already known for his fine computer concordances to Shakespeare, T. H. Howard-Hill has recently turned his attention to suggesting an "ideal" computer-aided text editing scheme that is feasible with current computer technology.[35] He goes further than Gilbert in proposed uses for an interactive computer in editing. For example, only one text, a "provisional copy text," needs to be permanently stored in the machine. A typist then prepares another text at an interactive CRT terminal, so that it appears on the screen. As it is encoded, the new text is compared to the provisional copy text by a computer program. When the texts do not agree, the computer signals the typist that a variant has been found. The typist visually confirms whether the variant is a genuine one or merely represents a typing mistake. Only true variants are recorded in a magnetic tape file. The comparison procedure, which could be one of those already described, should be carried out on whole blocks of data at a time, so that there is enough text to decide whether variations represent significant rewriting. If the machine loses its place, the operator can restart the comparison at an appropriate place.

Howard-Hill is proposing a complete "computer systems" approach to collation with man-machine interaction. He foresees "a close flexible relationship between the editor and the computer where the first does what he is good at (perceiving and evaluating the significance of com-

[35] T. H. Howard-Hill, "A Practical Scheme for Editing Critical Texts with the Aid of a Computer," *Proof*, 3 (1973), 335–56. A followup article expands further on the present state of hardware for editing: "Computer and Mechanical Aids to Editing," *Proof*, 5 (1977), 217–35.

plex differences and making judgments), the second does what it was designed for (speedy manipulation of large quantities of data, retention and accurate copying of data sets, creation and updating of extensive records), and the functions of each complement each other."[36] He takes issue with Petty and Gibson's desire to have a totally automatic collation program because the mind is superior to the machine in fine discriminatory judgments. Some of Project OCCULT's mistakes bear out this contention. A totally interactive collation procedure proposed by Howard-Hill does not currently exist, but it is feasible with existing technology and deserves experiment.

Howard-Hill is suggesting a "completely integrated" system for man-machine cooperation in all phases of textual editing. Besides collation, he discusses the role of the computer in later aspects of the editing process—collection of variants, emendation, and printing of the final edited text. Once the variant file contains the results of collations of several texts with the provisional copy text, the editor can call them up on the CRT screen beside the copy text. He can decide there whether variations are accidental or substantive and make appropriate emendations. He will then have a pre-final, emended copy text in computer-readable form. Now the computer can prepare a concordance to this text; with it the editor can do additional orthographic analysis. For instance, he may want to make further spelling emendations if the concordance reveals two spellings of the same word at different places in the text. Phillip de Lacy has already shown the efficacy of consulting a computer concordance to make emendations in his provisional text of the Roman physician, Galen.[37]

When the edited text is in final form, the computer can prepare it and a concordance to it for publication at the same time. Machine collation of the final emended text with the copy text will yield a collation record which can be printed along with the other variants as critical apparatus of the scholarly edition. Howard-Hill argues for photocomposition of the text and apparatus directly from machine-readable form in order to avoid introducing errors in the typesetting process. His own handsome computer concordances to Shakespeare are evidence of the flexible type fonts and page formats which photocomposition offers. Wilhelm Ott at the University of Tübingen has already reported a system which produces photocomposed scholarly text with notes automatically inserted at the bottom of each page.[38] Indeed, the technology for producing an

[36] Howard-Hill, *Proof*, 3, 345.
[37] See note 23, Chapter 4.
[38] Wilhelm Ott, "The Emancipated Input/Output," in Jones and Churchhouse, pp. 30–31.

automated textual edition based on a machine-readable critical text is already available.

Related to the process of emendation is development of the genealogy of several versions of a text. A number of scholars have pioneered in using a computer to work up a *stemma* of texts, particularly important for manuscript materials. Yet all of these studies are based on analysis of variants gathered by conventional collation methods. There is much disagreement over models suitable for letting the computer construct a stemma to illustrate the line of descent of manuscripts.[39] In this regard, Eric Poole has made the telling point that, without external evidence to order the texts, a stemma can be drawn with any point in the family tree as the origin of the texts without destroying the logic of the variant data.[40] It seems best to let the computer carry out the complicated sorting and cross-tabulating of variants between versions of the same text and leave the job of establishing their genealogy to the scholar, drawing upon his educated, subjective judgment and whatever external evidence is available. For scholars concerned with computer applications in classifying manuscript variants, the work of James M. Peavler with Chaucer manuscripts, the extensive statistical studies of the Greek New Testament by Wilhelm Ott, and the convincing "near neighbor" cluster analyses of John G. Griffith applied to Juvenal and New Testament manuscripts are worth consideration, as well as Poole's studies of medieval English texts.[41]

[39] See, for example, Froger's extensive discussion of stemmatic relationships in his *La Critique des textes et son automatisation*, especially pp. 244–60 on computer assistance. Jürgen Mau and his associates at Göttingen have developed a series of computer routines called AFFILI to develop stemma on Froger's principles. See Jürgen Mau, "Affiliation Programs," R.E.L.O. *Revue*, No. 3 (1972), pp. 63–76, and Heinz-Jörg Ahnert, "Affiliation Programs (Part II) Using the Program 'AFFILI,'" R.E.L.O. *Revue*, No. 4 (1972), pp. 34–54. Dom H. Quentin's *recensio* method of making family trees has been investigated for computer adaptation by G. P. Zarri in "Algorithms, *stemmata codicum* and the Theories of Dom H. Quentin," in Aitken, pp. 225–37, and "A Computer Model for Textual Criticism?" in Jones and Churchhouse, pp. 133–55. Vinton A. Dearing's recent book on editing is primarily concerned with developing genealogical relations between texts, including the use of computer models: *Principles and Practice of Textual Analysis* (Berkeley: University of California Press, 1974).

[40] Eric Poole, "The Computer in Determining Stemmatic Relationships," *CHum*, 8 (1974), 207.

[41] See James M. Peavler, "Analysis of Corpora of Variations," *CHum*, 8 (1974), 153–59; Wilhelm Ott, "Computer Applications in Textual Criticism," in Aitken, pp. 199–223; and John G. Griffith, "A Taxonomic Study of the Manuscript Tradition of Juvenal," *Museum Helveticum*, 25 (1968), 101–38, and "The Interrelations of Some Primary MSS of the Gospels in the Light of Numerical Analysis," in *Studia Evangelica VI*, ed. E. A. Livingstone (Berlin: Akademie-Verlag, 1973), pp. 221–38.

At the present time, the computer's use in textual editing, especially collation, remains experimental and tentative, compared to its widespread adoption for concordances or bibliographical searching. Yet much computerized work in text editing is innovative and suggestive for future applications. Theoretically most of the collation projects which have been described are sound. Experimentally they have been successful in proving that machine collation is possible, even though a few trouble spots remain. For other phases of the editing process—displaying variants for analysis and cross-tabulating them for many texts—the computer has offered proven assistance to the scholar. Photocomposition of machine-readable materials produces fine quality printing of the final text with fewer errors than traditional letterpress methods. Why then has the day of widespread computerized editing not yet come? Methods of getting text into the computer remain the largest stumbling block. Even with the newest optical scanners, which seem capable of reading almost any type font, input costs continue to be expensive for the average editor.

T. H. Howard-Hill has done textual editors a favor in envisioning a "compleat" computer-aided editing system. Most of his suggestions for collation, analysis of variants, emendation, and preparation of the scholarly edition are already possible with current computer theory and hardware. He closes his analysis by calling for a practical test on a large editorial project in order to see how feasible the integrated approach is and to identify problems that need further analysis. Let us hope that soon the input impasse can be resolved so that scholars can put the idea of an integrated editing system to the test on a major critical edition.

FOR FURTHER READING

Cannon, Robert L., Jr. "OPCOL: An Optimal Text Collation Algorithm." *CHum*, 10 (1976), 33–40.

A theoretical computer scientist puts well-known methods of prose collation through efficiency tests and proposes a new scheme designed to maximize effectiveness in comparing words between two texts.

Howard-Hill, T. H. "A Practical Scheme for Editing Critical Texts with the Aid of a Computer." *Proof*, 3 (1973), 335–56.

A reasonable manifesto arguing the feasibility of man-machine interaction with today's technology to develop a total editing system from input to final production of a critical edition.

Love, Harold. "The Computer and Literary Editing: Achievements and Prospects." *The Computer in Literary and Linguistic Research*. Ed. Roy A. Wisbey. Cambridge: Cambridge University Press, 1971. Pp. 47–56.

Practical discussion of ways computers can aid the several phases of textual editing by the designer of an automated collation program for poetry.

Ott, Wilhelm. "Bibliographie: Computer in der Editionstechnik." *ALLC Bulletin*, 2, No. 1 (1974), 73–80.

Most complete published bibliography of computer usage in editing, divided into two parts: computers in textual criticism and in automated book production.

Ott, Wilhelm, Hans Walter Gabler, and Paul Sappler. *EDV—Fibel für Editoren*. Tübingen: Max Niemeyer Verlag, and Stuttgart: Frommann-Holzboog, 1982.

A German monograph to introduce scholarly editors and publishers to the new technology as it affects the editorial process. The authors are a computer expert in the humanities, a literary editor of James Joyce, and a publisher.

La Pratique des ordinateurs dans la critique des textes. Colloques internationaux du Centre National de la Recherche Scientifique, No. 579. Paris: Centre National de la Recherche Scientifique, 1979.

The single most important collection of papers on textual criticism with computers from a 1978 Paris colloquium, with contributions from most of the significant projects. More emphasis on genealogy of texts and variants in manuscripts than on modern printed books.

Poole, Eric. "The Computer in Determining Stemmatic Relationships." *CHum*, 8 (1974), 207–16.

A recent, lucid assessment and critique of computerized research on genealogy of texts leads into Poole's own method.

CHAPTER 7

Stylistic Analysis

WHEN A SCHOLAR CHOOSES to study that quality of literary works called "style," he is opening Pandora's box. Since Plato and Aristotle, critics have attempted to define and characterize this elusive phenomenon. Most tend to agree that thought and expression come together in style and have argued over separating content and form for stylistic analysis. While the critic must always be concerned with this organic connection between form and content, he needs methods to describe and sort out style in order to avoid impressionism and vague descriptions of what he senses about an author's style. The advent of the computer, with its ability to count, classify, and categorize materials with accuracy and speed, soon led to its adoption for stylistic investigations and the debut of the subdiscipline of computer-assisted literary analysis dubbed "computational stylistics" by early pioneers Sally and Walter Sedelow in 1964.[1]

Compared to computer applications discussed previously—concordances, collation, automated bibliography and dictionary making—computer-assisted stylistics aims to be itself a partner in the scholarly practice of literary criticism instead of a means to produce tools helpful to the scholar in his various tasks. A critic may use the machine to generate a poetic concordance to Emily Dickinson in order to study her everyday imagery; the machine makes the stylistic study easier but does not itself point out the salient words to be investigated. Similarly textual collation, excerpting of dictionary citations, and retrieval of books published in the seventeenth century are means to grander scholarly ends. Computational stylistics, on the other hand, is usually adopted for its own

---

[1] See Sally Y. Sedelow and Walter A. Sedelow, Jr., "A Preface to Computational Stylistics," originally published as System Development Corporation Document SP–1534 (February 17, 1964); rpt. in *The Computer and Literary Style*, ed. Jacob Leed (Kent, Ohio: Kent State University Press, 1966), pp. 1–13.

sake to test a stylistic hypothesis—who wrote a disputed pamphlet or what elements constitute the uniqueness of a particular writer's style.

Strategies for using the computer often include counting some lexical or syntactic characteristics and then applying statistical methods in order to test and validate the significance of the results. Even so, there is little agreement or uniformity about the methods employed. The scholar must be wary that the literary aspects of style not be lost amid a pile of statistical tables and formulas. Sometimes reams of statistics are presented without the benefit of a covering hypothesis. A group of scholars at the University of Montreal had the machine search for and present in graph form the forty-four most frequent nouns in thirty plays of Molière, a project "concerned with describing a particular statistical technique, not with offering conclusions about the works of Molière."[2] Without any stylistic motivation, the encoding of over 340,000 words of Molière and writing programs to analyze them does not seem worth the time, trouble, and money involved.

Granted that admissions like this one making no pretense of stylistic importance are exceptional, applications in computerized stylistics have been, though many and varied, of a mixed quality, often of the nature of pilot studies, and rarely of generality and suitability for use by others. Despite the lack of wide acceptance of textual collation by machine, no one claims that the methodology is unsound, that computers cannot find variations among texts. Computer methods have also led to great successes in the other areas already discussed. Yet the methodologies of machine stylistic studies remain controversial, tentative, and unsettled; and the results are frequently negative or disappointing. Not surprisingly the work can be divided into the two general subheads which make up style—studies of content and of form—along with a specialized subgroup devoted to resolving cases of disputed authorship. Authorship problems usually rely on formal analyses of texts, but their assumptions differ somewhat from studies of individual authors or literary periods and suggest separate treatment. In order to understand the application of machines to their first creative literary task, let us focus on each of the three areas of stylistics in turn and examine their assumptions, methods, successes, and problems.

Two early authorship studies now universally acknowledged as successes represent different approaches to the authorship problem, the case of several anonymous *Federalist* papers solved by Frederick Mos-

---

[2] Paule Sainte-Marie, Pierre Robillard, and Paul Bratley, "An Application of Principal Component Analysis to the Works of Molière," *CHum*, 7 (1973), 137.

teller and David L. Wallace and Alvar Ellegård's analysis of the Junius letters written in Britain before the American Revolution. Under the best circumstances there are only two claimants as author of a disputed work. Mosteller and Wallace had this favored situation; they set out to discover whether Alexander Hamilton or James Madison wrote the twelve disputed *Federalist* papers.[3] As statisticians, they sampled to find vocabulary or syntactic evidence that distinguished either author in his known works. Among several features tested, sentence length was early abandoned, for it was virtually identical for both men; earlier, noncomputerized studies had had success with word length, but this measure varied more in the known works than in the disputed ones.[4] Using a computer concordance and hand counts to papers by both authors, Mosteller and Wallace finally settled on a pool of function words, not dependent on the subject of the papers like content words, as good discriminators between Hamilton and Madison. For instance, out of his sample of eighteen papers, Hamilton used the word *enough* in fourteen of them, while Madison never did in fourteen papers. Hamilton preferred the conjunction *while* but Madison regularly chose *whilst*. *Upon* was another Hamilton favorite rarely used by Madison. Not interested in the overall style of the writers, Mosteller and Wallace wanted only good telltale clues; and for their texts function words of high frequency made the best cases.

Statistically they did a lot of sampling and tried a number of statistical tests to validate their numerical results, the most powerful of which was a long-neglected technique based on Bayes Theorem (1763). Basically it uses the known probability of an event (say the frequency of *while* in Hamilton) to infer the probability of finding *while* in the unknown papers. The results all tended to the same conclusion: with very high odds Madison proved to be the author of all the twelve troublesome papers. The two papers most in doubt by modern historians proved sta-

[3] For full mathematical discussion of the project, consult Frederick Mosteller and David L. Wallace, *Inference and Disputed Authorship: "The Federalist"* (Reading, Mass.: Addison-Wesley, 1964). Most literary scholars can get the relevant information without all the complicated statistical apparatus in Ivor S. Francis, "An Exposition of the Statistical Approach to the *Federalist* Dispute," in Leed, pp. 38–78.

[4] For discussions of sentence length as a stylistic indicator, see C. B. Williams, *Style and Vocabulary: Numerical Studies* (London: Charles Griffin, 1970), pp. 52–63; and W. C. Wake, "Sentence-Length Distributions of Greek Authors," *Journal of the Royal Statistical Society*, Series A, 120 (1957), 331–46. Claude S. Brinegar used word-length frequencies to show that Mark Twain did not write ten letters in the *New Orleans Daily Crescent* (1861), published under the pseudonym of Quintus Curtius Snodgrass (see "Mark Twain and the Quintus Curtius Snodgrass Letters: A Statistical Test of Authorship," *Journal of the American Statistical Association*, 58 [1963], 85–96). Other evidence, both internal and external to the letters, later corroborated Brinegar's statistical findings.

141

tistically to fall heavily in Madison's favor. Since the Mosteller and Wallace study, there have been no serious attacks on their findings for at least two reasons: they experimented with a variety of variables before deciding on a list of discriminating words peculiar to their authors and their several statistical analyses were well chosen to check on each other. On the other hand, their conjecture that the distribution of function words may be a general fingerprint for authorship has been questioned, most recently by Fred J. Damerau, who used a computer to look for words occurring at least five times per 10,000 words in large samples of *Vanity Fair* and three American novels. Damerau's program found great diversity among the most frequent words in the various novelists and concluded that using function words as a general discriminator appears suspicious.[5] The lesson seems clear not only for function words but for authorship word studies in general: particular words may work for specific cases such as the *Federalist* papers but cannot in general be counted on for other analyses.

Alvar Ellegård had a more complicated situation than Mosteller and Wallace—the anonymous Junius letters, often thought to have Sir Philip Francis as author; besides Francis, there are no serious contenders. Ellegård decided to compare the Letters (157,000 words) to the writings of Francis (231,300 words) and other eighteenth-century English writers, a sample of over a million words.[6] Like Mosteller and Wallace, he examined several variables and rejected them as discriminators. Based on his own cursory reading of the letters and the other texts, he drew up a preliminary list of 458 vocabulary items and expressions—mainly content words—of "plus" and "minus" significance in Junius, and then recalculated their presence in all the samples. The computer came into use only in tabulating and analyzing statistical relationships. In the end, Ellegård found Francis to be very close to Junius and was able to eliminate all the other authors. Although Francis' vocabulary fit Junius best, he cannot be certainly identified because there may be other untested or unknown authors whose work would match the Letters as well. Even so, no one has seriously questioned the results of this study.

In terms of method, Ellegård's work in the early 1960s failed to use the machine for his most tedious task—picking the "plus/minus" words from Junius and counting them in all the large samples of texts. More

---

[5] Fred J. Damerau, "The Use of Function Word Frequencies as Indicators of Style," *CHum*, 9 (1975), 271–80.

[6] Ellegård's full description of picking the samples, choosing the test words, and doing the statistical analyses appears in his book, *A Statistical Method for Determining Authorship: The "Junius" Letters 1769–1772*, Gothenburg Studies in English, No. 13 (Gothenburg, Sweden: University of Gothenburg, 1962).

recently, Warren B. Austin has also adopted the concept of "plus" words to test whether the *Groatsworth of Wit* (1592) was written by Robert Greene or was a Greene forgery composed by Henry Chettle (Austin's contention).[7] To pick out his words, Austin had the computer prepare concordances to large samples of both writers: 40,000 words of Chettle and 100,000 of Greene. With the printout of words in front of him, Austin merged all spelling variants and inflectional forms of the same word together, then had the machine pick out high-frequency words for each author, his "plus" words. The plan for choosing word candidates depended on three numerical criteria:

1. The word must occur at least ten times in one author.
2. The frequency per 1000 words in one author must exceed the corresponding frequency in the other by 1.5—the differential ratio.
3. The ratio of variation within the body of works of one of the authors must be lower than the differential ratio.

The word *able* met Austin's second formula; it occurred 27 times in Greene and 65 times in Chettle; the differential ratio was 2.41 (65 divided by 27). In all, 103 words fitted the first criteria as potential markers; after variation within each author was checked, Austin whittled the list of words down to 50 good markers—29 for Greene and 21 for Chettle. Upon examination of the *Groatsworth of Wit*, Austin's comparisons of frequency matched with Chettle's other works, not with Greene's; and he announced the work as a literary hoax intended to capitalize on public interest in Greene after his death. Austin's focus on "plus" words resembled Ellegård's and the choice of function words by Mosteller and Wallace; yet he used the computer more completely than either earlier study to do preliminary screening of words as well as to carry out numerical comparisons. In fact, Austin's work is typical of the kinds of computer assistance to be expected in automated authorship studies: using the machine to look for some stylistic aspect of discriminating power in large bodies of texts, collecting evidence in the works under dispute, and carrying out numerical and statistical analyses to test validity of the findings.

No study of computerized authorship would be complete without consideration of the highly controversial work of the Reverend Andrew

[7] Warren B. Austin, "The Authorship of Certain Renaissance English Pamphlets: An Informal Account of Work in Progress," in *Proceedings: Computer Applications to Problems in the Humanities*, ed. Frederick M. Burelbach, Jr. (Brockport, New York: SUNY College at Brockport, 1970), pp. 93–99. Henceforth, the *Proceedings* will be denoted as Burelbach.

Q. Morton with Greek authors—the Pauline Epistles in the New Testament and a variety of classical Greek texts. Morton first made headlines in 1963 by announcing that his computer study of sentence length and Greek function words like *kai* (*and*—the most common word form in Greek) "proved" that St. Paul wrote only four of the New Testament epistles—Romans, I and II Corinthians, and Galatians—which show a consistency in style lacking in the others.[8] Morton decided on sentence length and *kai* after testing these variables on a number of samples of Greek prose. Immediately Morton began to receive criticism, not for his use of computers but from biblical scholars for his choice of test criteria and from statisticians for his methods of statistical validity.

Both sets of adversaries put telling dents in Morton's early arguments. Using Morton's same variables with English, the Reverend John Ellison decided that James Joyce's *Ulysses* had at least five authors and that Morton's own essays must have been written by several different people.[9] When Morton appeared before the Royal Statistical Society to present his findings in 1965, his remarks sparked heated debate and rebuttal, principally over his use of average sentence length as an important discriminant. Since Morton encoded printed texts with modern punctuation, his figures were suspect; in addition, sentence length has been shown to fluctuate enough within random samples to question the significance of Morton's findings.[10] He seems initially to have been too eager to report his shocking conclusions and suffered embarrassment when his figures came under serious criticism.

Undaunted, Morton continued to collect large samples of classical Greek texts and to refine the characteristics he applied to them. In recent years he has become more interested in other Greek writers, trying to define a "new stylometry," a foolproof authorship method, and has secured the assistance of competent mathematical and computer advice from Sidney Michaelson of the University of Edinburgh. Gradually new

---

[8] First reported in the New York *Times*, 7 November 1963, pp. 1, 17. Morton also included Philemon as Pauline, because of its similarity to the other four books, although its length was too short for adequate sample. The complete case is presented in Morton and James McLeman, *Paul, the Man and the Myth: A Study in the Authorship of Greek Prose* (New York: Harper and Row, 1966).

[9] John W. Ellison, "Computers and the Testaments," in *Computers for the Humanities?* (New Haven: Yale University Press, 1965), pp. 72–74.

[10] Morton's paper, "The Authorship of Greek Prose," *Journal of the Royal Statistical Society*, Series A, 128 (1965), 169–224, presents a clear picture of his early findings for Paul compared to forty other Greek authors. Equally important are the remarks which his presentation elicited from statisticians and linguists (pp. 224–33), including the scathing rebuttal from the eminent linguist, Gustav Herdan.

stylistic criteria were suggested and tested: classes of words that occur last in a Greek sentence, the interval between successive occurrences of *kai*, and genitive versus nongenitive occurrences of the Greek pronoun *autos*.[11] Perhaps Morton's most surprising new claim was definitely to deny the authorship of the disputed Seventh Letter to Plato based on the proposition that an author's writing habits are consistent over long years but not necessarily across genre lines (the Seventh Letter was compared to Plato's undisputed *Apology*). Again he was rebutted with some of his own arguments. A noted Plato scholar, Leonard Brandwood, pointed out that the *Apology* is an oration and the Seventh Letter a narrative; tested with Plato's *Laws*, another narrative, the Seventh Letter shared Platonic characteristics, point for point, that Morton's studies had denied in comparison with the *Apology*.[12] Despite the disclaimers, Morton has continued to do research, gather new associates, and publish in reputable journals.[13]

Surrounded by academic skeptics, Morton, in 1975, reached new heights of public respectability for his stylometric criteria of authorship in London's historic Old Bailey courtroom. An inmate of Brixton Prison, Steve Raymond, had somehow heard of Morton's work and asked his aid in proving that statements allegedly made by him were, in fact, forged by the police to frame him. Comparing the statements to known writings of Raymond using a new technique, Morton convinced the court that there was more than one author because of stylistic inconsistencies; and Raymond was acquitted of all criminal charges based on the documents. The new strategy uses a computer to look at collocations of words occurring together in texts—pairs like "of course" and "as if" in English. Morton claims that authors are consistent in their use of pairs within their own work but differ from other writers. After the machine produces a concordance of some text, the investigator can select the "fingerprint" pairs from the alphabetical word list with context. Mor-

---

[11] See three articles by Sidney Michaelson and A. Q. Morton, "Last Words: A Test of Authorship for Greek Writers," *New Testament Studies*, 18 (1972), 192–208; "The Spaces in Between: A Multiple Test of Authorship for Greek Writers," R.E.L.O. *Revue*. No. 1 (1972), pp. 23–77; and "The New Stylometry: A One-Word Test of Authorship for Greek Writers," *Classical Quarterly*, 22 N.S. (1972), 89–102.

[12] For both sides of the question, see Michael Levison, A. Q. Morton, and A. D. Winspear, "The Seventh Letter of Plato," *Mind*, 77 (1968), 309–25, and Leonard Brandwood, "Plato's Seventh Letter," R.E.L.O. *Revue*, No. 4 (1969), pp. 1–25.

[13] P. F. Johnson, another disclaimer, in "The Use of Statistics in the Analysis of the Characteristics of Pauline Writing," *New Testament Studies*, 20 (1973), 92–100, attacks the idea of finding consistency in last words in Paul's sentences because they are often determined by style and context.

ton's studies with a number of English authors satisfy him that collocations are the new answer for authorship problems.[14]

As might be expected, Morton has not gathered a large academic following, despite his newfound celebrity as an expert trial witness. Over the years, his bold revelations have sent shocks throughout the scholarly world. In his Greek studies, he has tried recently to be more careful in testing new variables which buttress his case. Nevertheless, serious classical and biblical scholars have labored to refute his points and discredit his methods. Morton was surely one of the pioneers in adapting the computer as a full partner in authorship studies; criticism of his work has always centered on his stylistic markers and statistical analyses, not on his computer usage. With his new studies in English successful in breaking up a trial, Morton is once again back in the public eye. Only time will reveal whether his new collocation technique with word pairs gains him general scholarly acceptance. Compared to many literary scholars, Morton lacks caution in speaking out boldly for his findings, no matter how shocking. He seems prepared to accept criticism and ready to defend his assertions and the methods behind them.

A contrasting, more cautious scholarly attitude was taken by Daniel L. Greenblatt in a recent analysis of the disputed Renaissance elegy, "The Expostulation," attributed to both John Donne and Ben Jonson.[15] Instead of vocabulary analysis, rejected because the samples of lyric poetry were too small, Greenblatt used the computer to look at deviations from normal metrical stress of the English iambic pentameter line, as defined by Morris Halle and Samuel J. Keyser (*English Stress: Its Form, Its Growth, and Its Role in Verse*, New York: Harper and Row, 1971). With ten stresses to examine in each line, 640 lines of verse chosen from Donne and Jonson love lyrics yielded a sample of over 6000 items for analysis. Greenblatt included one extra Donne poem as a control to test the homogeneous nature of the sample. He analyzed the metrical scansion himself, marking features like stress and syntactic boundaries, and then encoded the patterns for computer sorting and statistical testing. Three main indexes were then compared: line complexity, defined as exceptions to the Halle-Keyser rules of metrical stress; points of stress prominence; and a ratio of these two variables. For each measure Donne's verse showed up unlike "The Expostulation" and Jonson's very similar; different statistical measures appropriate to each sort of

[14] See Nigel Hawkes, "Word Detective Proves the Bard Wasn't Bacon," London *Observer*, 14 March 1976, p. 4.

[15] Daniel L. Greenblatt, "Generative Metrics and the Authorship of 'The Expostulation,'" *Centrum*, 1 (1973), 87–104.

test were carefully chosen to check the validity of the findings. On the basis of his metrical study, Greenblatt rejected Donne as the author of the poem; but more cautious than Morton has ever been, he claimed only that Jonson *may* be the author. Although his work treats a small problem compared to some others, Greenblatt worked out his methodology with a careful rationale. His focus on metrical patterns is uncommon in authorship studies and utilized the important Halle-Keyser metrical theory; his choice of each statistical test is defended as the best for its purpose. And his conclusions are guarded and tentative, since "The Expostulation" may have some unknown author other than Ben Jonson. We only regret that Greenblatt had to do all of his metrical analysis by hand before submitting it to the computer.

More extensive authorship problems usually require the selection of multiple criteria in order to distinguish a trend in favor of one writer, as well as careful choice of samples and control texts.[16] Representative of the kinds of decisions which must be made is the work of Geir Kjetsaa and a Norwegian-Swedish research team currently at work on one of the most intriguing authorship puzzles in modern literary history—whether Soviet Nobel Prize-winning novelist Mikhail Sholokhov plagiarized from a minor Cossack novelist, Fyodor Kryukov, for much of his masterpiece, *The Quiet Don*.[17] Although rumors about Sholokhov's plagiarism date back to 1928, the issue has recently heated up again with the publication in Paris in 1974 of a work by an anonymous Russian critic, identified only as "D*," arguing for Kryukov as the author of *The Quiet Don* and Sholokhov as "co-author." The fact that Alexander Solzhenitsyn endorsed the claims of the book in a special preface has added fuel to the controversy in Western and Communist literary circles.

In 1975 Kjetsaa and his associates decided that detailed stylistic

---

[16] Two well-known authorship studies encompassing multiple aspects of an author's style include Yehuda T. Radday, "Isaiah and the Computer: A Preliminary Report," *CHum*, 5 (1970), 65–73; and Bernard O'Donnell, *An Analysis of Prose Style to Determine Authorship: "The O'Ruddy," a Novel by Stephen Crane and Robert Barr* (The Hague: Mouton, 1970). Although neither study is innovative in computer usage (basically statistical calculations), each suggests a variety of vocabulary and linguistic elements that might be adaptable to other authorship disputes in prose. Although he began with the assumption of only one author of the Book of Isaiah, Radday's results suggested that there were probably at least three, with the author of some text sections still inconclusively identified. O'Donnell sampled eighteen variables—about sentences, words, syntactic elements, punctuation, parts of speech, metaphor, and dialogue—in *The O'Ruddy* and three novels each by Crane and Barr in order to see where Crane's manuscript left off at his death and was completed by Barr. O'Donnell's stylistic conclusions agreed completely with the traditional opinions of Crane scholars.

[17] Geir Kjetsaa, "Storms on the Quiet Don: A Pilot Study," *Scando-Slavica*, 22 (1976), 5–24.

comparison of *The Quiet Don*, over 1700 pages in length, with a large sample of secure text by both writers would help to clear up some of the impassioned arguments on both sides. The initial study examined 3000 sentences chosen at random from authorial narrative prose (excluding dialogue and characters' internal thoughts)—500 each from two novels by Sholokhov and Kryukov and from the first two volumes of *The Quiet Don*, singled out by "D*" for their heavy Kryukov influence. First, raw averages for sentence length proved too similar, but grouping the sentences by percentages based on their number of words showed that Sholokhov's work tended to coincide with *The Quiet Don*, whereas the Kryukov texts diverged from both. This pattern became clearer when a breakdown on several parts of speech was carried out on large samples of 10,000 words from each author and the novel. Except for pronouns, whose presence is determined by context, the Sholokhov and novel samples were very close for six parts of speech; using the chi-square test of goodness of fit, Kjetsaa was able to reject the hypothesis that Kryukov and *The Quiet Don* were from the same population of parts of speech, whereas the same test between Sholokhov and the novel could not be dismissed.

A third broad category of investigation involved the position of particular parts of speech in the sentence, which seemed an especially good measure for Russian with its allowed freedom of word order. Earlier Russian studies indicated that the first two positions in a sentence and the last three discriminated an author's style. In the present case, Sholokhov again showed greater kinship to *The Quiet Don* in sentence openings and closings in terms of parts of speech. Kjetsaa then looked more closely at syntactic constructions in these outer sentence positions in samples of 1000 sentences from each text. Whereas Kryukov preferred to start his sentences with the sequence, "subject + verb," the other texts began with "preposition + substantive" most often. Among the fifteen most frequent combinations of openers in *The Quiet Don*, only one is not among Sholokhov's top fifteen; five of Kryukov's do not appear in the list of fifteen for the novel. Parts of speech in three-word endings of sentences repeat the same relations more obviously. Sholokhov and the novel have almost the same list of fifteen most frequent constructions, while Kryukov uses more different and various concluding elements in his sentences. As always before, Kryukov's work is easily differentiated from the other two sets.

Despite all this evidence from the initial pilot study to contradict Solzhenitsyn and his anonymous friend, Kjetsaa and his colleagues have continued to expand the size of the samples and the stylistic variables to

148

include vocabulary items. By 1977 they had analyzed about 140,000 words from the three sources, including new material from Volume IV of *The Quiet Don*.[18] With different but similar texts from Kryukov and Sholokhov, they chose 1000 word samples, again at random within limits, to test type-token ratios, ratios of unique word forms found in the text compared to the lexical dictionary forms they represent. Heavily inflected Russian seemed especially appropriate for this variable; again Sholokhov tended to match the novel with many more vocabulary forms than Kryukov. Finally lexical spectra of the vocabularies were examined—the frequency of words used once, twice, etc., in the samples. For this last check, Kjetsaa was applying a statistical test favored in earlier Russian stylistic studies to check the significance of the by-now expected result—Sholokhov and *The Quiet Don* opposed to Kryukov. As with every criterion that had been tried, Kryukov could be rejected as the author; but Sholokhov could not be excluded. These subsequent investigations only add supporting evidence to the original conclusion of the pilot study: although Sholokhov may have relied to some extent on some Kryukov materials to compose his masterpiece, "the language seems to reveal that he wrote his own work, in which case the charge of plagiarism is null and void."[19]

To conclude the discussion of computer-assisted authorship disputes, Kjetsaa's study of *The Quiet Don* has been treated in considerable detail because the subject is an important, current literary controversy and, more importantly, because the analysis itself illustrates careful, conscientious planning and execution. The problem was well-defined at the outset: Whose work was most like *The Quiet Don*, Kryukov's or Sholokhov's? Given the restriction that the texts be authorial material, sampling was carried out at random instead of being chosen from any predetermined bias. Several of the variables chosen for sampling were particularly appropriate for texts in Russian, a highly inflected language with very free word order; they represented a spread of syntactic and vocabulary categories, indicative of the broad basis of the study. Whenever the data warranted them, statistical methods to test the significance of the findings were applied. With the evidence of eight tests all in agreement, Kjetsaa's rhetoric, unlike that of enthusiasts like Morton, remained free of dogmatic assertion and open to qualification in the same spirit as his statistical tests: Sholokhov cannot be excluded as the author. Scholars contemplating authorship studies can get valuable ad-

[18] Geir Kjetsaa, "The Battle of *The Quiet Don*: Another Pilot Study," submitted to *CHum* for publication.

[19] Kjetsaa, *Scando-Slavica*, p. 24.

vice from the model of this modest project—its principles, methods, and gradual growth and development.

Even among the computerized authorship problems that have focused on vocabulary, few have looked at content words for their own sake. Mosteller and Wallace noted long ago that content words are not usually good authorship discriminators because they relate to the meaning of the document instead of the stylistic habits of the writer. Other literary studies, however, focus on that side of style which is content. How convenient it would be if the computer could read a text and produce a list of its themes in an objective, scientific fashion, as an aid to the scholar's subjective judgment of the work. Since World War II, procedures with this goal have been developed mainly in the social sciences under the rubric of "content analysis." The pioneering computer application, called the General Inquirer and developed by the Harvard Laboratory of Social Relations in the early 1960s, has been described as

> . . . a set of computer programs to (a) identify systematically, within text, instances of words and phrases that belong to categories specified by the investigator; (b) count occurrences and specified co-occurrences of these categories; (c) print and graph tabulations; (d) perform statistical tests; and (e) sort and regroup sentences according to whether they contain instances of a particular category or combination of categories.[20]

Central to the General Inquirer system is automation of the first process. Prior to text submission, the computer has stored in it a dictionary of loaded terms coded for content categories. The Harvard Psychosociological Dictionary contains over 3500 words classified according to more than eighty semantic groups such as male or female role, orientation toward self or others, and cultural settings or objects. Each word is given a "first-order" semantic tag denoting its main meaning and several "second-order" tags relating to connotative meanings. The case of the word *teacher* suggests the process; it has one first-order category, job role, and two second-order ones, higher status and academic. Other dictionaries have been developed for analyzing political documents and

---

[20] Philip J. Stone, Dexter C. Dunphy, Marshall S. Smith, and Daniel M. Ogilvie, *The General Inquirer: A Computer Approach to Content Analysis* (Cambridge, Mass.: MIT Press, 1966), p. 68. For information about more recent versions of the General Inquirer system of programs in PL/I, see Dennis J. Arp, J. Philip Miller, and George Psathas, "An Introduction to the Inquirer II System of Context Analysis,"*CSHVB*, 3 (1970), 40–45; and Sandra Rice, "Inquirer III (Edinburgh Version): A Computer-Based System for Content Analysis," *CHum*, 10 (1976), 332.

folktales in anthropology.[21] Given the dictionary prepared by scholars, the computer automatically lemmatizes words into their root forms and then assigns content tags to them. It takes into account the possible effect of a negative word within the sentence (it concludes that "he is never a good teacher" reverses the affirmative senses of the word *good* applied to *teacher*) and applies tags to pronouns whose antecedents have been added to the input text (a bothersome instance of pre-editing before encoding). The machine then tabulates the trends of meaning categories, performs graphic and statistical analyses, and retrieves sentences loaded with significant content words for the user's perusal.

Heralded as an automated way to analyze meaning in documents when it was announced, the General Inquirer has been used most successfully in the social sciences; with literary texts, its usage has been minimal, and the results often disappointing. Of course, the discriminating power of the method depends entirely on the excellence of the tagging of content categories in the computer dictionary—a manual process that precedes machine analysis of the text. An early, experimental application using the Harvard Psychosociological Dictionary examined *Huckleberry Finn* in terms of the hero's relation to death and death imagery.[22] Sentences containing words embodying the death theme associated with Huck showed up in every chapter, often related to concepts of family. Yet few qualitative judgments were made about the relation of the theme to the novel. As James D. Merriman pointed out in a telling critique of this study, scholars have no standard by which to judge whether the computer's findings are normal or excessive. He questioned whether the discovery of death imagery, some of which seems more psychoanalytically than critically interesting, was worth the effort of time and energy involved in encoding the text for the analysis.[23]

A more recent analysis by Ralph Dengler of six Roman Catholic catechisms from before the Council of Trent (1566) to the present had much better results using the Harvard Psychosociological Dictionary.[24]

---

[21] See the fine discussion on General Inquirer dictionaries in Ole R. Holsti, *Content Analysis for the Social Sciences and Humanities* (Reading, Mass.: Addison-Wesley, 1969), pp. 156–60.

[22] Allan B. Ellis and F. André Favat, "From Computer to Criticism: An Application of Automatic Content Analysis to the Study of Literature," in Stone et al., pp. 628–38.

[23] See Charles Kadushin, Joseph Lovett, and James D. Merriman, "Literary Analysis with the Aid of the Computer," *CHum*, 2 (1968), 177–202; this article is a review symposium of the General Inquirer. George Psathas, a designer of revisions in the method, responded in "The General Inquirer: Useful or Not?" *CHum*, 3 (1969), 163–74.

[24] Ralph Dengler, "A General Inquirer Analysis of Sixteenth Century and Contemporary Catechisms," *CHum*, 8 (1974), 5–19.

151

Analyzing a random sample of 15 percent of each book, the computer was clearly able to distinguish differences of emphasis between the early and modern catalogs of Roman Catholic doctrine. The sixteenth-century texts, developed during the Counter-Reformation have an authoritarian tone, rigid morality, and defensive stance. Two current catechisms produced since Pope John's Second Vatican Council show awareness of the environment and technology; sensitivity to modern political and social realities; and positive, progressive tone. Dengler's impressive results are probably due more to the relationship between the nature of his texts and the psychological and sociological biases of the machine dictionary than to improvements in the General Inquirer system of computer routines.

Howard P. Iker and his associates have criticized the central weaknesses of the General Inquirer, the *a priori* category systems of meaning that underlie the making of dictionaries and the need to pre-edit the texts. In their system of automated PL/I procedures, called WORDS, the computer has no predetermined dictionary; it takes the documents themselves and isolates the most frequent content words, after deleting function words and lemmatizing others into their root forms.[25] Based on information retrieval principles, Iker's programs depend on the redundancy of language, since his early research with psychoanalytic interviews of patients indicated that repeated concepts contain the significant information. More recently his program called SELECT carries out several machine correlation techniques on the list of frequent words the computer has discovered in text segments like the paragraph in order to choose a final, associationally "rich" set for thematic analysis. Tests using Konrad Lorenz's important book, *On Aggression*, show that SELECT can ferret out major themes.[26] Besides psychological materials, WORDS has been applied to themes recurring in the exercises of Soviet history textbooks; performing cluster analysis on sets of high-frequency words that it picked out, the computer revealed the stages of student awareness of concepts like socialism and workers' revolutionary movements.[27] Only preliminary literary analysis of important terms in *The Wiz-*

[25] For a description of Iker's modular series of computer programs, consult Howard P. Iker and Robert H. Klein, "WORDS: A Computer System for the Analysis of Content," *Behavior Research Methods and Instrumentation,* 6 (1974), 430–38.

[26] See Iker's two recent articles about this routine: "SELECT: A Computer Program to Identify Associationally Rich Words for Content Analysis. I. Statistical Results," *CHum,* 8 (1974), 313–19; and "SELECT: A Computer Program to Identify Associationally Rich Words for Content Analysis. II. Substantive Results," *CHum,* 9 (1975), 3–12.

[27] Charles D. Cary, "Natural Themes in Soviet School History Textbooks," *CHum,* 10 (1976), 313–23.

ard of Oz has been tried with Iker's automatic methods,[28] and a much larger, more serious project seems warranted to see if paragraphs containing the content words chosen by the machine without any dictionary from unedited text are as comparatively significant for thematic study as the passages of content revealed by the General Inquirer. Certainly the idea of automated searching directly from unprepared literary text is as appealing as starting with one of the General Inquirer's dictionaries of tagged words with its built-in bias.

Probably more familiar to literary scholars is the work in computational stylistics by Sally Y. Sedelow and her colleagues, most well-known for their VIA (Verbally-Indexed Association) computer programs written in PL/I for thematic analysis of English text.[29] Compared to the General Inquirer, VIA enters texts into the machine in unedited form, a much preferred situation, given the problems inherent in the input of large textual files. Like the other content analysis routines, VIA includes procedures for canonizing content words into their base forms by removing suffixes and prefixes, counting them, and printing them out for the user's inspection. He decides on a cutoff point of word frequency above or below which the computer will continue its searches for more clues to meaning. To this point Sedelow's work closely resembles that of Iker in defining a list of content words worth further study.

Sedelow's more novel approach then has the computer consult machine-readable files of thesauri, synonym dictionaries, and the immediate context of the selected words in the texts. The thesaurus search seems especially appropriate, for it is organized to reveal semantic similarity among words in terms of closely related concepts. Basic to the method is the assumption that "theme is a function of semantic content and textual context."[30] The computer collects all words associated with the head words on lists which form the basis of a special computerized thesaurus for the text being studied. Tracing through the associated word lists, the machine looks for occurrences of these new-found words in the original text and gradually develops a set of conceptually related

[28] Howard P. Iker and Norman I. Harway, "A Computer Systems Approach Toward the Recognition and Analysis of Content," in *The Analysis of Communication Content*, ed. George Gerbner, Ole R. Holsti, Klaus Krippendorff, William J. Paisley, and Philip J. Stone (New York: John Wiley and Sons, 1969), pp. 394–401.

[29] For more information about the VIA system, see Sally Y. Sedelow, "The Computer in the Humanities and Fine Arts," *Computing Surveys*, 2 (1970), 93–96, or Sally Y. Sedelow and Walter A. Sedelow, Jr., "Stylistic Analysis," in *Automated Language Processing: The State of the Art*, ed. Harold Borko (New York: John Wiley and Sons, 1967), pp. 201–03.

[30] Sedelow and Sedelow, in Borko, p. 201.

words or "themes." When new words are chosen for analysis as more input text is read, the program consults its stored thesaurus for their earlier appearance; in other words, it uses the information already isolated to focus in on repeated concepts. The final result is a cross-referenced thesaurus to the original literary text produced automatically by the several steps of the VIA process.

Like the previously discussed methods of content analysis, the Sedelows' VIA programs have only been tested on a limited basis, most notably on themes in *Hamlet* by Sally Sedelow herself. Taking act by act, the computer picked out 65 primary words repeated at least ten times in one act as candidates for analysis. It comes as no surprise that "night" was primary in Act I, and "drink" in Act V, which contains the poisoned cup. Family members changed prominence throughout the play: Father (Act I), Daughter (Act II), Mother (Act III), and Father (Act IV). Act V had no significant family terms, suggestive of the breakup of the family groups in the final multiple murders; instead, more general concepts of "man" and "king" give the end of the play a more universal, impersonal tone. The theme of death shows up at the end linked through the thesaurus to fourteen content words in Act V, including "bleed," "murderous," and "slain." In sum, the program discovered obvious content elements as well as some that were not so readily expected.[31] Since these results were preliminary, the VIA system seems attractive for more extensive content analysis, especially for its convenience of unedited literary text, if the scholar is willing to accept the assumptions about interconnected chains of meaning that the thesaurus embodies.

Related in conception to the Sedelow method but not developed on so grand a scale is the semantic analysis of poetry carried out by Ellen Spolsky at the University of New Mexico.[32] Whereas the VIA programs incorporate several thesauri and synonym dictionaries, Spolsky relies on ordinary dictionary definitions to get behind the vocabulary of a poem. She assumes a framework of meanings much like Noam Chomsky's concept of semantic features: "Each word in a poem can be assumed to be the surface realization of a group of semantic features. The features of a word include all the referents of a word, denotative and

---

[31] More discussion of the *Hamlet* analysis is contained in Sally Y. Sedelow's article, "Communicating with a Computer about Humanistic Research," in Burelbach, pp. 52–56. See also, with Walter A. Sedelow, Jr., her "Categories and Procedures for Content Analysis in the Humanities," in Gerbner et al., pp. 487–99.

[32] Spolsky's work is reported in two articles: "Computer-Assisted Semantic Analysis of Poetry," *CSHVB*, 3 (1970), 163–68; and "Dictionaries and the Semantic Analysis of Poetry," *SIGLASH Newsletter*, 7, No. 3 (June 1974), 5–8.

connotative."[33] To zero in on these features, a problem that continues to vex linguists, Spolsky chose dictionary definitions; replacing each word in a poem by its several definitions results in a construct that is "semantically equivalent" to the original work. In tests with three dictionaries, the *New English Dictionary* (*OED*), *Random House Dictionary of the English Language*, and *Webster's Seventh Collegiate Dictionary*, Spolsky keypunched as text all the definitions of the words in a short poem; the computer then prepared a concordance from these, omitting the usual function words like *the* and *at*. Instances of the same words in definitions, the criteria for finding themes, turned up in the printed concordance alphabetized together. Listed with each definitional word was the actual word in the poem which included it among its definitions. Because of its extensive definitions, the printout for the *OED* analysis of Emily Dickinson's eight-line poem, "I Like a Look of Agony," was three inches thick, and much of it was useless. More manageable was the output from the other two dictionaries. Cross-tabulating the concepts revealed by the computer in the Random House dictionary with the content words of the poem (Figure 26), two kinds of results are apparent. The themes of *appearance, eye, truth*, and *pain and suffering* are important to the poem; *appearance* gets twelve references in the definitions of seventy of the twenty-four content words in the poem. Reading across the table reveals the words in the poem itself dense with important associations—*agony, sham*, and *feign*. Considering the simplicity of the method, the Spolsky routine does a fine job of focusing attention on the significant content of the poem. Similar results were also achieved in looking at other short poems of Yeats, Eliot, and Hopkins.

Spolsky's experiments contain several *caveats*. High on the list of words in the concordances for every poem were terms like *state, having, cause*, and *act*; their presence was inevitable as words commonly used in making dictionary definitions. Sometimes a key concept would not show up significantly because of the problem of language polysemy; the Random House dictionary defined *simulate* and *sham* without reference to *deceit* or *imitate*, other important concepts in the Dickinson poem, whereas the *OED* picked up these distinctions (noted by the asterisks in the table). In addition, Spolsky's method seems impractical for poetry of any length, since analysis of the enormous bulk of printout would be almost unmanageable and perhaps not worth the effort of encoding all the definitions. Spolsky herself makes no claims for revolu-

---

[33] Spolsky, *SIGLASH Newsletter*, p. 5.

	appearance [12]	pain & suffering [7]	truth [9]	pretense (pretend) [5]	violence [5]	death [5]	deceitfulness [3]	eye [12]	imitation	outburst [2]	necklace [3]	perceive (perception) [3]	struggle [3]	
I														
like	+													
a look	+							+						
of agony		+			+	+				+		+		
because														
I														
know				+								+		
it's true				+			+							
men														
do not														
sham	+			+			*+	+						
convulsion					+					+				
nor														
simulate	+			+				*+						
a throe		+		+									+	
The eyes	+							+				+		
glaze	+													
once														
and that is death						+								
impossible			+											
to feign	+			+			+	+						
the beads											+			
upon the forehead								+						
by homely														
anguish		+												
strung											+			

FIGURE 26. Spolsky's computer-generated analysis of concepts embodied in the vocabulary of Emily Dickinson's "I Like a Look of Agony." The two asterisks indicate connotations (*deceitfulness* and *imitation*) not found in the *Random House Dictionary* definitions but picked up by the machine using *OED* definitions. (*Reproduced courtesy of Ellen Spolsky*)

tionary discoveries with her program; the informed reader's judgment about the poem must confirm or dismiss the findings of the semantic model, a model which she finally decided was insufficient as a basis for understanding poetry. Nevertheless, considering the simplicity of the design, the machine's discovery of many of the important concepts in the poems analyzed was comparable in quality to the kinds of critical insights gleaned from the far more complicated content analysis procedures previously described.

Somewhat like the Sedelows' thematic system in concept but designed to analyze French texts is the package of interactive PL/I computer programs called THEME and developed by Paul Fortier and Colin McConnell at the University of Manitoba.[34] Starting with a concordance to a text in the KWIC format, the user sitting at terminal edits into the file base forms (root stems) of the words and their parts of speech, from which the machine produces a grammatical concordance. The scholar later types in synonym entries for a theme word from his consultation of several standard dictionaries of French synonyms. The computer produces a primary synonym list headed by the text forms and a secondary list organized under the synonyms themselves. Finally the user requests the machine to search through the file for instances of a particular theme; output options include graphs, tables, lists of selected words annotated with parts of speech and frequencies, and selective concordances limited to single themes.

Trial runs have succeeded in isolating a thematic relation between water and stone in a Camus short story, "La Pierre qui pousse," and the relationship of doubt, a common theme in the conversations of the two main characters in Beckett's *En attendant Godot*, with many terms for hesitation in the play's stage directions—a rough indication of unity of content and form in Beckett's masterpiece. Fortier and McConnell took pains to defend the time involved in using their system compared with manually consulting a keyword concordance with a lot of false starts; once the text has been enhanced into the final theme list, the scholar can rapidly check different thematic hypotheses sitting at the terminal on the whole text or subsections as he desires. Compared to the Sedelows' VIA procedure for English, THEME for French is more modular and

---

[34] Details of the THEME programs are presented in two papers by Paul A. Fortier and J. Colin McConnell: "Computer-Aided Thematic Analysis of French Prose Fiction," in Aitken, pp. 167–81; and "Computer-Aided Thematic Analysis of French Prose Fiction: II. Analysis of Texts and Preparation Costs," in Jones and Churchhouse, pp. 215–22. A user's manual for THEME prepared by Fortier and McConnell is now available: *THEME: A System for Computer-Aided Theme Searches of French Texts*, Research Report No. 1 (Winnipeg: University of Manitoba Department of French and Spanish, 1975).

less automatic in assigning synonyms through interactive computing rather than through stored thesauri. Ignoring the language differences, neither has been tested sufficiently to reveal the superiority of its method in showing more than tentative, sometimes obvious symbolic patterns.

For the study of theme as an aspect of literary style, none of the computer methods of content analysis that have been discussed has produced more than experimental or pilot results. Only occasionally have they discovered new content in their texts which was previously unnoticed by seasoned literary scholars. No doubt skeptics about the computer's intrusion into the realm of literary criticism are pleased that no automated method seems likely to become a substitute for the informed critical intelligence in the near future. Why have none of these schemes been more successful? One answer can be found in noticing that all of the content analysis programs define content in terms of the words of a document or other word associations suggested by them. Other frames of reference, such as irony, metaphor, idiom, and punning, are harder or perhaps even impossible to define so that a rational algorithm can be devised for computer analysis. Witness all the failures in machine translation because of the inadequate linguistic formulation of the semantic dimensions of language. In addition, the computer has neither the background knowledge nor the expectations that an author takes for granted in his readers. Indeed, Sally Sedelow herself, whose system is as good as anybody's, put her finger on the bottleneck in quantitative analyses of content in style when she remarked as recently as 1976:

> This reviewer continues to hope that in time it will be possible to define variables so accurately, operationally, and thoroughly as to be recognizable by computer, thus eliminating the weakest link in all statistical studies of literature so far: precoding the text on the basis of definitions which are often vague. Statistics, at best, are not better than the data they describe.[35]

Words are only partial clues to meaning, and the quantitative judgments content analysis produces based on the words appearing in a text remain experimental and tentative even when they are suggestive. Whether Sedelow's hope will be realized remains a problem for the future, probably contingent on better linguistic foundations of meaning.

A more quantitative and statistical emphasis is found in studies of

---

[35] Sally Y. Sedelow, rev. of *Toward a Quantitative Methodology for Stylistic Analyses*, by Agnes M. Bruno, *Style*, 10 (1976), 302.

form in style than in those of content, no matter what aspects of form are isolated—lexicon, grammar, or metrical patterns. Sometimes there seems more point to doing the counting and analyzing than to assessing the practical value of the results for stylistic study. Take, for instance, the work of Barron Brainerd, a respected professor of mathematics interested in statistical features of language. In one study, he sampled 51 texts, 2500 words each, looking for clues that would discriminate between genres—drama, belles lettres, and expository prose.[36] Comparing counts of articles and pronouns, he found that drama was high in pronouns and low in articles, with the reverse being true of exposition. Belles lettres, including novels and stories, fell in between. In the English language, the number of articles seems to vary inversely with the number of pronouns; this statistical correlation makes sense, since articles modify nouns, whereas pronouns replace nouns. Brainerd found the same kind of separation between realistic novels and romances, suggested by a remark in the *Theory of Literature* by René Wellek and Austin Warren (3rd ed., New York: Harcourt, Brace, and World, 1956) that novels developed out of letters and diaries (dramatic writing) and romances out of medieval romance (more expository, less dramatic writing).[37] In the main, the same situation obtained; novels had more pronouns, and romances more articles. Brainerd compared his results with literary materials in the million-word Brown Standard Corpus of American English[38] and found essential validity of his findings in these larger samples of text. Throughout Brainerd's analyses, there is a serious commitment to proper sampling sizes and methods and appropriate statistical tests of significance, a concern often lacking in other stylistic studies conducted by nonstatisticians.[39] Although the results may be interesting, many literary scholars will question the stylistic meaning of Brainerd's work. Seldom has a count of pronouns and adjectives been needed to tell a memoir from a novel. Definitions of "novel" and "romance" will continue to elicit criti-

[36] Barron Brainerd, "An Exploratory Study of Pronouns and Articles as Indices of Genres in English," *Language and Style*, 5 (1972), 239–59.

[37] Barron Brainerd, "On the Distinction between a Novel and a Romance: A Discriminant Analysis," *CHum*, 7 (1973), 259–70.

[38] See note 6, Chapter 5.

[39] Brainerd's continuing concern for linguistic and literary studies adequately based in statistical methods has led to his writing a book, *Weighing Evidence in Language and Literature: A Statistical Approach* (Toronto: University of Toronto Press, 1974). See also his article, "Statistical Analysis of Lexical Data Using Chi-Squared and Related Distributions," *CHum*, 9 (1975), 161–78. Norman D. Thomson published a series of six similar articles on literary statistical topics in early issues of *ALLC Bulletin* from 1973 to 1975: 1, No. 3 (1973), 10–14; 2, No. 1 (1974), 10–15; 2, No. 2 (1974), 42–47; 2, No. 3 (1974), 55–61; 3 (1975), 29–35; and 3 (1975), 166–71.

cal discussion on grounds other than distribution of parts of speech. Brainerd made few critical claims for his exploratory genre results, and one wonders how else they can be used except as models of statistical sampling with language texts.

The quantitative work of Louis Milic and his followers in studying style in prose and poetry is based on the assumption that grammatical categories reflect the mind and art of an author in a consistent way. According to Milic, syntax in a writer's style is more unconscious than word choice, not particularly subject to genre or content, and likely to be more uniform over a writer's career than other elements. For assessing Jonathan Swift's prose style, Milic manually marked samples for machine input from Swift and four comparable writers into traditional word classes adapted from the categories developed by Charles C. Fries (*The Structure of English*, New York: Harcourt, Brace, 1952): Parts of Speech, including nouns, verbs, adjectives, and adverbs; and Function Words, primarily pronouns, conjunctions, and intensifiers.[40] The computer then cataloged Swift's preferences for specific word classes and sequences of word classes, including a variable called the "D value," the number of arrangements of different three-word patterns suggestive of an author's varied or similar syntactic habits. With this measure and many others such as the use of series and catalogs and the penchant for opening a sentence with a connective, Swift led all the control authors. Milic was then able to make stylistic claims for Swift's variety, fertile imagination, and logical arguments based on the masses of syntactic evidence sifted and arranged into usable categories by the computer. Milic's book on Swift is more than a decade old, but it remains a landmark computer study of style. Although the machine revealed much syntactic evidence of little significance, it did discover writing patterns about Swift and others that literary scholars using traditional methods would never have noticed. Its major drawback was the practice of deciding on parts of speech manually before typing their numerical codes into the machine, an onerous task of syntactic analysis that Milic in 1967 noted "is beyond the present ability of both programmers and computers."[41]

Milic's success with syntactic categories of style soon gathered followers anxious to apply his methods to other authors. William Cherubini

[40] See Louis T. Milic, *A Quantitative Approach to the Style of Jonathan Swift* (The Hague: Mouton, 1967), pp. 142–49.

[41] Milic, p. 143. More recently two methods have been devised to automate at least some syntactic analysis in English: the interactive EYEBALL programs of Donald Ross, Jr., and Robert H. Rasche (see Chapter 8) and the research of Robert L. Oakman: "Carlyle and the Machine: A Quantitative Analysis of Syntax in Prose Style," *ALLC Bulletin*, 3 (1975), 100–14.

decided to refine C. S. Lewis' description of "Golden" Elizabethan verse through close analysis of Sir Philip Sidney's *Astrophel and Stella*.[42] Adopting several of Milic's measures and adding some he devised especially for his work, Cherubini had the computer look at patterns in Sidney's sonnets and control samples from the well-known sonnet sequences of Spenser and Shakespeare. He was able to classify several aspects of Renaissance "Goldenness" that bear out Lewis' critical impressions: "dense" verse, denoted by a high index of nonfunction words; an active verse in which "a great deal happens" (Lewis), exemplified by a high ratio of verbs to nouns and frequent use of attributive participles such as "killing care"; and syntactic complexity, signaled by a high "D value" of word-class sequences.

Much more extensive in adaptation of Milic's model is the impressive research of Robert Cluett and his colleagues, who have compiled the York Computer Inventory of Prose Style, an enormous library of English literary prose with hand-marked parts of speech (a modified version of the Fries categories) for over a hundred writers from Roger Ascham and Lancelot Andrewes to Northrop Frye and Marshall McLuhan.[43] Each sample of approximately 3500 words is analyzed by a FORTRAN IV program into multiple categories—frequencies and percentages of word classes, types of prepositional phrases, Milic's "D value" statistic of syntactic variety, clusters that open and close sentences, word parallelisms, sentence lengths, etc. In great detail, Cluett first organized his results around elements of the sentence and types of styles, i.e., nominal, verbal, modifying; then focused on four particular stylistic investigations: Sir Philip Sidney and Elizabethan novelists, Hemingway's plain style, Carlyle and the Victorian baroque, and a historical development of English literary prose. Throughout his book, Cluett bombards the reader with charts, tables, and statistics for the plethora of syntactic studies he undertakes. His wealth of results and stylistic generalizations, too numerous to suggest even their flavor in digested form, resembles in kind those of Milic earlier but is much more broadly suggestive over the whole history of English prose. Certainly Cluett's work is a monument of stylistic study that cannot be ignored by future scholars. In whatever way Cluett wanted the computer to rearrange or reorder his word cate-

---

[42] William Cherubini, "The 'Goldenness' of Sidney's *Astrophel and Stella*: Test of a Quantitative-Stylistics Routine," *Language and Style*, 8 (1975), 47–59.

[43] The complete list of samples is given in Appendix B, pp. 284–91, of Cluett's *Prose Style and Critical Reading* (New York: Columbia University Teachers College Press, 1976). See also Cluett's earlier study of Restoration "plain" style: "Style, Precept, Personality: A Test Case (Thomas Sprat, 1635–1713)," *CHum*, 5 (1971), 257–77.

gories, it did so with speed and accuracy. Too bad he and his associates had to mark all the word classifications manually before the machine went to work. No one else is likely to go to that much trouble again soon.

Darrell Mansell's attempt to place the writing of Ernest Hemingway's *The Old Man and the Sea* chronologically with his earlier works long before its publication in 1952 resembles the Milic approach in manual coding of a variety of stylistic features prior to machine analysis.[44] Although Mansell devised his own syntax codes through trial and error, he defended them as consistent for comparing his Hemingway samples, even if they were more intuitively based on a critical sense than grammatically rigid. For *The Old Man* and four other texts composed by Hemingway between 1933 and 1951 (thirty subsamples), Mansell looked at eight variables, including average number of syllables per word; the number of words of one, two, three, etc., syllables; ratio of main verbs to adjectives and adverbs; and the average number of words between the first word of a sentence and the main verb. Using the "F-test" statistical measure of validity, the computer suggested seventeen cases in which another text was similar to *The Old Man*; and in twelve of these the match was with the long short story, "The Capital of the World" (1936). Acknowledging some of the shortcomings of his tentative analysis, Mansell was, nevertheless, pleased to have verifiable internal evidence of his original critical hypothesis: that *The Old Man* was written about 1935 or 1936. Like the best of the authorship studies, Mansell chose to examine stylistic elements that seemed significant to his literary mind; he got professional advice about statistical testing; and he came to a guarded conclusion. In common with Milic and Cluett, his most onerous task was surely hand marking the texts, even though he had a much smaller total of 22,500 words (4500 from each of five Hemingway works) than either of the other two projects.

Whereas these scholars focused on syntax as an unconscious element of style, a number of others have chosen vocabulary as a valid stylistic variable for their purposes and relied on computer-produced concordances and indexes to assist their analyses. Unexpectedly Sister Dolores M. Burton found it helpful to concord 300 function words (articles, prepositions, conjunctions, auxiliary verbs, and pronouns) which comprise about half of language texts, in order to compare the styles of

[44] Darrell Mansell, "*The Old Man and the Sea* and the Computer," *CHum*, 8 (1974), 195–206.

Shakespeare's *Antony and Cleopatra* and *Richard II*.[45] Indicative of the kind of stylistic judgments revealed by analysis of the computer printout was Philo's description of Cleopatra with "a tawny front," "a gypsy's lust," and "a strumpet's fool" in the opening scene of the play. Choice of the indefinite article *a* over the definite article *the* by a character who dislikes Cleopatra, Burton contends, detracts from her uniqueness before she appears on stage (*a* gypsy vs. *the* gypsy).[46] Like other practitioners of quantitative stylistics, Burton finds many such distinctions in her concordance materials; without the machine, she would probably not have even considered function word analysis by traditional means.

Joseph Raben's early research into vocabulary similarity between Milton's *Paradise Lost* and Shelley's *Prometheus Unbound* represents a simple but ingenious use of a computer algorithm to solve a problem practically impossible without machine assistance. Since it is known that Shelley was reading Milton while writing *Prometheus*, Raben wanted to check the amount of assimilation, if any, of Milton's epic vocabulary into Shelley's poem.[47] He decided to check for the appearances of two or more content words in one poetic sentence in *Prometheus* (about 20,000 words long) which also occur within one poetic sentence in *Paradise Lost* (about 80,000 words). First his computer made a word index to each poem, essentially a concordance without context, with function words omitted and with sentence numbers attached to each content form. The most recent version of the program then requires the scholar to canonize words into base forms before sorting them alphabetically again.

Two computer scientists, Seymour Goodman and Raymond D. Villani, suggested a way for merging the two lemmatized indexes, presented as a flowchart in Figure 27.[48] The machine reads a word from Index I (for Milton, let us say) and sees if it is in Index II (Shelley). If

[45] Dolores M. Burton, *Shakespeare's Grammatical Style* (Austin: University of Texas Press, 1973). See also Burton's earlier article, "Some Uses of a Grammatical Concordance," *CHum*, 2 (1968), 145–54.

[46] Burton, *CHum*, pp. 148–49.

[47] See two Raben discussions of this project: "A Computer-Aided Study of Literary Influence: Milton to Shelley," in *Proceedings of a Literary Data Processing Conference, September 9–11, 1964*, ed. Jess B. Bessinger, Jr., Stephen M. Parrish, and Harry F. Arader (New York: Modern Language Association, 1964), pp. 230–74; and Joseph Raben and David Lieberman, "Text Comparison: Principles and a Program," in Jones and Churchhouse, pp. 297–308. The second article documents two current versions of the program in both FORTRAN and PL/I.

[48] Seymour Goodman and Raymond D. Villani, "An Algorithm for Locating Multiple Word Co-occurrence in Two Sets of Text," *Proceedings of a Literary Data Processing Conference, September 9–11, 1964*, pp. 275–92.

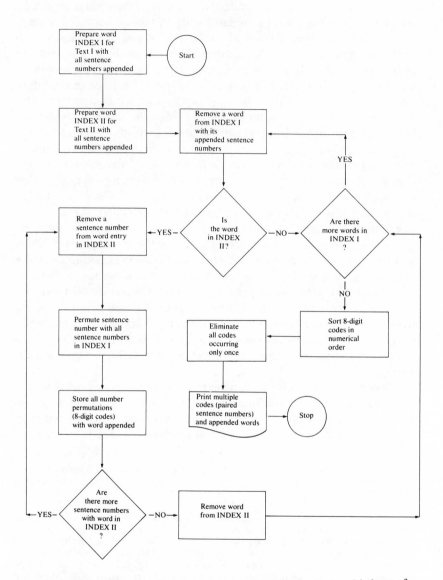

FIGURE 27. A flowchart for a computer program to merge the word indexes of two literary texts to reveal vocabulary similarity between them. Raben used this method to show extensive similarity of word choice in Milton's *Paradise Lost* and Shelley's *Prometheus Unbound*.

not, the word is erased from memory to economize on storage, and the next word is tried. When a word occurs in both indexes, the computer permutes all the sentence numbers from Index I with all those in Index II, then stores the permutation as an eight-digit code number along with the associated word. For instance the permutation code for pairing sentences 100 in Milton and 579 in Shelley would be 01000579. Continuing to form permutations for identical words in both indexes, the machine has stored a code number for every word which appears in both epics. Treating the eight-digit codes as numbers and sorting all of them in numerical order—a standard computer task—clusters together all the context words that co-occur in one pair of Milton-Shelley sentences. Eliminating all cases of only one word in common per sentence pair, the machine then prints out the words and sentence numbers for the multiple instances, in numerical order of most frequent pairs if desired. The scholar can then locate the passages in the poems by sentence numbers and check to see if the contexts are as similar as the vocabulary items. Raben's project discovered thousands of correspondences, including one pair of sentences sharing seventeen words in common; in many cases the content of the passages showed similarities of subject matter. By cleverly adapting common numerical sorting to the special code numbers, the algorithm got the computer to reveal to Raben a wealth of information about both poets' word choices that he would never have noticed in these two long epic poems. It seems surprising that since this technique was announced more than a decade ago no other scholars have apparently taken advantage of it for comparable investigations.

Concordances have also been very useful in studying early oral formulaic poetry in both Old English and Old French. Probably Joseph J. Duggan's work with the *Chanson de Roland* and other medieval French romances and *chansons de geste* represents the most automated method.[49] Duggan had the computer produce concordances of his French texts with the occurrences of each word arranged in alphabetical order of the following words in each line of verse. When printed out, oral formulas of at least two words were listed side by side under both words and could be easily noticed by inspection. Because Old French spelling is

[49] Joseph J. Duggan, *The Song of Roland: Formulaic Style and Poetic Craft* (Berkeley: University of California Press, 1973). Donald C. Green looked at syntactic frames, not repeated words, in his "Formulas and Syntax in Old English Poetry: A Computer Study," *CHum*, 6 (1971), 85–93. He had to mark metrical stresses and syntactic types by hand before input; the machine was used primarily for sorting and counting. A more complex, automated approach employing cluster analysis to examine formulaic devices in Greek oral poetry is documented with results in Cora A. Sowa and John F. Sowa, "Thought Clusters in Early Greek Oral Poetry," *CHum*, 8 (1974), 131–46.

seldom standard, however, word formulas spelled *barons franceis* and *baruns franceis* often did not appear on the same page of the printed concordance under *b*; they would be near each other under the entry for *franceis*. Duggan found that often formulas were easiest to spot under the entries for function words like *il*, *de*, or *le*, since their spellings were much more set than content words. In order not to count the same formula twice (under *b* and *f* for *barons franceis*), Duggan had each line of context with its appended location prepared from the machine on a punchcard as well as printed in the concordance. As he found a formula in the printed version, he pulled the corresponding card out of the deck; when he finished, the cards were sorted alphabetically, and duplicates removed, leaving one card per formula. Duggan succeeded with this simple machine-assisted procedure in showing that the entire *Roland* had about 35 percent of its half lines as formulas, almost the same percentage as his earlier analysis of the *Couronnement de Louis* (37 percent)[50] and fewer than earlier samples from the work had indicated. Even the disputed "Baligant" episode matched the rest of *Roland* in formulaic practice, despite other evidence that it may have been added later.[51] Duggan's book-length study of *Roland* and other Old French poems certainly has validated the success of computer assistance in proving the extent of oral formulaic practices, a long-standing critical issue of great controversy.

Methods of computational stylistics have been applied in a number of studies of the novel, but most have used the same methods already discussed for other genres to study vocabulary, syntax, imagery, or rhetorical devices: hand analysis of input samples of text into categories to be investigated and computer assistance in sorting, counting, and doing statistical tests on the findings.[52] A suggestive technological advance adopted by John B. Smith for his analysis of hand-marked, computer-

---

[50] Joseph J. Duggan, "Formulas in the *Couronnement de Louis*," *Romania*, 87 (1966), 315–44.

[51] John R. Allen's preliminary computer analysis of other aspects of this problem suggested divergent results: "On the Authenticity of the Baligant Episode in the *Chanson de Roland*," in Mitchell, pp. 65–72.

[52] See, for example, Mitchell A. Leaska's *Virginia Woolf's Lighthouse: A Study in Critical Method* (New York: Columbia University Press, 1970), which looks for stylistic differences between nine narrators in the novel. Karl Kroeber in *Styles in Fictional Structure: The Art of Jane Austen, Charlotte Brontë, George Eliot* (Princeton: Princeton University Press, 1971) studied three fictional elements on a quantitative basis: vocabulary; "total design," which included time, setting, characters, and kinds of action; and distinctions between dialogue and narration.

sorted image patterns in James Joyce's *Portrait of the Artist as a Young Man* was the presentation of two- and three-dimensional diagrams produced at an ADAGE graphics terminal to illustrate peaks of image intensity at epiphanal moments in the novel.[53]

A structural study by Christiane and Claude Allais of an epistolary novel, *Les Liaisons dangereuses* by Pierre Laclos, was based on patterns of similarity and difference within the ten two-week time periods in which the letters of the novel were written.[54] For each time period, the significant variable, the pairs of letter writers and recipients—who wrote whom—were recorded; in all, twenty-eight possible exchanges of letters were tallied for each of the ten periods—some very numerous with letters, others sparse. Patterns of exchange in certain periods were statistically more similar than in other periods, so that the Allaises were able to group the periods together as points on a graph. The points on the graph clustered neatly into five groups; distances between clusters were proportional to similarity of exchanges between periods. The investigators speculated that the clusters displayed a five-part structure of the novel over its ten time periods. Like Smith, the analysis yielded graphic representation of one aspect of the novel, its temporal relations, amenable to study in a straightforward epistolary novel. The Allaises suggested that similar numerical relations could be calculated and graphed for interactions of characters in drama, but no one seems to have taken up the idea. Acceptance of graphic representation of novel elements seems to depend more on critical reception of the variable under study as significant than on computer analysis, statistical results, or technological elegance.

With one important exception, stylistic investigations of poetry and meter represent little advance in automated methods over earlier prose applications. Usually the material must be pre-edited to mark elements under study, whether meter, rhyme, syntax, imagery; then the machine performs its usual functions of sorting, counting, grouping, and applying

---

[53] John B. Smith, "Computer Generated Analogues of Mental Structures from Language Data," in *Proceedings of the International Federation for Information Processing Congress 1974*, ed. Jack L. Rosenfeld (Amsterdam and London: North-Holland, 1974), pp. 842–45. For more substantive discussion of the project itself, see Smith's "A Computational Analysis of Imagery in James Joyce's *A Portrait of the Artist as a Young Man*," in *Proceedings of the International Federation for Information Processing Congress 1971*, ed. C. V. Freiman (Amsterdam and London: North-Holland, 1972), pp. 1443–47.

[54] Christiane and Claude Allais, "A Method of Structural Analysis with an Application to *Les Liaisons dangereuses*," R.E.L.O. *Revue*, No. 2 (1968), pp. 13–33.

statistical tests.[55] Robert J. Dilligan has, however, programmed the computer to do integral portions of phonetic and metrical analysis itself, based on a machine-readable version of Daniel Jones' *English Pronouncing Dictionary* (New York: E. P. Dutton, 1927).[56] To study Robert Bridges' experiments in quantitative verse, Dilligan encoded Bridges' translation of Book VI of the *Aeneid* in English hexameter. With minimal editing, the computer program consulted the dictionary, produced "a fairly broad phonetic transcription of the text,"[57] and sorted and cross-referenced patterns of assonance and alliteration for Dilligan's perusal.

More recently, along with Todd K. Bender, Dilligan has reported a series of computer routines in both PL/I and FORTRAN V to perform automatic metrical scansion of English iambic pentameter based on the well-known model of Morris Halle and Samuel J. Keyser, mentioned earlier in connection with Greenblatt's authorship attribution work.[58] A computer concordance punches out the lexicon of a poem, one word per card, onto which is now keypunched a phonemic transcription of the word. Apparently the automatic "broad" transcription done for Bridges was not accurate enough for the later, expanded machine operations now included in the system. The scanning process itself works with the transcribed text a line at a time; its repertoire of functions is extensive: determining stressed vowels, counting syllables, and listing vowels and initial consonant clusters. Later, parts of the program can decipher patterns of assonance and alliteration and pick out points of stress maxima and deviations from metrical regularity before printing out impressive lists and graphs of numerical counts, as well as lines and transcriptions if desired. Tested with early verse of Gerard Manley Hopkins, the computer found that Hopkins' famous metrical license did not apply before 1876; twenty poems had only five unmetrical lines. Cases of elision in early work represent the kind of strain against conventional metrics usually expected in late Hopkins. Although these tests were only partial,

---

[55] The work of two scholars on sonnets suggests the usual methods and patterns of computer assistance: Judith A. Vanderbok, "Developing a Quantitative Poetic: E. E. Cummings and his Sonnets," *SIGLASH Newsletter*, 9, No. 4 (September 1976), 2–9; and Joseph Leighton, "Sonnets and Computers: An Experiment in Stylistic Analysis Using an Elliott 503 Computer," in Wisbey, pp. 149–58; also "Automatic Analysis of Simple Rhetorical Devices in Seventeenth Century German Sonnets," in Jones and Churchhouse, pp. 246–54.

[56] Robert J. Dilligan, "*Ibant Obscvri*: Robert Bridges' Experiment in English Quantitative Verse," *Style*, 6 (1972), 38–65.

[57] Dilligan, p. 40.

[58] Robert J. Dilligan and Todd K. Bender, "The Lapses of Time: A Computer-Assisted Investigation of English Prosody," in Aitken, pp. 239–52. For Halle and Keyser, see note 15.

they suggest the power of the scansion algorithm to discover prosodic features for the scholar, unmarked by him, that would be extremely tedious to catalog by traditional methods.

It is reassuring to be able to close the discussion of computational stylistics with work like Dilligan's, which employs the machine to do more than its usual tasks to analyze the formal properties of verse. Unlike most literary scholars, Dilligan has had much experience in writing computer programs for himself; he understands how to analyze metrics into a series of algorithmic processes so that a computer program can do much of the analysis for him. On the other hand, the great majority of stylistic work that has been described originated with literary scholars with little or no prior computer experience. Many of these projects adapted conventional computer tasks—sorting, searches, word indexes, calculations—to their own stylistic purposes; a few developed suggestive new measures to apply to style. The best of the quantitative studies display concern for choosing proper samples and validating the results with appropriate statistical tests. In 1973 Joseph Raben, editor of *Computers and the Humanities*, assessing the current state of computerized stylistic analysis, warned against the powerful seductive pull of the "objective aspects" of stylistic analysis with the machine—often "counting for its own sake."[59] The most suggestive work has more to offer than a collection of facts and numbers; instead it provides verifiable, empirical evidence of stylistic habits or trends about a writer, his works, or literary genres under study. As with its earlier applications to literary research, the machine must keep its proper place—a powerful, accurate, and speedy assistant, and sometimes even partner, with the scholar—in the enterprise of stylistic analysis. When properly used, the computer can reveal patterns that men would never notice or would rarely take the trouble to ferret out. If the results are disappointing—more show than substance—the failure reflects more on the person behind the scheme— his inadequate theories of linguistics, thematics, or stylistics; his methods of applying them; or his assessment of the results—than on his computer tool.

[59] Joseph Raben, "The Humanist in the Computer Lab: Thoughts on Technology in the Study of Literature," *ALLC Bulletin*, 1, No. 1 (1973), 7.

FOR FURTHER READING

Doložel, Lubomír, and Richard W. Bailey, eds. *Statistics and Style.* New York: American Elsevier, 1969.

Collection of essays by various hands on statistical elements of vocabulary, sentences, and poetics suitable for stylistic application, including a critique of computerized authorship studies by Richard Bailey.

Holsti, Ole. *Content Analysis for the Social Sciences and Humanities.* Reading, Mass.: Addison-Wesley, 1969.

Currently the best introduction to the theory and practice of content analysis, including a long section on computer usage. Holsti emphasizes more applications in the social sciences than the humanities.

Gerbner, George, Ole R. Holsti, Klaus Krippendorff, William J. Paisley, and Philip J. Stone, eds. *The Analysis of Communication Content.* New York: John Wiley and Sons, 1969.

Most influential collection of papers on content analysis and its applications, with contributions by Stone, Iker, Sedelow, Raben, and others on computerized approaches.

Kemp, Kenneth W. "Personal Observations on the Use of Statistical Methods in Quantitative Linguistics." *The Computer in Literary and Linguistic Studies.* Ed. Alan Jones and Robert F. Churchhouse. Cardiff: University of Wales Press, 1976. Pp. 59–77.

Practical advice from a statistician on carrying out a quantitative stylistic study, including sampling and appropriate statistical models for language text.

Leed, Jacob, ed. *The Computer and Literary Style.* Kent, Ohio: Kent State University Press, 1966.

Useful collection of papers focusing on early computerized stylistic studies, especially of authorship attribution. Contributions include discussion of the work of the Sedelows, Milic, O'Donnell, Morton, and Mosteller and Wallace among others.

Morton, A. Q. *Literary Detection: How to Prove Authorship and Fraud in Literature and Documents.* New York: Charles Scribner's Sons, 1978.

The latest word on Morton's theory of stylometry for languages, both inflected (Greek) and uninflected (English). English test cases from Shakespeare and Jane Austen to Conan Doyle conclude with remarks about the surprise ending of the Steve Raymond case and its implications.

Spraycar, Rudy S., and Lee F. Dunlap. "Formulaic Style in Oral and Literate Epic Poetry." *Perspectives in Computing,* 2 (December 1982), 24–33.

Excellent survey of all the arguments about oral formulaic verse, folk and literary, with telling comments on the inadequate statistical validity of the early studies of Parry and Lord and recommendations about sample size and technique for future work.

Tallentire, D. R. "The Mathematics of Style (Thinking by Numbers, 2)." *Times Literary Supplement,* 13 August 1971, pp. 973–74.

A careful, negative assessment of the study of vocabulary as a discriminator of style with well-chosen illustrations of refutation.

Widmann, R. L. "Computers and Literary Scholarship." *CHum,* 6 (1971), 3–14.

_____. "Recent Scholarship in Literary and Linguistic Studies." *CHum,* 7 (1972), 3–27.

_____. "Trends in Computer Applications to Literature." *CHum,* 9 (1975), 231–35.

Most recent of several detailed surveys of developments in literary study published by *Computers and the Humanities.* Widmann's articles range widely and offer summary with incisive criticism, as well as excellent bibliographies.

CHAPTER 8

Further Considerations: Archives, Packages, and Future Prospects

TO CONCLUDE THE SURVEY of major trends in literary computing, we shall examine both texts in machine-readable form and program aids already available for scholarly use and then suggest problems and potentials for future development. There should be no need for one scholar to go to the trouble of encoding a copy of a literary text a second time if someone else has previously prepared it for machine input. Yet, without careful planning or knowledge of available textual archives, just that situation can happen. Along the same lines, a scholar setting out to prepare a new text should think about the possibility of someone else's using it later for other study. If feasible, he should encode it in a form and medium that retain its accuracy, can be readily transported from one place to another, and are likely to be readable by others' computer equipment.

For these purposes, magnetic tape, both seven and nine track, has been the most favored medium, with punchcards and paper tape also used. Magnetic tape holds its information intact over long periods of time and can easily be mailed. Punchcards tend to warp after several months and then may jam when read into a reader; in addition, they are bulky and require more storage space than more compact magnetic tapes holding literally millions of characters on one reel. Compared to punchcards, paper tape is more ephemeral and easy to damage or tear; consequently, it has been the least popular medium for sharing machine-readable texts. No matter what input method is used initially, at most computer centers the text can usually be converted onto magnetic tape for permanent storage or later distribution.

More than anyone else, Stephen V. F. Waite of Dartmouth College has had experience in the collection of literary texts donated by scholars, their storage, and later dissemination to other scholars throughout the world. Begun in 1969 as the American Philological Association Repository of Classical Texts in Machine-Readable Form, Waite's archive has grown from modest beginnings to include donated selections from more than forty classical authors of works in both Greek and Latin, including major holdings of Homer, Virgil, the Greek New Testament, and St. Augustine. By 1976, several large files of modern English text, including the collected poetry of Robert Frost and T. S. Eliot and several plays of Sean O'Casey, had been added to the collection, now called Project LIBRI (Literary Information Bases for Research and Instruction).[1]

Waite's guidelines for accepting and distributing texts are flexible and practical, with the overall goal of conserving all kinds of texts and making them available to others at a minimal cost of reproduction and shipping. The recipient must acknowledge the original preparer of the text in any subsequent use of it. Waite serves only as repositor and distributor; he cannot guarantee accuracy of the texts. Upon receipt of a donated text, he tries to verify it before sending it out, normally on magnetic tape or, if necessary, on punched cards. For persons beginning to prepare text ultimately to be housed in the Repository, Waite suggests one of two common magnetic tape formats and a coding scheme for languages like Greek with a nonroman alphabet, which can be adapted for reading on a great variety of modern computer systems. Because of his long experience in running a clearinghouse for machine-readable texts, scholars continue to contribute materials to Waite's center, averaging about 60,000 to 80,000 new lines per year. Certainly his success in archiving texts for many classical authors and more recently for modern languages, all produced originally by scholars for their own use but then donated for the use of others, marks Waite's Repository and Project LIBRI as models for other textual archives that may be started in the future.

At present there is no universally agreed-upon standard even for encoding literary text in magnetic tape format. Some texts were prepared as long ago as 1960, when the computing technology available throughout the world offered very limited input possibilities, typically punched cards and paper or magnetic tape, with no international cooperation on standardization in either machinery or scholarly endeavors. Joan and L. M. Smith at the computation center at the University of Manchester have had more experience than most other humanists in trying to salvage texts by converting them into a modern, compatible format from whatever exotic early encoding form they were originally prepared in.[2]

---

[1] A complete listing of available texts is available from Waite, Kiewit Computation Center, Dartmouth College, Hanover NH 03755. New items added to the collection are reported in the bimonthly issues of *CALCULI*.

[2] See Joan M. and L. M. Smith, "The Availability of Texts in Machine-Readable Form: Practical Considerations," *ALLC Bulletin*, 3 (1975), 19–28, for full, even gruesome details of some of their conversion problems.

For instance, most British literary texts were prepared in the early days on paper tape of various types (five, six, seven, and eight track) and differing character codes. To make them into the modern standard eight-track paper tape, the Smiths used a tape reader with adjustable slides for various widths and wrote programs to map all the original character codes into a common standard. The situation with magnetic tape was equally confusing; there were tapes of different widths (from one-quarter to one inch) and a variety of track widths on which the information was encoded (from the usual seven and nine tracks to an old-style sixteen-track tape used by a computer long ago phased out). Where possible, the Smiths located old machinery to carry out interim conversion to a normal half-inch tape in either seven or nine tracks. Based on the Smiths' complicated, tedious experiences in trying to retain valuable texts encoded initially for now outdated machinery, the moral for the scholarly community is obvious: the future encoding of texts should adhere, if at all possible, to as compatible a modern medium and character coding scheme as is available.

As noted, there exists no worldwide, agreed-upon modern standard for encoding texts. Given the situation of widely dispersed scholars using whatever brand of equipment they have available to them, universal conventions for preparing texts, even for languages using the roman alphabet, are probably unattainable. However, there are gradually developing guidelines pointing toward compatibility of text formats over international boundaries. Project LIBRI, for instance, initially settled on a standard of seven-track magnetic tape, readable on many models of computing machinery, and a common character set allowing 64 different codes. More recently Waite has also developed an optional nine-track magnetic tape format. In Europe, the enormous Italian data bank of literary texts, over one hundred million words coded in one format, is headquartered at Pisa under the guidance of Antonio Zampolli of the Centro Nazionale Universitario di Calcolo Elettronico (CNUCE).[3] In recent years French scholars have agreed to adopt the Italian standards—seven-track magnetic tape with a character set of 120 codes—for their work, a possible move toward a common European standard. The similarities of tape format between the Waite and Zampolli standards, along with the friendly contacts already existing between these centers, sug-

---

[3] A list of the many Italian texts available from Pisa and the Accademia della Crusca in Florence—all encoded in the same format—appears in *CHum*, 2 (1968), 133–44; 6 (1972), 172–75; and 7 (1973), 177–81. For current information about the holdings of the Italian archive and its encoding standards, contact Professor Antonio Zampolli, CNUCE, Via S. Maria 36, 56100 Pisa, Italy.

gest the possibility of compatible conversion of materials within these large data archives.

Scholars setting out on a large-scale project would do well to consider these developing international guidelines for permanent magnetic tape storage of their large quantities of literary text in machine-readable form, no matter what encoding medium is used initially. Most computer centers today can convert materials into these magnetic tape formats from cards, paper tape, optical scanners, or direct input at a terminal keyboard. Proper planning prior to the actual encoding of texts can today avoid many of the conversion headaches of the past.

Besides Project LIBRI and the large Italian repository at Pisa, several other archives with large holdings of literary texts in Western languages deserve mention. Often the texts were originally compiled as source materials for the great historical dictionary projects being carried out in several European countries. In this category fall the collection of modern French texts available from the files of the *Trésor de la Langue Française* under the direction of Professor Paul Imbs at Nancy and a variety of Older Scottish texts used by A. J. Aitken and his colleagues at the University of Edinburgh for the *Dictionary of the Older Scottish Tongue*.[4] German texts have been archived in several centers, including Mannheim, Bonn, Los Angeles, and Cambridge University; the Institut für Deutsche Sprache in Bonn and the University of Southern California serve jointly as clearinghouses for Early German materials.[5]

At Cambridge, the Literary and Linguistic Computing Centre (see Chapter 2) has literary texts in modern IBM tape format for a variety of modern and classical languages; it is especially strong in Early German, the research field of its founder, Roy Wisbey, and offers a sampling of English texts, from Aelfric homilies in Old English to Spenser's *Faerie Queene* from the Renaissance to modern short stories by Katherine Mansfield and Virginia Woolf.[6] Very recently the Computing Laboratory at Oxford University has decided to become a central archive for English literature; its initial brochure lists texts collected or promised for donation by early 1977. Authors from the Renaissance to the present are

---

[4] Listings of texts available several years ago appeared in *CHum*: for modern French, *CHum*, 3 (1969), 225–39, and for Old Scottish, *CHum*, 5 (1971), 172. For up-to-date files, contact Professor Paul Imbs, Directeur, Centre pour un Trésor de la Langue Française, 44 Avenue de la Libération, 54-Nancy, France, and Professor A. J. Aitken, *Dictionary of the Older Scottish Tongue*, 27 George Square, Edinburgh 8, Scotland.

[5] For information about German texts, see *CHum*, 5 (1971), 171–72 (Mannheim); *CHum*, 7 (1973), 253–56 (Bonn and Los Angeles); and *ALLC Bulletin*, 4 (1976), 179–80 (Cambridge).

[6] Recent details about the Cambridge holdings and their technical description and availability appear in *ALLC Bulletin*, 4 (1976), 178–81.

175

represented, including novels by Fielding, Scott, Conrad, and Woolf; poetry by Pope, Coleridge, Keats, T. S. Eliot, Robert Graves, and Dylan Thomas; and drama by Marlowe, Samuel Beckett, and Thomas Randolph. Like LIBRI, the Oxford Archive collects texts prepared in various formats by different scholars around the world and then makes them available to others for the small cost of postage and handling and assurance of due acknowledgment of the original source.[7]

For classical Greek texts, the enormous files being encoded by the Thesaurus Linguae Graecae (TLG) at the University of California at Irvine deserve special attention. Unprecedented in literary study, this project set out in 1972 to encode in computer-readable form essentially all of the extant classical Greek materials. By 1976, the center, under the direction of Theodore F. Brunner at Irvine, contained about 18,000,000 words of text, including most writers before A.D. 200 and more than 5,000,000 words of medical works to A.D. 800. All of this material is encoded in one format: one text per file on nine-track magnetic tapes in the widely used EBCDIC character set. In order to distribute these texts, the governing board of the TLG has developed guidelines similar in concept to other clearinghouses. Texts may be purchased on magnetic tape for the cost of reproduction and shipping for nonprofit use by scholars; in addition, the center can provide concordances, frequency indexes, etc., with similar cost provisions. Eventually the TLG plans its own nonprofit publishing agency to produce concordances and other indexes for its great wealth of Greek materials.[8] The Thesaurus is unique among the great language archives in being privately endowed rather than state sponsored. It is well that classical scholars now can have access to its enormous resources, all prepared with a common format and character code that can be readily accepted as input by much modern computer machinery.

In addition to possibly finding a copy of a text already prepared in computer-readable form, the scholar starting out with a typical literary computing job may also be lucky enough to borrow a program package developed by someone else that will do his work for him. Under the best circumstances, he would be able to send away and get copies of his text and a general-purpose program, both probably on magnetic tapes; carry them to his local computer center; and have a technician run them for

---

[7] For information about policies and textual files at Oxford, contact The Archive, Oxford University Computing Laboratory, 19 Banbury Road, Oxford OX2 6NN, England.

[8] Guidelines for distribution of TLG materials appeared in *CALCULI* (January 1976), p. 241. Complete information about the project is available from Professor Brunner, Thesaurus Linguae Graecae Project, University of California at Irvine, Irvine CA 92717.

him so that within a short time he would have his printed output. Practically this scenario is almost impossible, although it is technologically feasible. Perhaps the "canned" program prepared elsewhere is written in a programming language unavailable on his local computer; even if it will run, the format it requires for input of text may not match the text format in the borrowed magnetic tape. Thus, before the program can accept it, the input text must be converted to the form desired by the program package; a conversion program will be required, perhaps written by someone at the computer center. Of course, if the scholar is going to prepare his own text from scratch, he will be able to set it up according to the demands of a prepared program he is planning to use.

It should be clear that using others' programs or prepared texts is seldom as easy as it might seem. For one reason or another (incompatible programming language, incompatible hardware requirements, or incompatible input format) the scholar who wants to adapt programs done by someone else for his own purposes will certainly be, as Colin Day puts it, "dependent on the goodwill of the programmer who created the package, and on the assistance of local computer centre staff to help implement it."[9] Without good cooperation, the "canned" program may be useless, despite the fact that it is designed for the very job needed by the scholar. Designers of the most successful program packages have thought carefully about such issues as the choice of a common programming language, kinds of input requirements, and optional features within the programs themselves, in order to make their products portable from one computer installation to another and accessible for a variety of literary uses.

The most frequently requested computer routine of literary application is a program to generate a concordance, given the text as input. Features of several prepared concordance schemes have already been mentioned in Chapter 4. One of them will serve, however, as an excellent example of a well-conceived, general-purpose program of wide applicability—the current version of the COCOA concordance generator developed at the Atlas Laboratory in Britain. Completed in 1973, CO-COA, an acronym for Count and Concordance generation on Atlas, is written in USASI Standard FORTRAN, a version of the language acceptable throughout the world, in order to make the program machine-independent; it is distributed on punched cards. Apropos of its portability, I know an American friend who had COCOA running within fifteen minutes on a computer on which it had never previously been tried.

[9] A. Colin Day, "The State of Software," *ALLC Bulletin*, 3 (1975), 43.

177

Besides this remarkable adaptability, the designers of COCOA have provided an assortment of useful program options and a readable user's manual with explicit instructions and lots of examples for the computer novice.[10] For instance, COCOA can produce concordances arranged in KWIC format, word counts, and word-frequency information for material in any language as long as its characters can be encoded on the implementing computer. Arrangements for word counts are flexible: alphabetical, reverse alphabetical, or frequency order. The user can define his alphabetical order so that the *ll* in Spanish can be treated as a separate letter or *é* in French (punched as "e/" on a card) will be alphabetized with unaccented e's. The program is capable of concording only words occurring above a certain frequency threshold or located in specific sections of a longer text (such as one act of a Shakespeare play).

To activate these and numerous other options, all chosen to give CO-COA more general application than a stripped concordance program, the scholar prepares special control cards read in before his text. The operator's manual clearly describes all of these facilities with actual, easy-to-follow illustrations of typical input and output. All in all, the evolution of COCOA to its present state represents a serious effort on the part of its designers to see what kinds of jobs, related to the concordance process, literary scholars want done, to write their programs in the most universal version of the popular FORTRAN language, and to explain how to use them in a well-written manual. To date, COCOA has been successfully adopted by scholars throughout the world; its wide acceptance indicates the success of its authors in carrying out these carefully planned, practical aspects of the project.

Several other "general" programs represent modifications of the concordance process. Developed at the University of Montreal, JEU-DEMO, a clever bit of mnemonic "word play," adds to a COCOA-based program more features for information retrieval.[11] The program and its user's manual were tested for simplicity of use by fifty scholars in the process of development; by having only a few commands the designers intended to help the inexperienced humanist over the problems of programming. In its current form, JEUDEMO accepts text prepared on punched cards or Flexowriter paper tape; an interactive version is planned for running on a CDC Cyber 74 computer system, the machine

---

[10] Godelieve L. M. Berry-Rogghe and T. D. Crawford, *COCOA: A Word Count and Concordance Generator* (Chilton, Didcot: Atlas Computer Laboratory, and Cardiff: University College, 1973).

[11] See two articles by Paul Bratley, Serge Lusignan, and Francine Ouellette: "JEU-DEMO: A Text-Handling System," in Mitchell, pp. 234–49; and "JEUDEMO, A Package for Scholars in the Humanities," *SIGLASH Newsletter*, 7, No. 3 (June 1974), 15–19.

on which it was originally designed. The program incorporates all of the flexible options of COCOA and the ability to request searches containing complicated expressions with *and*—a basic searching choice in information retrieval (see Chapter 5). The user first defines his own hierarchies of text—word, sentence, paragraph, chapter, etc. Then, using its pattern-searching features, JEUDEMO can look for two words, like "boy" and "dog," occurring in the same sentence, in the same paragraph, or with a proximity of ten words from each other in the whole text, according to the scholar's request. These pattern-matching capabilities make JEUDEMO potentially more useful than COCOA.

However, problems of adaptability of JEUDEMO to most computer systems still remain. Although its developers had portability in mind for the program, the fact that some of its programming is done in a computer language peculiar to the CDC Cyber 74 system (the rest uses CDC-compatible FORTRAN IV) will limit its use in present form to scholars with access to this hardware. Of course, other scholars can borrow the JEUDEMO programs and rewrite or replace the particular CDC routines with equivalent ones for their computer systems. But often that process is as difficult, troublesome, and time-consuming as developing one's own programs from the start. Compared to COCOA, its forerunner, JEUDEMO offers attractive additional features and a few easy commands that humanists can learn to use quickly. Yet it is not likely to be as widely accepted because of its annoying, partial programming in a language specific to one computer manufacturer's machinery.

Two PL/I program packages have been reported that are intended for tasks typically requested by literary scholars. CLAS, the Computerized Language Analysis System announced several years ago from Pennsylvania State, adds to the typical concordancing options some facilities for performing standard statistical tests on literary texts.[12] Given the text on punchcards, the program can produce an index of its words and then generate a variety of numerical facts about the passage: total numbers of words processed, sentences, lines, questions, exclamations, and punctuation marks (listed individually). Mean word lengths and sentence lengths are also calculated, along with standard deviations. The computer prints out a bar graph displaying the frequency distributions of word lengths in the text (what percentage of words have one letter, two, three, etc.) as well as a graph displaying type/token ratios (the

---

[12] George A. Borden and James J. Watts, "A Computerized Language Analysis System," *CHum*, 5 (1971), 129–41. Franklin M. Waltman has recently reported using CLAS for a medieval Spanish authorship study: "C.L.A.S. and the *Cantar de Mio Cid*," *CHum*, 10 (1976), 145–52.

number of word types in the text as a percentage of the total number of words). It also punches cards with more numerical data suitable for later correlation studies. The scholar who is interested in quantitative aspects of his text and has access to PL/I on an IBM 360/370 system may find that CLAS offers many of the features he requires, although it does not carry out an exhaustive quantitative analysis of a literary text.

Another PL/I program called PROVIDE resembles CLAS in its numerical characteristics but lacks the usual concordance features including context. Thus, it aims to do less than CLAS: to supply "a set of measured characteristics of a text . . . useful in quantitative stylistics,"[13] broken down by word type, word token, and sentence. For the appropriate level it provides figures such as frequency of word type, words per sentence, and the number of letters, vowels, and syllables per word and sentence. The routine to count syllables works only for English, although PROVIDE is intended for a general audience desiring text analyses. The user can request the table of word types with location— essentially a word index, almost a concordance—printed in either alphabetical or descending frequency order, as well as all the other numerical measures. Like CLAS, the system is designed for use by the novice with a short, readable user's manual. Input codes are flexible; and output can be on printer, cards, tape, magnetic disk, or microfilm. On the surface, PROVIDE seems to be more efficient in terms of computer time than CLAS; yet it requires more memory storage space and produces primarily numerical and tabular data.[14] No clear recommendation between the two programs is apparent for the scholar having a computer that runs

---

[13] Boyd K. Swigger, "PROVIDE—A Preliminary Program for Text Analyses," *SIG-LASH Newsletter*, 6, No. 5 (December 1973), 3.

[14] Granted that comparisons of efficiency between programs run at different locations with hardware differences are approximate at best, CLAS carried out all of its routines on a sample of 1000 words in 100 seconds on an IBM 360/67 machine in 1971 using only a small amount of memory, whereas PROVIDE printed all of its analyses for 500 words on an IBM 360/65 in 12 seconds and for 2000 words in 40 seconds but required much more computer storage. A third PL/I textual system developed by John B. Smith at Pennsylvania State ("RATS: A Middle-Level Text Utility System," *CHum*, 6 [1972], 277–83) is aimed at a more experienced programmer than the typical literary scholar. Basically it produces three interrelated files compiled from a text encoded on punchcards: a dictionary list of words with frequency, separate occurrences of every word arranged in alphabetical order, and a copy of the text (a linear order of words from beginning to end). Programs in RATS then compress or expand the files according to the user's needs (see examples in Smith's article). Although Smith has shown admirable concern for achieving efficiency in computer storage, his programs seem, by and large, too complex for most inexperienced literary scholars to use with ease. Practically, one of the other PL/I program packages may be more convenient for the novice.

PL/I. He should look at the features of both to see which better fits his analytical needs and hardware constraints.[15]

As noted in Chapter 3, FORTRAN, the most commonly used language in the world today, is very cumbersome for carrying out textual manipulations. Experienced computer scholars such as the designers of COCOA were willing to accept the inconvenience of programming in FORTRAN in order to capitalize on its efficiency and portability; they produced a wonderful tool that can be used worldwide. To meet the needs of literary scholars with little computing experience and only FORTRAN available on their computer, A. Colin Day at the University of London has devised a package of routines called FISHER (FORTRAN Implemented String Handling and Editing Routines) in universally accepted Standard FORTRAN to carry out many of the operations built into more text-oriented programming languages like SNOBOL4 or PL/I.[16] Typical features of FISHER enable the computer to compare

[15] For strictly statistical analyses, there exist a number of well-known computer program packages available at every large university computer center. Most of these programs accept the information for analysis in numerical form and then count, tabulate, and perform basic and advanced statistical processing on the results. The scholar usually must quantify his material prior to submission to the computer. One such package—probably the most widely used in the social sciences today—is called SPSS (Statistical Package for the Social Sciences) and has been adopted occasionally for literary analyses (see Judith A. Vanderbok, "Developing a Quantitative Poetic: E. E. Cummings and His Sonnets," *SIGLASH Newsletter*, 9, No. 4 [September 1976], 2–9; and Nona Newman, "The Use of General Purpose Statistical Packages in Linguistics Research," *ALLC Bulletin*, 2, No. 3 [1974], 4–6). Vanderbok hand-marked poetic features like rhyme, meter, and typography into numeric codes for all 212 Cummings sonnets and then had SPSS programs create tables cross-tabulating two or more of the features to suggest their relationships. Newman describes using SPSS to study medieval French rhymed verse; initially she encoded the poetic lines in alphabetic form, including the recoding of diphthongs as single characters, so that the program could compare and classify rhyme elements. Of course, she then had to convert the machine's findings to numerical codes prior to getting SPSS to carry out statistical tests.

Although general-purpose statistical packages like SPSS are more widely available and often more efficient of computer time and storage than text-based packages like CLAS and PROVIDE, their bias in favor of numerical coding usually forces the scholar to do a lot of hand analysis of the literary text before computer input. Despite its facilities for some alphabetic sorting, the designers of SPSS make a point of urging users to employ numerical values for coding data if possible (see the standard user's manual for SPSS: Norman H. Nie et al., *Statistical Package for the Social Sciences*, 2nd ed. [New York: McGraw-Hill, 1975], p. 22). Because hand analysis is tedious, time-consuming, and even error producing, the advantages to the scholar of using literary packages that accept unedited text and produce statistical results may easily outweigh their liabilities—provided the user can run the programs on his computer.

[16] Christine Allwright describes and assesses Day's programs in "FISHER: A String-Handling Package," *CHum*, 10 (1976), 297–98. Full information about the package and its implementation can be secured directly from Dr. A. Colin Day, Computer Centre, University College London, 19 Gordon Street, London WC1H OAH, England.

strings of characters, look for particular character patterns (such as the word *love*, treated as a pattern of 4 letter-characters), and conjoin or delete character strings (such as excluding the word *the* from a computer concordance). Using FISHER's commands resembles programming in PL/I; the process of putting them together in order to carry out a major job like a word index of a text is similar to programming in a more textually compatible language. Even with the helpful user's manual, the inexperienced scholar will find the going rough at first. Compared to a program package like JEUDEMO or CLAS, in which the computer can be instructed in a few commands to do a complete index, in terms of convenience FISHER comes out in second place, although it is probably more machine efficient. On the other hand, for people whose only option is FORTRAN, Day has already done much of the hard work of modifying the language for text processing. For these scholars, FISHER could make the difference in being able or not being able to carry out any analysis with a computer.

Many universities and colleges offer interactive computing in the BASIC programming language—like FORTRAN, not initially amenable to text processing. Recently Ben R. Schneider, Jr., founder of the *London Stage* Information Bank, along with Reid M. Watts announced a text processing package called SITAR (System for Interactive Text-Editing, Analysis, and Retrieval) that can run on any computer having a Dartmouth BASIC time-sharing system.[17] In its present form, only the input/output routines depend on the particular computers on which SITAR was originally designed—the Digital Equipment PDP-11/20, /35, /40, /45 series. These procedures in Digital Equipment's version of BASIC-PLUS would require modification for other machinery. Unlike some program packages discussed earlier, SITAR is intended primarily for information retrieval but includes other pattern-finding features as well. Already Schneider's students have used SITAR for calling up entries for about 15,000 pages of *The London Stage* on CRT video terminals for interactive checking and editing. SITAR's few commands are expressed in English—EDIT, SHOW, FIND, and PRINT are suggestive—and allow the user to call up a textual file, perhaps a bibliographical reference or a short poem, and edit it for spelling errors or search it for a word or set of characters. The file can then be replaced in computer storage for later use or sent to a printer for a hardcopy version. SITAR's most convenient feature for literary use is asking the computer to look for any

---

[17] Ben R. Schneider, Jr., and Reid M. Watts, "SITAR: An Interactive Text Processing System for Small Computers," *Communications of the ACM*, 20 (1977), 495–99.

pattern (a letter, a word, a word stem, even a complete phrase) among its stored files and then to display its finding on the CRT screen. In effect, the user can query his textual data files to produce an ad hoc concordance. Unlike a typical concordance package like COCOA, SITAR responds directly to the user sitting at the terminal; COCOA users run the program on cards in batch mode and wait for printout. Compared to the many other general-purpose editing routines available on an interactive basis, SITAR has two appealing characteristics for literary use: it was designed by a literary scholar aware of what computer jobs he and others like himself need for their research and was implemented in BASIC, the most common interactive programming language in service today. Scholars lacking access to other general computer editing programs—WYLBUR from Stanford, various systems available from computer manufacturers[18]—but having a BASIC computer system at their computer center might do well to investigate SITAR's feasibility for their problems.

To conclude our selected sample of programs for literary data processing, we must examine two ambitious projects coded in FORTRAN: CONSTAT, the product in its present form of Louis A. Ule and associates at the University of Southern California, and EYEBALL, a joint production of Donald Ross, Jr., and Robert H. Rasche. Ule set out in the late 1960s to investigate the issues of disputed authorship for several anonymous Renaissance plays sometimes attributed to Christopher Marlowe; out of his needs evolved a suite of computer routines that produce textual and statistical measures of style potentially valuable for authorship discrimination.[19] The program accepts both punchcards or magnetic tape as input; its output options include cards, magnetic tape, printer, and a plotter to draw graphs of statistical relations. CONSTAT's text-indexing routine—in fact, a KWOC index, not a complete concordance generator—aims to be fast and inexpensive to run; for a typical Renaissance drama, an index costs about ten dollars to produce on Ule's IBM 370 system. The following list suggests other kinds of analytical results the program produces after processing the text: typical summary statistics (number of words, sentences, paragraphs, and vocabulary size, plus figures on standard deviation and covariance), frequency-distribution curves (on plotter) of the various statistical features or of any

---

[18] For an early, comparative tutorial on common text editors available on computers, see Andries van Dam and David E. Rice, "On-Line Text Editing: A Survey," *Computing Surveys*, 3 (1971), 93–114.
[19] Louis A. Ule, "The Use of CONSTAT in Authorship Investigations," *ALLC Bulletin*, 3 (1975), 211–25.

word list requested by the user, frequency lists in alphabetical or numerical order, and percentages of words used once, twice, etc., relative to total vocabulary. The frequency-distribution lists of such features as letters of the alphabet and common function words can then be fed into programs for cluster analysis, a statistical measure to illustrate closeness between two texts. Because a scholar might expect works by the same author or within the same genre to cluster together, cluster analyses of alphabets or function words, according to Ule, seem especially suitable for authorship groupings. Ule has even been tentatively able to graph clusters of Elizabethan plays in three-dimensional form with his plotter, a process suggesting several Renaissance dramas by other playwrights with affinities to the Marlowe canon.[20] In comparison to CLAS and PRO-VIDE, which also produce statistical results, CONSTAT offers more comprehensive statistics, has facilities for graphical display as well as printed results, and is probably more capable of adaptation to different computer systems because it is written in FORTRAN instead of PL/I.[21]

Last among the program packages to be considered is the EYE-BALL system of Donald Ross, Jr., and Robert H. Rasche.[22] In many ways EYEBALL is the most innovative in conception; built neither on the model of a concordance generator nor on a statistical base, its several parts are primarily designed to take unedited English literary text and analyze its sentences linguistically into their parts of speech and syntactic functions as an aid to stylistic analysis.[23] Available in two ver-

[20] Alone among scholars, Ule has argued on the basis of his cluster analyses that Marlowe is the author of the anonymous Elizabethan play, *Woodstock*. He presents his controversial contention in "Cluster Analysis and the Authorship of *Woodstock*," R.E.L.O. *Revue*, No. 1 (1976), pp. 1–34.

[21] Currently, versions of CONSTAT exist in FORTRAN for running on IBM 360/370 machines and Control Data 7600 systems. The latter implementation was done by Morris Smith of the University of Manchester Regional Computer Centre.

[22] Three important references jointly authored by Ross and Rasche contain the essential information for EYEBALL: "EYEBALL: A Computer Program for Description of Style," *CHum*, 6 (1972), 213–21; "Beyond the Concordance: Algorithms for Description of English Clauses and Phrases," in Aitken, pp. 85–99; and the indispensable *Description and User's Instructions for EYEBALL*, Revised Ed. (Minneapolis: University of Minnesota Department of English, 1974).

[23] By 1976 Ross had published three stylistic analyses of short texts using EYEBALL, but they present more quantitative textual features revealed by the computer than qualitative critical judgments about the works. See "An EYEBALL View of Blake's *Songs of Innocence and of Experience*," in Mitchell, pp. 94–108; "Emerson and Thoreau: A Comparison of Prose Styles," *Language and Style*, 6 (1973), 185–95 [comparison of a short section on "Discipline" in Emerson's *Nature* with "Spring" in *Walden*]; and "Stylistic Contrasts in Yeats's Byzantium Poems," *Language and Style*, 8 (1975), 293–305.

sions of FORTRAN, for IBM 360/370 systems or CDC 6600 machines, EYEBALL is distributed on punchcards by Ross from the University of Minnesota for a nominal fee of $10.00 to cover postage and handling; by 1976 more than twenty-five copies of EYEBALL had been sent out throughout the world. The user's manual illustrates typical control cards needed to make the programs work on either the IBM or CDC equipment and then describes, in sections sometimes hard to follow, each of the programs and how they work and what they produce.

Organized into three sequential programs, EYEBALL requires intermediate action between parts by the user to add additional information about syntactic structures or to correct erroneous computer analyses. To begin with, the PHASE 1 program takes literary text encoded in an unedited form without any precoding by the scholar, certainly a great convenience, and structured in punchcard format (textual units of up to 80 characters). Consulting a small dictionary of about 200 function words, PHASE 1 indexes the text with locations into the function word categories pioneered by Charles Fries and modified by Louis Milic in his computer study of Jonathan Swift (see Chapter 7). The computer marks all the other words, about half the text, as content words. It records the number of syllables of the function words and estimates the syllable count for content words. Like many other programs, it produces at this time several numerical characteristics of the text, such as frequencies of function and content words, type/token counts for words in the text, and sentence and clause lengths, along with a variety of statistical measures calculated from these figures. The final segment of PHASE 1 called GUESS attempts to parse the partially analyzed sentence by means of the concept of syntactic frames; for instance, the sequence "preposition + article + content word" usually signals a prepositional phrase. Finally the machine sends its word-by-word and phrasal analyses to some form of output for the scholar's inspection.

Before entering the second program of EYEBALL, called SYNTAX, the user must check the machine's markings of phrases and clauses and make corrections where the ambiguities of English have led to incorrect parsing. In effect, EYEBALL requires medial editing. Ross and Rasche intentionally planned to have this interim human intervention, since no automatic method for syntactic analysis looking only at function words and syntactic frames can achieve complete success at parsing. Many years of automated syntactic analysis as part of research on mechanical translation have shown that programs using word forms and frames, with no component for meanings, inevitably generate some mistaken analyses.[24]

Along with marking the final word in each prepositional phrase, the scholar adds functional information about words that are subjects, predicates, and complements in all clauses to the word and phrase files produced in PHASE 1; normally the new information is added to punchcards that have been produced at the end of PHASE 1. The SYNTAX program then completes the analysis of the sentence for all phrases and clauses, subordinate and independent. Its output lists sequentially every word in the text, its part of speech, and function in the sentence. The user has the option of getting the results on punchcards, one word per card, or on magnetic tape.

EYEBALL's third phase, designated STYLE 1, carries out statistical analyses on the results of SYNTAX. Any residual errors the machine has made in assigning word classes or functions need to be corrected by the user before the start of STYLE 1. This program essentially counts every kind of information already assembled, about words, phrases, and clauses. It produces matrices that break down the count of nouns into those that are subjects, objects of prepositions, complements (including direct objects), etc. Ratios of nominal word classes to verbal ones are calculated, as are percentages of content and function words. The program presents syllabic analyses of the words in the text, even though some of its syllabic counts for content words have been estimated and are probably in error. In summary, STYLE 1 deluges the scholar with masses of quantitative detail about his literary text; if he can decipher it all, perhaps he will find meaningful stylistic patterns. Meanwhile, he has the completely augmented word file produced by SYNTAX for other stylistic investigations.

Certainly the EYEBALL approach of syntactic analysis to aid stylistic study is very ambitious; its results are more varied and comprehensive than those of any other package that has been discussed. Yet, from personal experience I know that users of EYEBALL have difficulties getting it to run at their local computer centers.[25] Adapting EYEBALL to

[24] Another approach to computerized syntactic analysis allows the whole parsing process to be completed by the machine automatically for each sentence without interim user interaction. The scholar must then go over his printout to sort out the errors before compiling his statistical results. One such stylistic analysis of syntax with no medial editing is described in my article, "Carlyle and the Machine: A Quantitative Analysis of Syntax in Prose Style," *ALLC Bulletin*, 3 (1975), 100–14.

[25] These remarks apply to a stylistic analysis of Joseph Conrad's *Heart of Darkness* with EYEBALL as part of a dissertation research project by Elizabeth A. Sikes under my supervision (see "Conrad's Conscious Artistry: A Computer-Assisted Exploration of Style in *Heart of Darkness*," Diss. South Carolina 1976).

local conditions was frustrating and time-consuming; the experience serves as a useful case study of the problems and discouragements to be expected in borrowing a program package designed elsewhere and sent out for general use, albeit only for English literary text. The fact that the programs are coded in FORTRAN argued for their easy adaptability. Yet the local IBM 370 computer refused to read the program because several errors were found in the IBM version of the FORTRAN rules distributed on punchcards. When those had been corrected by computer center personnel, PHASE 1 refused to analyze more than about 1000 words of running text at one time. After repeated inquiries, neither Ross nor Rasche could determine why the program limited the number of words it could handle at one time; consequently, segments of *Heart of Darkness* no more than 1000 words long had to be submitted to the program individually. Three paragraphs longer than 1000 words had to be broken up for partial analyses; in a few bad cases analyses done by hand had to replace parts of the EYEBALL routine. Quirks in the programs also had trouble with some punctuation marks, which had to be deleted before processing. Because of annoyances like these, the text had to be submitted piecemeal on punchcards rather than on faster, more convenient magnetic tape. A job for which the text was not excessively long (*Heart of Darkness* contains almost 40,000 words) was dragged out over many months of separate computer runs. With manual editing and occasional hand analysis in place of some of EYEBALL's programs, its syntactic and statistical results were finally compiled; and the job of deciphering the masses of material for a useful stylistic profile of *Heart of Darkness* could begin.

The moral of this frustrating experience applies to other program packages as well as to EYEBALL. Ross and Rasche set out to make up a set of stylistic computer routines unlike any other available ones; their system seems to work fine for their purposes on their computer systems. Yet borrowing EYEBALL for other similar analyses to be carried out elsewhere on comparable computer hardware caused problems. Because the user's manual proved hard to follow or silent about particular situations, the help provided by Ross and Rasche by mail was indispensable but necessarily delayed implementation of the full set of programs. It is reasonable to expect some similar headaches with other borrowed programs.

Only with the COCOA concordance package have many scholars reported getting the program to run locally with little trouble and time delay. The present version of COCOA represents improvements and refinements of at least two earlier concordance routines and was designed by computer scientists, not exclusively literary scholars, who were knowledgeable about the needs of the concordance user. They thought through most of the potential problems, such as choosing a widely used programming language, before developing the programs themselves, and their planning has paid off in the wide adoption of CO-COA throughout the world. The COCOA model provides a standard of planning and practical execution worthy of study by any scholars setting out to design new literary program packages. For users of packages already developed, I suspect that my personal experience with EYE-BALL represents typical implementation headaches. Of course, scholars should continue to borrow programs fit for their purposes; however, let them not be surprised if problems of local adaptation arise.

What then of the state of the art in literary computing in the late 1970s and the prospects for the future? A decade ago wild claims that the computer would revolutionize literary study were not uncommon. In 1965 Louis Marder predicted in *Shakespeare Newsletter* that computer adaptation to literary study will mean that "ignorance may become impossible . . . limited [only] by human ability and reason."[26] Marder went on to catalog fifty computer research projects on Shakespeare, including assignment of plays to genres based on stylistic features and even deciding "what [Shakespearean] metaphor and vocabulary is common to all dramatists [perhaps he means only in the English Renaissance] and therefore not valid for evidential purposes."[27] Clearly Marder was unaware of the costs and time involved in encoding "all" dramatic texts, then finding and correcting the attendant errors that would ensue.

The intervening years have shown that such glowing, naive predictions are uninformed and even ill-founded. As computer knowledge and applications have increased, the number of similar remarks has dropped off sharply. Scholars have grown to appreciate the speed, accuracy, and applicability of machines to their concerns, but they have often learned the lessons of proper data structuring, input/output headaches, and program complexities slowly through frustrating, painful steps of trial and error. Even as late as 1973, however, Fred R. MacFadden, Jr., was still proposing the computer as a panacea of incredible opportunity in Shakespeare studies.[28] More fanciful than Marder, though somewhat indebted to him, MacFadden listed more than sixty ways the machine could make

[26] Louis Marder, "Computer Scholarship in Shakespearean and Related Studies," *Shakespeare Newsletter*, 15 (December 1965), 52.

[27] Louis Marder, "A Guide to 50 Computer Projects in Shakespeare," *Shakespeare Newsletter*, 15 (December 1965), 53.

[28] Fred R. MacFadden, Jr., "Report on Opportunities for Teaching and Researching the Literature of Shakespeare Using the Computer," *CSHVB*, 4 (1973), 3–8.

Shakespeare studies come alive by adapting subfields of computer science to research problems. Representative entries on the list include decision-simulation games for plots of the plays, machine translation of the complete works into Basic English to see if Renaissance idioms can be universalized, and phonetic research with a sound spectroscope to test Shakespeare's accuracy relative to his fellow dramatists in transcribing dialect words. MacFadden seems to have leafed through current research literature in computer science and thought that every new technique would fit Shakespeare. Practically he seems unaware about how to proceed, and there is no evidence that his suggestions have been more than pipedreams for Shakespearean scholarship.

An apocryphal anecdote overheard at a conference bears more resemblance to the world of realities. As the story goes, sometime in the near future three graduate students in English, trained in the developing discipline of literary computing during their graduate studies, completed their doctoral degrees and departed to their first jobs at widely separated geographical locations. The employment aspect of the story seems definitely optimistic; no doubt their interdisciplinary training in literature and computing made the three more attractive for employment than most Ph.D.'s in English. Concerned about eventual tenure and promotion at their institutions, the three bright new scholars ordered copies of each other's dissertations for their school libraries and then began routinely assigning readings from them for their students. By this date, academic libraries were totally automated and connected through a national computer network so that they could produce on a daily basis an analysis of the national demand for scholarly books. Gradually chairmen of departments and promotion committees came to rely on these reports to see how often the work of their faculty colleagues was being called for. The enterprising threesome were soon promoted because of the heavy demand for their original dissertation research. If that was so significant, imagine what productive careers lay before the clever trio!

Although this story is set in the future, two aspects of it—library automation and computer networks—are already technologically feasible, not out of the bounds of possibility. Large university libraries now commonly subscribe to automated bibliographical services activated through computer terminals. Regional library consortia such as OCLC, Inc., are already sharing cataloging tasks.[29] As the explosion of knowl-

---

[29] An excellent overview and critique of OCLC, its accomplishments, problems, and plans for the future recently appeared in a special section of several articles in *American Libraries*: "A Primer on OCLC for all Librarians," 7 (May 1976), 258–75.

edge continues, libraries of the future are definitely going to have to rely more on computers to automate many of their services in order to cope efficiently and economically with the glut of information that threatens to inundate them.

On a limited basis, the interconnection of a number of computers together into a network within which computer programs and files of data can be exchanged among machines already exists. The ARPANET project, developed with funds from the Advanced Research Projects Agency of the U.S. Department of Defense, has shown that different computers can be joined through telephone connections to share resources. Drawing on this precedent, Sally and Walter Sedelow at the University of Kansas have been working for several years to lay the groundwork for a national network of computer centers committed to language research, of which an important component would be literary and linguistic analysis. Their proposed recommendations, based on a comprehensive survey of scholarly interest, technological capacity, and language-related research areas, suggest a two-part development for the network concept.[30] A national center for language analysis using computers could organize conferences and develop standard program packages with wide applicability. At a later stage, a series of university computer centers organized on a geographical or topical basis could be linked into a network to share programs and textual materials with each other and the original national center. Funding through government agencies and member institutions has so far not been forthcoming and remains problematical for the near future. Even so, if national computer networks become economically feasible, the foundations have already been laid for the importance of all kinds of language research within such a framework. Although practically it may not be worth the cost of development, it is entirely possible that some day national interest in a local scholar's works can be ascertained through a network of interconnected library files as forecast by the story.

Today the most limiting constraint for massive literary research using computers remains the input headache of getting the text in a correct copy into the machine. The scholar now has to use some keyboarding technique—whether to keypunch cards or magnetic tape or to type directly at an interactive terminal. Even the capacity to enter text at a

---

[30] Sally Y. Sedelow and Walter A. Sedelow, Jr., *Language Research and the Computer: A Study of the Concept of a National Center or Network for Computational Research on Language (Ce/NCoReL)* (Lawrence, Kansas: University of Kansas, 1972). Included with this report is an excellent and extensive bibliography on all facets of language relationships with computers (pp. 219–458).

keyboard and then to correct and edit it displayed on a CRT screen, one of the most convenient methods available, lacks the speed and efficiency that a multifont optical character reader provides. Of course, the scholar can get his text scanned rapidly if he types it over with special typeballs that can be read by character readers, although with any keyboard technique typing will necessarily introduce error into the text. The multifont scanner that can theoretically be "taught" any character set through programming is already operational (see Chapter 2), but its cost remains prohibitively expensive for the typical budget of a literary project, even with funding assistance. If the cost of purchasing such a scanner or contracting for its services ever becomes reasonable, we can expect that soon most of the world's classical texts will become available in computer-readable form for analysis and editing. Given the variety of applications that have already been done to literary works with current input problems, the advent of reasonable, accurate optical scanning will cause literary computing to mushroom in quantities unexpected by traditional scholars more accustomed to thinking of library books and index card files as the paraphernalia of scholarship.

Some scholars with early computer achievements like Todd K. Bender at the University of Wisconsin have already begun to forecast that versions of literary texts in electronic computer storage may soon represent the definitive, most correct form for their existence.[31] Bender notes that modern textual editors normally examine several versions of a text and emend their copy text—in fact, creating a conflated version which is supposed to represent the author's "final intentions" but in reality was never published in this form. Because of the very complicated textual history of many texts, Bender argues that the most accurate form of the work would be a computer-readable copy of all the relevant editions stored one behind the other as layers of machine memory. The textual history of a nineteenth-century English novel published in both Britain and America might easily exist in more than ten significant versions, "a constantly shifting, dynamic work, nowhere represented adequately in a physical text. . . ." As Bender sees it, "The 'real' repository of information is the electronic data. Any printed expression of that data is merely one among many possible provisional, incomplete, and arbitrary formats of information which exists in its fullest and most flexible form in electronic memory."[32] With all the texts in

---

[31] See Bender's two articles on "electronic texts": "Literary Texts in Electronic Storage: The Editorial Potential," *CHum*, 10 (1976), 193–99; and "Computational Bibliography," in Jones and Churchhouse, pp. 329–37.

[32] Bender, *CHum*, pp. 194–95.

memory, all words and variants surrounded by any amount of context wanted for concordance, collation, or stylistic purposes become available for retrieval at terminals or in printed form. Bender predicts that it is only a matter of time until machine versions of texts will be considered as the basic permanent records for scholarly work; if that time comes, much modern editing theory and practice will have to be revised or reformulated.

Bender's concept of the electronic book is workable today, but realistically the vision of scholarly analysis of machine-coded literary texts becoming more commonplace than traditional habits of having the book physically in hand probably belongs to the realm of science fiction. There will remain resistance (sometimes well-founded, considering a few of the experiences we have reported) by some humanists to the encroachments of the machine into hallowed literary scholarship. As this book has made clear, many scholars already rely on their computers to aid in time-honored research tasks like concordancing, collation, and dictionary making. New approaches to stylistic investigations and information retrieval have grown up with literary computing. It would be nice if by the 1980s there were program packages and accessible text archives to allow scholars sitting at their own terminals to do all kinds of tasks reported here through a worldwide computer network. In this hypothetical world, graduate students might receive routine computer orientation as part of their literary courses of study. From the perspective of the late 1970s, predictions like these seem fairly safe for the near future. Computer applications have already shown their worth in literary research and will continue to grow and expand in complexity and sophistication. More power to the machine and its minions, so long as the importance of the literature itself remains the central focus of study instead of the all-powerful electronic tool and its methodologies. Meanwhile, the individual scholar can best try to understand how the computer can help him and come to appreciate the decisions he must make in order to use this remarkably flexible and accurate tool to his advantage. To these ends this book has been dedicated; if it has served these purposes it has met its goals.

FOR FURTHER READING

Brier, Alan, and Ian Robinson. *Computers and the Social Sciences.* London: Hutchinson, 1974.

A survey book designed to introduce computer fundamentals to social scientists, of interest to literary scholars for its discussion of program packages for statistical methods, information retrieval, and content analysis.

Howard-Hill, T. H. "A Common Shakespeare Text File for Computer-Aided Research: A Proposal." *CSHVB*, 4 (1973), 53–56.

The editor of the Oxford old-spelling Shakespeare concordances assesses the needs and problems in collecting computer-readable text files and argues for a university center for Shakespeare study with computers, as well as for programs and textual data structures adaptable to various machines.

Smith, Joan M., and L. M. Smith. "The Availability of Texts in Machine-Readable Form: Practical Considerations." *ALLC Bulletin*, 3 (1975), 19–28.

The authors' extensive, frustrating experiences in trying to convert literary texts prepared in obsolete machine-readable forms to more modern storage methods leads them to recommend common international standards for encoding future large text archives.

Turn, Rein. *Computers in the 1980's.* New York: Columbia University Press, 1974.

From the perspective of the early 1970s, a Rand Corporation computer systems analyst forecasts technological advances in computers in the next decade, including microcomputers, massive memories, and input/output improvements applicable to large-scale literary processing.

Waite, Stephen V. F. "Steps Toward Making Literary Texts Available." *Facts and Futures: What's Happening Now in Computing for Higher Education.* Princeton, N.J.: EDUCOM, The Interuniversity Communications Council, 1974. Pp. 309–13.

Humorous report from Waite's firsthand experience in setting up and administering the American Philological Association's Repository of Classical Texts in Machine-Readable Form on the issues involved in sharing textual data files, especially troubles with incompatibility among university computer centers and the lack of standards for encoding all the characters encountered in literary texts.

A Selected Bibliography for Literary Computing *

I. General

Aitken, A. J. "The Literary Uses of Computers." *Times Literary Supplement*, April 21, 1972, p. 456.

Aitken, A. J., R. W. Bailey, and N. Hamilton-Smith, eds. *The Computer and Literary Studies*. Edinburgh: University of Edinburgh Press, 1973.

Boggs, Roy A. "Computer-Aided Studies of Middle High German Texts: A Report on the Mannheim Symposium." *CHum*, 6 (1972), 157–59.

Booth, A. D., ed. *Machine Translation*. New York: North-Holland, 1967.

Borko, Harold, ed. *Automated Language Processing: The State of the Art*. New York: John Wiley and Sons, 1967.

Bowles, Edmund A. "Computerized Research in the Humanities: A Survey." *ACLS Newsletter*, Special Supplement (June 1966).

————, ed. *Computers in Humanistic Research*. Englewood Cliffs, N.J.: Prentice-Hall, 1967.

————. "The Humanities and the Computer: Some Current Research Problems." *Computers and Automation*, 15 (1966), 24–27.

Bullough, Vern L., Serge Lusignan, and Thomas H. Ohlgren. "Computers and the Medievalist." *Speculum*, 49 (1974), 392–402.

Burelbach, Frederick M., Jr., ed. *Proceedings: Computer Applications to Problems in the Humanities: A Conversation in the Disciplines, State University College, Brockport, New York, April 4–5, 1969*. Brockport,

* Excludes items listed in Further Readings

194

N.Y.: Department of English, State University College at Brockport, 1970.

Burton, Dolores M. "*Respice Finem* and the *Tantum Quantum*: An Essay Review of Computational Stylistics for 1967–68." *CHum*, 3 (1968), 41–48.

Cohen, Doron J., and Peter C. Brillinger. *Introduction to Data Structures and Non-Numeric Computation*. Englewood Cliffs, N.J.: Prentice-Hall, 1972.

Computers for the Humanities? New Haven: Yale University Press, 1965.

Condon, Thomas J. "Computers, Traditional Scholarship, and the ACLS." *American Behavioral Scientist*, 10 (1967), 4–7.

Conference on the Use of Computers in Humanistic Research: Sponsored by Rutgers, The State University, and International Business Machines Corporation, December 4, 1964. White Plains, N.Y.: IBM, 1966.

Delatte, Louis. "Computers and the Classics." R.E.L.O. *Revue*, No. 4 (1967), pp. 97–103.

———. "Computers and the Classics: A Supplement." *CHum*, 2 (1968), 117–20.

Dénes, J. "A Bibliography on Non-Numerical Applications of Digital Computers." *Computing Reviews*, 9 (1968), 481–508.

Dillon, Martin. "The Quantitative Analysis of Language: Preliminary Considerations." *CSHVB*, 3 (1972), 191–207.

Dopping, O. *Computers and Data Processing*. Lund, Sweden: Student-litteratur, 1970.

Duro, Aldo. "Humanities Computing Activities in Italy." *CHum*, 3 (1968), 49–52.

Dyer, Robert R. "Towards Computational Procedures in Homeric Scholarship." R.E.L.O. *Revue*, No. 4 (1967), pp. 1–54.

Fogel, Ephim G. "Electronic Computers and Elizabethan Texts." *The Practice of Modern Literary Scholarship*. Ed. Sheldon P. Zitner. Glenview, Ill.: Scott, Foresman and Co., 1966. Pp. 364–77.

————. "The Humanist and the Computer." *Shakespeare Newsletter*, 15 (1965), 51.

Fortier, Paul A. "Etat présent de l'utilisation des ordinateurs pour l'étude de la littérature française." *CHum*, 5 (1971), 143–54.

Freeman, Robert R., Alfred Pietrzyk, and A. Hood Roberts, eds. *Information in the Language Sciences*. New York: American Elsevier, 1968.

Grayston, Kenneth. "Computers and the New Testament." *New Testament Studies*, 17 (July 1971), 477–80.

Hays, David G., ed. *Readings in Automated Language Processing*. New York: American Elsevier, 1966.

Hirschmann, Rudolf. "A Survey of Computer-Aided Research in Early German." *CHum*, 8 (1974), 279–84.

IBM Symposium on Introducing the Computer into the Humanities: Poughkeepsie, New York, June 30/July 2, 1969. Document G320–1044–0. White Plains, N.Y.: IBM Corp., Data Processing Division, 1969.

Jones, Alan, and R. F. Churchhouse, eds. *The Computer in Literary and Linguistic Studies*. Cardiff: University of Wales Press, 1976.

Lenders, Winfried. "Linguistic Data Processing and ALLC Activities in Germany." *ALLC Bulletin*, 2, No. 1 (1974), 24–27.

Lusignan, Serge, and John S. North, eds. *Computing in the Humanities*. Waterloo, Ont.: University of Waterloo Press, 1977.

McDonough, James F. "Computers and the Classics." *CHum*, 2 (1967), 37–40.

Marder, Louis. "Computer Scholarship in Shakespearean and Related Studies." *Shakespeare Newsletter*, 15 (December 1965), 51–52.

————. "A Guide to 50 Computer Projects in Shakespeare." *Shakespeare Newsletter*, 15 (December 1965), 53.

Martin, Willy. "Literary Computing at I.T.L." *ALLC Bulletin*, 2, No. 1 (1974), 28–34.

————. "On Uses of the Computer in Literary Research: A Congress Report." *Review of Institute of Applied Linguistics* (Louvain), 8 (1970), 3–8.

Milic, Louis. "Winged Words: Varieties of Computer Application." *CHum*, 2 (1967), 24–31.

Mitchell, J. L., ed. *Computers in the Humanities*. Edinburgh: Edinburgh University Press, 1974.

Morgan, Richard S. "Computers and Humanities in Britain." *CHum*, 4 (1969), 121–24.

Proceedings of a Literary Data Processing Conference, September 9–11, 1964. Ed. Jess B. Bessinger, Jr., Stephen M. Parrish, and Harry F. Arader. White Plains, N.Y.: IBM Corp., Data Processing Division, 1964.

Proceedings of the Second Annual Conference on Computers in the Undergraduate Curriculum, June 23, 24, 25, 1971, Dartmouth College, Hanover, New Hampshire. Hanover, N.H.: University Press of New England, 1971.

Raben, Joseph. "Alphabetic and Numeric Data Processing." *Information Processing 74*. Ed. Jack L. Rosenfeld. Amsterdam: North-Holland, 1974. Pp. 866–71.

———, ed. *Computer-Assisted Research in the Humanities: A Directory of Scholars Active*. Elmsford, N.Y.: Pergamon Press, 1977.

———. "Computers and Their Utility in Humanities Research." *ACLS Newsletter*, 23 (Winter 1972), 2–13.

———. "The Humanist in the Computer Lab: Thoughts on Technology in the Study of Literature." *ALLC Bulletin*, 1, No. 1 (1973), 3–9.

Raben, Joseph, and R. L. Widmann. "Information Systems Applications in the Humanities." *Annual Review of Information Science and Technology*, No. 7. Ed. Carlos A. Cuadra. Washington: American Society for Information Science, 1972. Pp. 439–69.

Reichardt, Jasia, ed. *Cybernetic Serendipity: The Computer and the Arts*. 2nd rev. ed. London: W. & J. MacKay and Co., 1968.

———. *Cybernetics, Art, and Ideas*. Greenwich, Conn.: New York Graphic Society, 1971.

Rustin, Randall, ed. *Natural Language Processing*. New York: Algorithmics Press, 1973.

Sedelow, Sally Y. "The Computer in the Humanities and Fine Arts." *Computing Surveys*, 2 (1970), 89–110.

———. "Language Analysis in the Humanities." *Communications of the ACM*, 15 (July 1972), 644–47.

Sedelow, Sally Y., and Walter A. Sedelow, Jr. *Language Research and the Computer: A Study of the Concept of a National Center or Network for Computational Research on Language (Ce/NCo/ReL).* Lawrence, Kansas: University of Kansas, 1972.

Smith, John B. "Computer Studies in the Humanities: Intellectual, Educational, and Social Implications." *Interdisciplinary Essays*, 4 (1975), 38–46.

Venezky, Richard L. "Computer-Aided Humanities Research at the University of Wisconsin." *CHum*, 3 (1969), 129–38.

Wachal, Robert S. "Humanities and Computers: A Personal View." *North American Review*, 8 (1971), 30–33.

———. "The Machine in the Garden: Computers and Literary Scholarship, 1970." *CHum*, 5 (1970), 23–28.

Waite, Stephen V. F. "Computers and Classical Literature: 1970–1971." *CHum*, 6 (1971), 31–34.

———. "Computers and Classical Literature: 1971–1972." *CHum*, 7 (1972), 99–104.

———. "Computers and the Classics." *CHum*, 3 (1968), 25–29.

———. "Computers and the Classics." *CHum*, 5 (1970), 47–51.

Whalley, George. "Literary Computing." *Bulletin of the Computer Society of Canada* (Summer 1967), pp. 9–13.

Wisbey, Roy A., ed. *The Computer in Literary and Linguistic Research: Papers from a Cambridge Symposium.* Cambridge: Cambridge University Press, 1971.

Wood, Gordon R. "Computer Research: An Adjunct to Literary Studies." *Papers on Language and Literature*, 4 (1968), 459–78.

Zampolli, Antonio. "Humanities Computing in Italy," *CHum*, 7 (1973), 343–60.

Zettersten, Arne. "Current Computing Activity in Scandinavia Related to Language and Literature Research." *CHum*, 3 (1968), 53–60.

———. "Current Scandinavian Computer-Assisted Language and Literature Research." *CHum*, 5 (1971), 203–08.

II. Hardware Considerations—Input and Output

Andersson, P. L. "OCR Enters the Practical Stage." *Datamation*, 17 (December 1, 1971), 22–27.

———. "Phototypesetting—a Quiet Revolution." *Datamation*, 16 (December 1, 1970), 22–27.

Casey, Richard G., and George Nagy. "Advances in Pattern Recognition." *Scientific American*, 224 (April 1971), 56–71.

Clutterbuck, D. "Prospects for the Reading Computer." *New Scientist*, 53 (2 March 1972), 485–88.

"Computer Typesetting." *ALLC Bulletin*, 1, No. 1 (1973), 32.

Froger, J. "Le Lecture automatique et l'analyse statistique des textes." R.E.L.O. *Revue*, No. 1 (1970), pp. 37–44.

Glickman, Robert J., and Gerrit J. Staalman. *Manual for the Printing of Literary Texts and Concordances by Computer*. Toronto: University of Toronto Press, 1966.

Hockey, Susan. "Input and Output of Non-Standard Character Sets." *ALLC Bulletin*, 1, No. 2 (1973), 32–37.

Irby, Charles H. "Display Techniques for Interactive Text Manipulation." *AFIPS Conference Proceedings*, 43 (1974 National Computer Conference and Exposition, May 6–10, 1974, Chicago). Montvale, N.J.: AFIPS Press, 1974. Pp. 247–55.

Kay, Martin. "Standards for Encoding Data in a Natural Language." *CHum*, 1 (1967), 170–77.

Lesk, Michael E. "Facilities for Data Manipulation in the Humanities." *Facts and Futures: What's Happening Now in Computing for Higher Education*. Princeton, N.J.: EDUCOM, The Interuniversity Communications Council, 1974. Pp. 305–08.

Mau, Jürgen. "Again: A Simple Means for Input and Output of Greek Texts on a Small IBM 1130 Outfit." R.E.L.O. *Revue*, No. 1 (1972), pp. 1–3.

Morgan, R. S. "Optical Readers." *CHum*, 3 (1968), 61–64.

——. "Optical Readers: 1970." *CHum*, 5 (1970), 75–78.

Nelson, Carl E. "Microform Technology." *Annual Review of Information Science and Technology*, No. 6. Ed. Carlos A. Cuadra and Ann W. Luke. Chicago: Encyclopaedia Britannica, 1971. Pp. 77–111.

Ott, Wilhelm. "Transcription and Correction of Texts on Paper Tape: Experience in Preparing the Latin Bible Text for the Computer." R.E.L.O. *Revue*, No. 2 (1970), pp. 51–67.

Packard, David W. "Publishing Scholarly Compilations by Computer." *CHum*, 4 (1969), 75–80.

Reagan, Fonnie H., Jr. "Should OCR Be Your Data Input Medium?" *Computer Decisions*, 3 (June 1971), 19–21.

Richmond, Phyllis A. "An Extended Character Set for Humanities Computer Output." *CHum*, 4 (1970), 247–50.

Robertson, John R. "A Rational Approach to COM." *Journal of Micrographics*, 3 (Winter 1970), 73–77.

Rudall, B. H., and C. Hall. "Literary Data Processing on a Small Store Computer." *Computer Bulletin*, 11 (1967), 131–34.

Schneider, Ben R. "The Production of Machine-Readable Text: Some of the Variables " *CHum*, 6 (1971), 39–47.

Sedgwick, Henry D. "Goodbye Hot Metal, Hello Cool Tape." *Datamation*, 16 (December 1, 1970), 32–35.

Smith, John B. "Encoding Literary Texts: Some Considerations." *ALLC Bulletin*, 4 (1976), 190–98.

Snyderman, Martin, and Bernard Hunt. "The Myriad Virtues of Text Compaction." *Datamation*, 16 (December 1, 1970), 36–40.

"A Survey of the OCR Scene." *Computer Decisions*, 3 (June 1971), 22–23.

Toll, D. C., and F. R. A. Hopgood. *GROATS: A Graphical Output Package on the 1906A Using the SC4020*. Chilton, Didcot: Atlas Computer Laboratory, 1973.

Walter, Gerald O. "Typesetting." *Scientific American*, 220 (May 1969), 61–69.

Whitaker, Richard E. "Computerized Video-Composition for the Humanist." *CHum*, 6 (1972), 153–56.

Wilks, Yorick. "The XGP Computer-Driven Printer at Stanford." *ALLC Bulletin*, 2, No. 2 (Summer 1974), 30.

Yerkes, Charles P. "Microfilm: A New Dimension for Computers." *Datamation*, 15 (December 1969), 94–97.

III. Software Considerations—Programming Languages, Techniques, and Packages

Addyman, A. M. "A Language for Literary Data Processing: I—The Choice of a Language." *ALLC Bulletin*, 4 (1976), 146–51.

———. "A Language for Literary Data Processing: II—Simple ALGOL68." *ALLC Bulletin*, 4 (1976), 238–44.

———. "A Language for Literary Data Processing: III—String Processing in ALGOL68." *ALLC Bulletin*, 5 (1977), 46–51.

———. "A Language for Literary Data Processing: IV—ALGOL68 Exposed." *ALLC Bulletin*, 5 (1977), 119–25.

Allwright, Christine. "FISHER: A String-Handling Package." *CHum*, 10 (1976), 297–98.

Barnett, Michael P. *Computer Programming in English*. New York: Harcourt, Brace and World, 1969.

———. "SNAP—A Programming Language for Humanists." *CHum*, 4 (1970), 225–40.

Borden, George A., and James J. Watts. "A Computerized Language Analysis System." *CHum*, 5 (1971), 129–41.

Bratley, Paul, Serge Lusignan, and Francine Ouellette. "JEUDEMO, A Package for Scholars in the Humanities." *SIGLASH Newsletter*, 7, No. 3 (June 1974), 15–19.

Brown, P. J. "SCAN: A Simple Conversational Programming Language for Text Analysis." *CHum*, 6 (1972), 223–27.

Cummings, L. A. "The Electronic Humanist: Computing at Waterloo in Canada." *ALLC Bulletin*, 3 (1975), 226–34.

Davis, Charles H. *Illustrative Computer Programming for Libraries: Selected Examples for Information Specialists*. Westport, Conn.: Greenwood Press, 1974.

Day, Arthur Colin. *FORTRAN Techniques: With Special Reference to Non-Numerical Applications*. Cambridge: Cambridge University Press, 1972.

———. "The State of Software." *ALLC Bulletin*, 3 (1975), 42–44.

De Tar, De Los F. *Principles of FORTRAN Programming*. Menlo Park, Cal.: W. A. Benjamin, Inc., 1972.

Dilligan, Robert J. "Introductory FORTRAN Textbooks: An Overview for Humanists." *CHum*, 7 (1973), 399–406.

Forte, Allen. *SNOBOL3 Primer: An Introduction to the Computer Programming Language*. Cambridge, Mass.: MIT Press, 1967.

Foster, J. M. *List Processing*. New York: American Elsevier, 1967.

Griswold, Ralph E. *The Macro Implementation of SNOBOL4*. San Francisco: W. H. Freeman, 1972.

———. *String and List Processing in SNOBOL4: Techniques and Applications*. Englewood Cliffs, N.J.: Prentice-Hall, 1974.

Heller, Jack, and George W. Logemann. "PL/I: A Programming Language for Humanities Research." *CHum*, 1 (1966), 19–26.

High Level Languages: International Computer State of the Art Report. Maidenhead, England: Infotech Information, 1972.

Higman, Bryan. *A Comparative Study of Programming Languages*. New York: American Elsevier, 1967.

Housden, Richard J. W. "Further Thoughts on SNAP." *CHum*, 7 (1973), 407–12.

———. "On String Concepts and Their Implementation." *Computer Journal*, 18 (1975), 150–56.

IBM System/360 Operating System: PL/I (F) Language Reference Manual. No. GC28-8201-4. Yorktown Heights, N.Y.: IBM Corporation, 1972.

Johnson, R. L. "On the Establishment of a Set of Standard ALGOL60 Procedures for Use in Automatic Language Processing." *Review of the ITL*, 10 (1970), 3–10.

Joyce, James. "Extensions of PL/I for Natural-Language Processing." *CHum*, 6 (1972), 271–75.

Kemeny, J. G., and T. E. Kurtz. *BASIC*. 6th ed. Ed. Stephen V. F. Waite and Diane G. Mather. Hanover, N.H.: University Press of New England, 1971.

———. *BASIC Programming*. 2nd ed. New York: John Wiley and Sons, 1971.

Koubourlis, Demetrius J. "Computer Sequencing and Non-Alphabetical Interference in Language Data Processing." *CHum*, 7 (1973), 149–55.

Levison, Michael. "A Programming Language for Textual Analysis." *SIGLASH Newsletter*, 6, No. 4 (October 1973), 4–5.

Lindsey, C. H. "ALGOL68 with Fewer Tears." *Computer Journal*, 15 (1972), 176–88.

Lindsey, Charles H., and S. G. van der Meulen. *Informal Introduction to ALGOL68*. Amsterdam: North-Holland, 1971.

Marateck, Samuel L. *BASIC*. New York: Academic Press, 1975.

Martin, William A. "Sorting." *Computing Surveys*, 3 (1971), 147–74.

Maurer, Ward D. *The Programmer's Introduction to SNOBOL*. New York: American Elsevier, 1976.

Meunier, Jean-Guy, Stanislas Rolland, and François Daoust. "A System for Text and Content Analysis." *CHum*, 10 (1976), 281–86.

Mullen, Karen A. "In-Core Sort-Search Methods in PL/I for Lexical Data." *SIGLASH Newsletter*, 6, No. 5 (December 1973), 4–8.

Newman, Nona. "The Use of General-Purpose Statistical Packages in Linguistics Research." *ALLC Bulletin*, 2, No. 3 (1974), 4–6.

Nie, Norman H., C. Hadlai Hull, Jean G. Jenkins, Karin Steinbrenner, and Dale H. Bent. *Statistical Package for the Social Sciences*. 2nd ed. New York: McGraw-Hill, 1975.

Oomen, Ursula. "New Models and Methods in Text Analysis." *Monograph Series on Languages and Literature*, No. 24. Ed. Richard J. O'Brien. Washington: Georgetown University Press, 1971.

Raskin, Jeffrey F. "FLOW: A Teaching Language for Computer Programming in the Humanities." *CHum*, 8 (1974), 231–37.

———. "Programming Languages for the Humanities." *CHum*, 5 (1971), 155–58.

Ross, Donald, Jr., and Robert H. Rasche. *Description and User's Instructions for EYEBALL*. Revised ed. Minneapolis: University of Minnesota Department of English, 1974.

———. "EYEBALL: A Computer Program for Description of Style," *CHum*, 6 (1972), 213–21.

Rudall, B. H. "The Design of Literary Data Processing Languages: Part I." *Journal of the Institution of Computer Science*, 2 (1971), 65–68.

Sammet, Jean E. *Programming Languages: History and Fundamentals*. Englewood Cliffs, N. J.: Prentice-Hall, 1969.

———. "Programming Languages: History and Future." *Communications of the ACM*, 15 (1972), 601–10.

———. "Roster of Programming Languages, 1970." *Computers and Automation*, 19, No. 6b (November 1970), 6–11, 21.

Schneider, Ben Ross, Jr., and Reid M. Watts. "SITAR: An Interactive Text Processing System for Small Computers." *Communications of the ACM*, 20 (1977), 495–99.

Silva, Georgette, and Cliff Bellamy. *Some Procedures and Programs for Processing Language Data*. Clayton, Australia: Monash University, 1969.

Smith, John B. "RATS: A Middle-Level Text Utility System." *CHum*, 6 (1972), 277–83.

Swigger, Boyd K. "PROVIDE—A Preliminary Program for Text Analyses." *SIGLASH Newsletter*, 6, No. 5 (December 1973), 1–3.

Sykes, J. M. "Programming Languages in ICI, Past, Present, and Future." *Computer Bulletin*, 11 (1967), 145–48.

Thomson, Norman D. "Literary Statistics I: On the Small Print of Statistics." *ALLC Bulletin*, 1, No. 3 (1973), 10–14.

———. "Literary Statistics II: On Probability Distributions." *ALLC Bulletin*, 2, No. 1 (1974), 10–15.

———. "Literary Statistics III: On Estimation." *ALLC Bulletin*, 2, No. 2 (1974), 42–47.

————. "Literary Statistics IV: On Hypothesis Testing." *ALLC Bulletin*, 2, No. 3 (1974), 55–61.

————. "Literary Statistics V: On Correlation and Regression." *ALLC Bulletin*, 3 (1975), 29–35.

————. "Literary Statistics VI: On the Future of Literary Statistics." *ALLC Bulletin*, 3 (1975), 166–71.

Ule, Louis A. "On the Use of CONSTAT in Authorship Investigations." *ALLC Bulletin*, 3 (1975), 211–25.

Valentine, S. H. "Comparative Notes on ALGOL68 and PL/I." *Computer Journal*, 17 (1974), 325–31.

van Dam, Andries, and David E. Rice. "On-Line Text Editing: A Survey." *Computing Surveys*, 3 (1971), 93–114.

Waite, William M. *Implementing Software for Non-Numeric Applications*. Englewood Cliffs, N.J.: Prentice-Hall, 1973.

Weizenbaum, J. "Symmetric List Processor." *Communications of the ACM*, 6 (1963), 524–44.

Yngve, Victor H. *Computer Programming with COMIT II*. Cambridge, Mass.: MIT Press, 1972.

IV. Concordances

Bedford, Emmett G., and Robert J. Dilligan, eds. *A Concordance to the Poems of Alexander Pope*. 2 vols. Detroit: Gale Research Co., 1974.

Bender, Todd K. "Gerard Manley Hopkins and His Circle of Literary Associates: Literary Data Bank at the University of Wisconsin." *Hopkins Quarterly*, 1 (1974), 77–91.

Berry-Rogghe, G. L. M. "COCOA: A Word Count and Concordance Generator." *ALLC Bulletin*, 1, No. 2 (1973), 29–31.

————. *COCOA Technical Manual*. Chilton, Didcot: Atlas Computer Laboratory, 1974.

Berry-Rogghe, Godelieve L. M., and T. D. Crawford. *COCOA—A Word Count and Concordance Generator*. Chilton, Didcot: Atlas Computer Laboratory, 1973.

Bessinger, J. B., Jr., ed. *A Concordance to "Beowulf."* Ithaca: Cornell University Press, 1969.

Bevan, E. Dean, ed. *A Concordance to the Plays and Prefaces of Bernard Shaw.* 10 vols. Detroit: Gale Research Co., 1971.

―――. "A Shaw Concordance." *Modern Drama*, 14 (1971), 155–68.

Burton, Dolores M. "Some Uses of a Grammatical Concordance." *CHum*, 2 (1968), 145–54.

Busa, Roberto. "Concordances." *Encyclopedia of Library and Information Science.* Ed. Allen Kent, et al. Vol. 5. New York: Marcel Dekker, 1971. Pp. 592–604.

―――. *Index Thomisticus: Sancti Thomae Aquinatis Operum Omnium Indices et Concordantiae. . . .* 23 vols. Stuttgart: Frommann-Holzboog, 1974.

Crennell, Kathleen M. "How to Use COCOA to Produce Indexes (To Both Book and Subroutine Libraries)." *ALLC Bulletin*, 3 (1975), 190–96.

Crosland, Andrew T., ed. *A Concordance to the Complete Poetry of Stephen Crane.* Detroit: Gale Research Co., 1975.

―――. *A Concordance to F. Scott Fitzgerald's "The Great Gatsby."* Detroit: Gale Research Co., 1975.

―――. "The Concordance and the Study of the Novel." *ALLC Bulletin*, 3 (1975), 190–96.

Dawson, J. L. "Textual Bracketing." *ALLC Bulletin*, 5 (1977), 148–57.

Dixon, J. E. G. "A Prose Concordance: Rabelais." *ALLC Bulletin*, 2, No. 3 (1974), 47–54.

Duggan, Joseph J. "The Value of Computer-Generated Concordances in Linguistic and Literary Research." R.E.L.O. *Revue*, No. 4 (1966), pp. 51–60.

Freeman, Bryant C., ed. *Concordance du théâtre et des poésies de Jean Racine.* 2 vols. Ithaca: Cornell University Press, 1968.

Hamilton-Smith, Neil. *CONCORD.* Edinburgh: Edinburgh Regional Computing Centre, 1972.

Hancock, Leslie, ed. *Word Index to James Joyce's "Portrait of the Artist."* Carbondale: Southern Illinois University Press, 1967.

Hines, Theodore C., Jessica L. Harris, and Charlotte L. Levy. "An Experimental Concordance Program." *CHum*, 4 (1970), 161–71.

Hockey, Susan M., and Vladimir A. Shibayev. "The Bilingual Analytical Literary and Linguistic Concordance—BALCON." *ALLC Bulletin*, 3 (1975), 133–39.

Howard-Hill, Trevor H. "The Oxford Old-Spelling Shakespeare Concordances." *Studies in Bibliography*, 22 (1969), 143–64.

————. "Shakespeare: The Clarendon Press Concordances." *Shakespeare Newsletter*, 17 (1967), 35.

Ingram, William. "Concordances in the Seventies." *CHum*, 8 (1974), 273–77.

Jacobson, Sibyl C., Robert J. Dilligan, and Todd K. Bender, eds. *Concordance to Joseph Conrad's "Heart of Darkness."* Carbondale: Southern Illinois University Press, 1973. 2 microfiche.

Jacobson, Sibyl C., James G. Parins, Robert J. Dilligan, and Todd K. Bender. "Report on the Project in Literary Applications of Computer Technology at the University of Wisconsin-Madison." *SIGLASH Newsletter*, 7, No. 3 (June 1974), 9–14.

Koubourlis, Demetrius J., ed. *A Concordance to the Poems of Osip Mandelstam.* Ithaca: Cornell University Press, 1974.

Ladner, Gerhart B., and David W. Packard. "Gregory the Great and Gregory VII: A Comparison of Their Concepts of Renewal." *Viator*, 4 (1973), 1–31.

Lathem, Edward Connery, ed. *A Concordance to the Poetry of Robert Frost.* New York: Holt Information Systems, 1971.

Misek, Linda D. *Context Concordance to John Milton's "Paradise Lost."* Cleveland: Andrew R. Jennings Computing Center, Case Western Reserve University, 1971.

Naugle, Helen H., ed. *A Concordance to the Poems of Samuel Johnson.* Ithaca: Cornell University Press, 1973.

Oakman, Robert L. "Concordances from Computers: A Review." *Proof*, 3 (1973), 411–25.

Packard, David W., ed. *A Concordance to Livy.* 4 vols. Cambridge: Harvard University Press, 1968.

Parrish, Stephen M., ed. *A Concordance to the Poems of Matthew Arnold*. Ithaca: Cornell University Press, 1959.

————. *A Concordance to the Poems of W. B. Yeats*. Ithaca: Cornell University Press, 1963.

Raben, Joseph. "The Death of the Handmade Concordance." *Scholarly Publishing*, 1 (1969), 61–69.

Reaver, J. Russell, ed. *An O'Neill Concordance*. 3 vols. Detroit: Gale Research Co., 1969.

Rosenbaum, S. P., ed. *A Concordance to the Poems of Emily Dickinson*. Ithaca: Cornell University Press, 1964.

Shinagel, Michael A., ed. *A Concordance to the Poems of Jonathan Swift*. Ithaca: Cornell University Press, 1972.

Smith, O. Romaine, Jr. "GENDEX: GENeral InDEXer of Words with Context—A Concordance Generator." *CSHVB*, 3 (1970), 50–53.

Smith, Philip H., Jr. "The State of the ICRH Concordance Generator." *ICRH Newsletter*, 4, No. 5 (January 1969), 1–4.

Spevack, Marvin. *A Complete and Systematic Concordance to the Works of Shakespeare*. 8 vols. Hildesheim, Germany: Georg Olms Verlag, 1968–75.

————. "Concordances: Old and New." *CSHVB*, 4 (1973), 17–19.

————. *The Harvard Concordance to Shakespeare*. Cambridge: Harvard University Press, 1973.

Venezky, R. L. *BIBCON: An 1108 Program for Producing Concordances to Prose, Poetry and Bibliographic References*. University of Wisconsin Computer Services Department, Technical Report Revised, No. 133, 1971.

Wisbey, Roy A. *A Complete Concordance to the Vorau and Strassburg "Alexander."* Leeds, England: W. S. Maney and Son, Ltd., 1968.

————. *A Complete Word-Index to the Speculum Ecclesiae (Early Middle High German and Latin)*. Leeds, England: W. S. Maney and Son, Ltd., 1969.

————. "Computers and Lexicography." *The Use of Computers in Anthropology*. Ed. Dell Hymes. The Hague: Mouton, 1965. Pp. 213–34.

————. "Concordance Making by Electronic Computer: Some Experiences with the 'Wiener Genesis'." *Modern Language Review*, 57 (1962), 161–72.

Young, Ione D., ed. *A Concordance to the Poetry of Byron*. 4 vols. Austin, Texas: Pemberton Press, 1965.

V. Information Retrieval: Lexicography

Aitken, A. J., and Paul Bratley. "An Archive of Older Scottish Text for Scanning by Computer." *English Studies*, 48 (1967), 60–61.

Alford, M. H. T. "The Computer and Lexicography." *ALLC Bulletin*, 1, No. 3 (1973), 8–9.

Bailey, Richard W. "Computer-Assisted Lexicography: A Preliminary Bibliography." *American Journal of Computational Linguistics*, Microfiche 1 (1974), pp. 9–15.

————. "Research Dictionaries." *American Speech*, 44 (1969), 166–72.

Bailey, Richard W., James W. Downer, Jay L. Robinson, with Patricia V. Lehman. *Michigan Early Modern English Materials*. Ann Arbor: Xerox University Microfilms, 1975.

Bailey, Richard W., and Jay L. Robinson. "MEMEM: A New Approach to Lexicography." *Source*, 4 (1974), 2–6.

Ben-Hayyim, Ze'ev. "A Hebrew Dictionary on Historical Principles." *Ariel* (A Review of the Arts and Sciences in Israel), No. 13 (1966), pp. 14–20.

Cameron, Angus, Roberta Frank, and John Leyerle, eds. *Computers and Old English Concordances*. Toronto: University of Toronto Press, 1970.

Danielsson, Bror. "Proposal for DEMEP: A Dictionary of Early Modern English Pronunciation 1500–1800 (Six Volumes)," *Neuphilologische Mittelungen*, 75 (1974), 492–95.

de Tollenaere, F. "Encoding Techniques in Dutch Historical Lexicography." *CHum*, 6 (1972), 147–52.

————. "The Leiden Thesaurus." *CSHVB*, 3 (1970), 169–72.

de Tollenaere, F., and W. Pijnenberg. "Processing a Corpus of Early Middle Dutch Texts." *ALLC Bulletin*, 2, No. 1 (1974), 16–23.

Dolby, J. L., and H. L. Resnikoff. *The English Word Speculum*. 5 vols. The Hague: Mouton, 1967.

Dubois, C. "Le traitement automatique de l'information lexicologique: realisations et projets." R.E.L.O. *Revue*, No. 3 (1971), pp. 235–39.

Duro, Aldo. "Analyse électronique de textes littéraires appliquée à la lexicographie en Italie." *Applications of Linguistics: Selected Papers of the Second International Conference of Applied Linguistics, Cambridge 1969*. Ed. G. E. Perren and J. L. M. Trim. Cambridge: Cambridge University Press, 1971.

————. "Les nouvelles méthodes du dictionnaire historique de la langue italienne." *Cahiers de Lexicologie*, 8 (1966), 95–111.

Fenton, A. Rev. of "A Dictionary of the Older Scottish Tongue." *Scottish Studies*, 10 (1966), 198–205.

Findler, Nicholas V., and Heino Viil. "A Few Steps Toward Computer Lexicometry." *American Journal of Computational Linguistics*, Microfiche 4 (1974).

Finkenstaedt, Thomas, and Dieter Wolff. *Ordered Profusion: Studies in Dictionaries and the English Lexicon*. Annales Universitatis Saraviensis, Band 13. Heidelberg: Carl Winter, 1973.

"France's Word Horde." *Times Literary Supplement*, 13 October 1972, p. 1229.

Frank, Roberta, and Angus Cameron, eds. *A Plan for the Dictionary of Old English*. Toronto: University of Toronto Press, 1973.

Greene, Barbara B., and Gerald M. Rubin. *Automatic Grammatical Tagging of English*. Providence: Brown University Department of Linguistics, 1971.

Hanon, Suzanne. "A Report on the Colloque sur L'analyse des Corpus Linguistiques (Strasbourg, Centre de Philologie et Littératures Romanes, May, 1973)." *ALLC Bulletin*, 1, No. 3 (1973), 18–19.

Hellberg, Staffan. "Computerized Lemmatization without the Use of a Dictionary: A Case Study from Swedish Lexicography." *CHum*, 6 (1972), 209–12.

Henderson, Michael M. T. "Use of an Interactive Program in Analyzing Data for a Dialect Dictionary." *CHum*, 9 (1975), 105–13.

Imbs, Paul. "Creating a New Dictionary." *CNRS Research*, 2 (1975), 44–48.

———, ed. *Trésor de la Langue Française: Dictionnaire de la langue du XIXe et du XXe siècles (1789–1960)*. Paris: Centre National de la Recherche Scientifique, 1971–.

Josselson, Harry H. "Lexicography and the Computer." *To Honor Roman Jakobson*, Vol. 2. The Hague: Mouton, 1967. Pp. 1046–59.

Kučera, Henry. "Computers in Language Analysis and in Lexicography." *The American Heritage Dictionary of the English Language*. Ed. William Morris. Boston: Houghton Mifflin, 1969. Pp. xxxviii–xl.

Kučera, Henry, and W. Nelson Francis. *Computational Analysis of Present-Day American English*. Providence: Brown University Press, 1967.

Lara, L. F. "On Lexicographical Computing: Some of the Aspects of the Work for a Mexican Spanish Dictionary." *ALLC Bulletin*, 4 (1976), 97–104.

Leonard, Rosemary. "Some Possible Uses of the Computer Archive of Modern English Texts." *ALLC Bulletin*, 2, No. 2 (1974), 13–19.

Leyerle, John. "'The Dictionary of Old English': A Progress Report." *CHum*, 5 (1971), 279–83.

Lowe, Pardee. "Information Retrieval and the Old Norse Dictionary." *Studia Linguistica* (Lund), 24 (1970), 87–113.

McDavid, Raven I., Jr., and Audrey Duckert, eds. *Lexicography in English*. Annals of the New York Academy of Sciences, Vol. 211. New York, 1973.

Revard, Carter. "On the Computability of Certain Monsters in Noah's Ark." *CSHVB*, 2 (1969), 82–90.

Sherman, Donald. "A New Computer Format for *Webster's Seventh Collegiate Dictionary*." *CHum*, 8 (1974), 21–26.

Smith, Raoul N. "Interactive Lexicon Updating." *CHum*, 6 (1972), 137–45.

Štindlová, Jitka, ed. *Les machines dans la linguistique.* The Hague: Mouton, 1968.

Urdang, Laurence. "The Systems Design and Devices Used to Process *The Random House Dictionary of the English Language.*" *CHum*, 1 (1966), 31–33.

Venezky, Richard L. "Storage, Retrieval, and Editing of Information for a Dictionary." *American Documentation*, 19 (January 1968), 71–79.

Zampolli, Antonio. "L'automatisation de la recherche lexicologique: état actuel et tendances nouvelles." *Meta*, 18 (1973), 103–38.

———, ed. *Linguistica Matematica e Calcolatori.* Accademia Toscana di Scienze e Lettere, Studi XXVIII. Florence: Leo S. Olschki, 1973.

Zgusta, Ladislav. *Manual of Lexicography.* The Hague: Mouton, 1971.

VI. Information Retrieval: Bibliography and Indexes

Bellos, David. "The *Bibliographie de la France* and Its Sources." *The Library*, 28 (1973), 64–67.

Burton, Dolores M. "Research-in-Idleness or Puck among Bibliographers: Reflections on a Fully Automated Shakespeare Bibliography." *CSHVB*, 4 (1973), 37–43.

Carroll, John M., and Robert Roeloffs. "Computer Selection of Keywords Using Word-Frequency Analysis." *American Documentation*, 20 (July 1969), 227–33.

Computers and Early Books. London: Mansell, 1974.

Crennell, K. M. "FAMULUS." *CHum*, 10 (1976), 233–34.

Donohue, Joseph, and James Ellis. "The London Stage 1800–1900: An Immodest Proposal." *Nineteenth Century Theatre Research*, 1 (1973), 53–56.

———, eds. *The London Stage 1800–1900 Newsletter.* No. 2 (April 1974).

———, eds. *The London Stage 1800–1900 Newsletter.* No. 3 (February 1975).

Hutchins, W. J. "Linguistic Processes in the Indexing and Retrieval of Documents." *Linguistics*, 61 (1970), 29–64.

Lehnert, Herbert, Frederick Ruecking, and Robert Porter. "The Thomas Mann Project: A Progress Report." *CHum*, 1 (1967), 65–71.

Litto, Frederic M. *American Dissertations on the Drama and the Theater*. Kent, Ohio: Kent State University Press, 1969.

McNamee, Lawrence F. *Dissertations in English and American Literature*. New York: Bowker, 1968.

Noel, J. "Linguistics and Mechanized Indexing of Legal Texts." R.E.L.O. *Revue*, No. 3 (1971), pp. 219–33.

Plotnik, Art, Barbara Jacobs, and Joe A. Hewitt. "A Primer on OCLC for All Librarians." *American Libraries*, 7 (May 1976), 258–75.

Pollin, Burton R. *Dictionary of Names and Titles in Poe's Collected Works*. New York: De Capo Press, 1968.

———. *Godwin Criticism: A Synoptic Bibliography*. Toronto: University of Toronto Press, 1967.

———. "Poe and the Computer." *ICRH Newsletter*, 3, No. 3 (1968), 2–3.

Reimers, Paul R., and Henriette D. Avram. "Automation and the Library of Congress: 1970." *Datamation*, 16 (June 1970), 138–43.

Roeming, Robert, ed. *Camus: A Bibliography*. Madison: University of Wisconsin Press, 1968.

Ryan, Vincent J., and Vinton A. Dearing. "Computerized Manuscript and Index Processing." *Scholarly Publishing*, 4 (1973), 333–50.

———. "Computerized Text Editing and Processing with Built-In Indexing." *Information Storage and Retrieval*, 10 (1974), 211–28.

Salton, Gerard. *Automatic Information Organization and Retrieval*. New York: McGraw-Hill, 1968.

———. *Dynamic Information and Library Processing*. Englewood Cliffs, N.J.: Prentice-Hall, 1975.

———. "A New Comparison between Conventional Indexing (Medlars) and Text Processing (SMART)." *Journal of the ASIS*, 23 (1972), 75–84.

———. "Recent Studies in Automatic Text Analysis and Document Retrieval." *Journal of the ACM*, 20 (1973), 258–78.

————, ed. *The SMART Retrieval System—Experiments in Automatic Document Processing.* Englewood Cliffs, N.J.: Prentice-Hall, 1971.

Sawin, Lewis. "The Integrated Bibliography Pilot Study in Retrospect." *ALLC Bulletin*, 3 (1975), 201–07.

Schneider, Ben R., Jr., and Will Daland. "The 'London Stage' Information Bank." *CHum*, 5 (1971), 209–14.

Sparck Jones, Karen, and Martin Kay. *Linguistics and Information Science.* New York: Academic Press, 1973.

VII. Textual Criticism and Editing

Ahnert, Heinz-Jörg. "Affiliation Programs (Part II) Using the Program 'AFFILI.' " R.E.L.O. *Revue*, No. 4 (1972), pp. 35–54.

Bender, Todd K. "Literary Texts in Electronic Storage: The Editorial Potential." *CHum*, 10 (1976), 193–99.

Berman, Lawrence V. "Preliminary Report on a Computer Aided Critical Edition of the Hebrew Version of Averroes' Middle Commentary on the *Nicomachean Ethics* with Sample Text." *Hebrew Computational Linguistics*, 4 (1971), 111–21.

Cabaniss, Margaret S. "Using a Computer for Text Collation." *CSHVB*, 3 (1970), 1–33.

Dearing, Vinton A. Rev. of *La Critique des textes et son automatisation*, by Dom Jacques Froger. *CHum*, 4 (1969), 149–54.

————. "Methods of Textual Editing." *Bibliography and Textual Criticism: English and American Literature 1700 to the Present.* Ed. O. M. Brack, Jr., and Warner Barnes. Chicago: University of Chicago Press, 1969. Pp. 73–101.

————. *Principles and Practice of Textual Analysis.* Berkeley: University of California Press, 1974.

————. "Some Routines for Textual Criticism." *The Library*, 5th series, 21 (1966), 309–17.

Dearing, Vinton A., Serge E. Brunet, John H. Hall, and R. Gill Tamarelli. "Dryden's *Heroic Stanzas* on Cromwell: A New Critical Text." *PBSA*, 69 (1975), 502–26.

de Lacy, Phillip. "Editing and Translating a Galenic Text." *Modern Methods in the History of Medicine*. Ed. Edwin Clarke. London: Athlone Press, 1971. Pp. 233–37.

Epp, Eldon J. "The Twentieth Century Interlude in New Testament Textual Criticism." *Journal of Biblical Literature*, 93 (1974), 386–414.

Evrard, Etienne. "La critique des textes et son automatisation: à propos d'un livre récent." R.E.L.O. *Revue*, No. 1 (1968), pp. 69–81.

Fischer, Bonifatius. "The Use of Computers in New Testament Studies, with Special Reference to Textual Criticism." *Journal of Theological Studies*, 21 (October 1970), 297–308.

Froger, Jacques. "La critique des textes et l'ordinateur." *Vigiliae Christianae*, 24 (1970), 210–17.

———. "The Electronic Machine at the Service of Humanistic Studies." *Diogenes*, 52 (1965), 104–42.

———. *La Critique des textes et son automatisation*. Paris: Dunod, 1967.

Gilbert, Penny. "Automatic Collation: A Technique for Medieval Texts." *CHum*, 7 (1973), 139–47.

Gottesman, Ronald, and Scott B. Bennett, eds. *Art and Error: Modern Textual Editing*. Bloomington: Indiana University Press, 1970.

Griffith, J. G. "The Interrelations of Some Primary MSS of the Gospels in the Light of Numerical Analysis." *Studia Evangelica VI*. Ed. E. A. Livingstone. Berlin: Akademie-Verlag, 1973. Pp. 221–38.

———. "Numerical Taxonomy and Some Primary Manuscripts of the Gospels." *Journal of Theological Studies*, 20 (1969), 389–406.

———. "A Taxonomic Study of the Manuscript Tradition of Juvenal." *Museum Helveticum*, 25 (1968), 101–38.

Herlihy, David. "Editing for the Computer: The Florentine Catasto of 1427." *ACLS Newsletter*, 22, No. 2 (1971), 1–7.

Howard-Hill, T. H. "Computer and Mechanical Aids to Editing." *Proof*, 5 (1977), 217–35.

Jacobson, Sibyl C., and Todd K. Bender. "Computer Assisted Editorial Work on Conrad." *Conradiana*, 5, No. 3 (Fall 1973), 37–45.

Mau, Jürgen. "Affiliation Programs." R.E.L.O. *Revue*, No. 3 (1972), pp. 63–76.

Mullen, Karen A. "Using the Computer to Identify Differences among Text Variants." *CHum*, 5 (1971), 193–201.

Najock, Dietmar. "Automatic Classification of Text by Methods of Multivariate Statistics." R.E.L.O. *Revue*, No. 2 (1973), pp. 31–54.

————. "Orientation of Text-Stems." R.E.L.O. *Revue*, No. 2 (1972), pp. 39–56.

Niță, Sorin Cristian. "Establishing the Linkage of Different Variants of a Romanian Chronicle." *Mathematics in the Archaeological and Historical Sciences*. Ed. F. R. Hodson, D. G. Kendall, and P. Tăutu. Edinburgh: Edinburgh University Press, 1971. Pp. 401–09.

Oakman, Robert L. "The Present State of Computerized Collation: A Review Article." *Proof*, 2 (1972), 333–48.

————. "Textual Editing and the Computer." *Costerus*, 4 (1975), 79–106.

Ott, Wilhelm. "Remarks on the Specialist Group for Textual Editing Techniques." *ALLC Bulletin*, 2, No. 1 (1974), 35–37.

Pappin, G., and Raoul N. Smith. "The Coded Manuscripts of Jonathan Fisher (1768–1847): Some Techniques of Generating and Editing Parallel Texts." *SIGLASH Newsletter*, 9, No. 4 (September 1976), 10–21.

Peavler, James M. "Analysis of Corpora of Variations." *CHum*, 8 (1974), 153–59.

Petty, George R., Jr., and William M. Gibson. *Project OCCULT: The Ordered Computer Collation of Unprepared Literary Text*. New York: New York University Press, 1970.

Sarna, David E. Y., and Lawrence H. Schiffman. "Computer-Aided Critical Editions of Rabbinic Texts." *Hebrew Computational Linguistics*, No. 2 (1970), pp. 47–63.

Schiffman, Lawrence H. "The Computer-Aided Critical Edition: Features and Extensions." *Hebrew Computational Linguistics*, No. 8 (1974), pp. E1–E8a.

216

Shaw, David J. "MSS—Manuscript Stemma Simulator." *ALLC Bulletin*, 2, No. 2 (1974), 27–29.

———. "A Sampling Theory for Bibliographical Research." *The Library*, 5th series, 27 (1972), 310–19.

Silva, Georgette, and Harold Love. "The Identification of Text Variants by Computer." *Information Storage and Retrieval*, 5 (October 1969), 89–108.

Spencer, Christopher. "Shakespeare's *Merchant of Venice* in Sixty-Three Editions." *Studies in Bibliography*, 25 (1972), 89–106.

Vidmanová, Anežká. "Les textes contaminés et l'ordinateur." R.E.L.O. *Revue*, No. 1 (1972), pp. 5–22.

Widmann, R. L. "Computer Collation." *CSHVB*, 4 (1973), 45–51.

———. "Shakespeare and the Computer." *ALLC Bulletin*, 1, No. 3 (1973), 22–26.

Zarri, G. P. "Il metodo per la 'recensio' di Dom H. Quentin esaminato criticamente mediante la sua traduzione in un algoritmo per elaboratore elettronico." *Lingua e stile*, 4 (1969), 161–82.

VIII. Stylistics: Authorship Studies

Adams, L. LaMar, and Alvin C. Rencher. "The Popular Critical View of the Isaiah Problem in Light of Statistical Style Analysis." *CSHVB*, 4 (1973), 149–57.

Allen, John R. "Methods of Author Identification Through Stylistic Analysis." *French Review*, 47 (1974), 904–16.

Austin, Warren B. "The Posthumous Greene Pamphlets: A Computerized Study." *Shakespeare Newsletter*, 16 (1966), 45.

Brainerd, Barron. "The Computer in Statistical Studies of William Shakespeare." *CSHVB*, 4 (1973), 9–15.

Brandwood, Leonard. "Plato's Seventh Letter." R.E.L.O. *Revue*, No. 4 (1969), pp. 1–25.

Brinegar, Claude S. "Mark Twain and the Quintus Curtius Snodgrass Letters: A Statistical Test of Authorship." *Journal of American Statistical Association*, 58 (1963), 85–96.

Coppens-Ide, H. "Authorship Problems and the Computer." R.E.L.O. *Revue*, No. 3 (1971), pp. 187–94.

Damerau, Fred J. "The Use of Function Word Frequencies as Indicators of Style," *CHum*, 9 (1975), 271–80.

Drake, Bryan. "Unanswered Questions in Computerized Literary Analysis." *Journal of Biblical Literature*, 91 (1972), 241–42.

Ellegård, Alvar. *A Statistical Method for Determining Authorship: The Junius Letters 1769–1772*. Gothenburg Studies in English, No. 13. Gothenburg: University of Gothenburg, 1962.

———. *Who Was Junius?* Stockholm: Almquist and Wiksell, 1962.

Erdman, David V., and Ephim G. Fogel, eds. *Evidence for Authorship: Essays on Problems of Attribution*. Ithaca: Cornell University Press, 1966.

Frautschi, Richard L. "The Authorship of Certain Unsigned Articles in the *Encyclopédie*: A First Report." *CSHVB*, 3 (1970), 66–76.

———. "A Project for Author Discrimination in the *Encyclopédie*." *South Atlantic Bulletin*, 32 (1967), 14–17.

Greenblatt, Daniel L. "Generative Metrics and the Authorship of 'The Expostulation.'" *Centrum*, 1 (Fall 1973), 87–104.

Johnson, P. F. "The Use of Statistics in the Analysis of the Characteristics of Pauline Writing." *New Testament Studies*, 20 (1973), 92–100.

Kemp, Kenneth W. "Aspects of the Statistical Analysis and Effective Use of Linguistic Data." *ALLC Bulletin*, 4 (1976), 14–22.

Kjetsaa, Geir. "Storms on the Quiet Don: A Pilot Study." *Scando-Slavica*, 22 (1976), 5–24.

Köster, Patricia. "Words and Numbers: A Quantitative Approach to Swift and Some Understrappers." *CHum*, 4 (1970), 289–304.

Levison, Michael, A. Q. Morton, and A. D. Winspear. "The Seventh Letter of Plato." *Mind*, 77 (1968), 309–25.

McKinnon, Alastair, and Roger Webster. "A Method of 'Author' Identification." *CSHVB*, 2 (1969), 19–23.

Michaelson, Sidney, and Andrew Q. Morton. "Identifying Aristotle." *Computer Calepraxis*, 1 (1972), 13–42.

————. "Last Words: A Test of Authorship for Greek Writers." *New Testament Studies*, 18 (1972), 192–208.

————. "The New Stylometry: A One-Word Test of Authorship for Greek Writers." *Classical Quarterly*, 22 N. S. (1972), 89–102.

————. "The Spaces in Between: A Multiple Test of Authorship for Greek Writers." R.E.L.O. *Revue*, No. 1 (1972), pp. 23–77.

Morton, Andrew Q. "The Authorship of Greek Prose." *Journal of the Royal Statistical Society*, Series A, 128 (1965), 169–224.

————. "The Authorship of the Pauline Corpus." *The New Testament in Historical and Contemporary Perspective*. Ed. H. Anderson and W. Barclay. Oxford: Blackwell, 1965. Pp. 209–35.

Morton, A. Q., and Michael Levison. "Literary Uses of the Computer." *New Scientist*, 39 (15 August 1968), 340–42.

Morton, A. Q., and James McLeman. *Christianity and the Computer*. London: Hodder and Stoughton, 1964.

————. *Paul, the Man and the Myth: A Study in the Authorship of Greek Prose*. Evanston, Ill.: Harper and Row, 1966.

Morton, Andrew, and Alban Winspear. *It's Greek to the Computer*. Montreal: Harvest House, 1971.

Mosteller, Frederick, and David L. Wallace. "Deciding Authorship." *Statistics: A Guide to the Unknown*. Ed. Judith M. Tanur, Frederick Mosteller, William H. Kruskal, et al. San Francisco: Holden-Day, 1972. Pp. 164–75.

————. *Inference and Disputed Authorship: The Federalist*. Reading, Mass.: Addison-Wesley, 1964.

————. "Inference in an Authorship Problem." *Journal of American Statistical Association*, 58 (1963), 275–309.

————. "Notes on an Authorship Problem." *Annals of the Computation Laboratory of Harvard University*, 31 (1962), 163–97.

O'Donnell, Bernard. *An Analysis of Prose Style to Determine Authorship: "The O'Ruddy," a Novel by Stephen Crane and Robert Barr*. The Hague: Mouton, 1970.

Posner, Rebecca. "The Use and Abuse of Stylistic Statistics." *Archivum Linguisticum*, 15 (1963), 111–39.

Radday, Yehuda T. "Isaiah and the Computer: A Preliminary Report." *CHum*, 5 (1970), 65–73.

————. "Two Computerized Statistical-Linguistic Tests Concerning the Unity of Isaiah." *Journal of Biblical Literature*, 89 (1970), 319–24.

————. *The Unity of Isaiah in the Light of Statistical Linguistics*. Hildesheim: H. A. Gerstenberg, 1973.

Radday, Yehuda T., and Haim Shor. "AND in Isaiah." R.E.L.O. *Revue*, No. 2 (1974), pp. 25–41.

Särndal, Carl-Erik. "On Deciding Cases of Disputed Authorship." *Applied Statistics*, 16 (1967), 251–68.

Ule, Louis. "Cluster Analysis and the Authorship of *Woodstock*." R.E.L.O. *Revue*, No. 1 (1976), pp. 1–34.

Waite, Stephen V. F. "Approaches to the Analysis of Latin Prose, Applied to Cato, Sallust, and Livy." R.E.L.O. *Revue*, No. 2 (1970), pp. 91–120.

Wake, W. C. "Sentence-Length Distributions of Greek Authors." *Journal of Royal Statistical Society*, Series A, 120 (1957), 331–46.

Waltman, Franklin M. "C.L.A.S. and the *Cantar de Mio Cid*." *CHum*, 10 (1976), 145–52.

Williams, C. B. *Style and Vocabulary: Numerical Studies*. London: Charles Griffin, 1970.

Yule, George Udny. *The Statistical Study of Literary Vocabulary*. 1944; rpt. Hamden, Conn.: Archon Books, 1968.

IX. Content Analysis

Arp, Dennis J., J. Phillip Miller, and George Psathas. "An Introduction to the Inquirer II System of Content Analysis." *CSHVB*, 3 (1970), 40–45.

Baird, J. Arthur. *Audience Criticism and the Historical Jesus*. Philadelphia: Westminster Press, 1969.

————. "Content Analysis and the Computer: A Case Study in the Application of the Scientific Methods to Biblical Research." *Journal of Biblical Literature*, 95 (1976), 255–76.

Carney, T. F. *Content Analysis: A Technique for Systematic Inference from Communications*. Winnipeg: University of Manitoba Press, 1972.

Cary, Charles D. "Natural Themes in Soviet School History Textbooks." *CHum*, 10 (1976), 313–23.

Damerau, Frederick J. "Automatic Parsing for Content Analysis." *Communications of the ACM*, 13 (1970), 356–60.

Dengler, Ralph, "A General Inquirer Analysis of Sixteenth Century and Contemporary Catechisms." *CHum*, 8 (1974), 5–19.

Fortier, Paul A. "From Objectivity to Convenience: Information Processing for Literary Study." *Proceedings of the International Federation for Information Processing Congress 1974*. Ed. Jack L. Rosenfeld. Amsterdam and London: North-Holland, 1974. Pp. 846–50.

Harway, N., and H. Iker. "A Computer Approach towards the Analysis of Content." *Behavioral Science*, 10 (1965), 173–83.

Holsti, Ole. "Computer Content Analysis for Measuring Attitudes: The Assessment of Qualities and Performance." *CSHVB*, 1 (1968), 200–16.

Iker, Howard P. "An Historical Note on the Use of Word-Frequency Contiguities in Content Analysis." *CHum*, 8 (1974), 93–98.

———. "SELECT: A Computer Program to Identify Associationally Rich Words for Content Analysis. I. Statistical Results." *CHum*, 8 (1974), 313–19.

———. "SELECT: A Computer Program to Identify Associationally Rich Words for Content Analysis. II. Substantive Results." *CHum*, 9 (1975), 3–12.

Iker, H., and N. Harway. "A Computer Systems Approach to the Recognition and Analysis of Content." *CSHVB*, 1 (1968), 134–54.

Iker, H., and R. Klein. "WORDS: A Computer System for the Analysis of Content." *Behavior Research Methods and Instrumentation*, 6 (1974), 430–38.

Kadushin, Charles, Joseph Lovett, and James D. Merriman. "Literary Analysis with the Aid of the Computer: Review Symposium." *CHum*, 2 (1968), 177–202.

Kelly, Edward F., and Philip J. Stone. *Computer Recognition of English Word Senses*. New York: American Elsevier, 1975.

McConnell, J. Colin, and Paul A. Fortier. *THEME: A System for Computer-Aided Theme Searches of French Texts*. Research Report No. 1. Winnipeg: University of Manitoba Department of French and Spanish, 1975.

Misek, L. D. *Automated Contextual Analysis of Thematic Structure in Natural Languages*. Cleveland: Case Western Reserve University, 1970.

Psathas, George. "The General Inquirer: Useful or Not?" *CHum*, 3 (1969), 163–74.

Rice, Sandra. "Inquirer III (Edinburgh Version): A Computer-Based System for Content Analysis." *CHum*, 10 (1976), 332.

Ross, Robert N. "Content Analysis: Quantitative Semantics in Literary Studies and Political Science." *Style*, 10 (1976), 442–66.

Sedelow, Sally Y. "The Use of the Computer for Stylistic Studies of Shakespeare." *CSHVB*, 4 (1973), 33–36.

Sowa, Cora A., and John F. Sowa. "Thought Clusters in Early Greek Oral Poetry." *CHum*, 8 (1974), 131–46.

Spolsky, Ellen. "Computer-assisted Semantic Analysis of Poetry." *CSHVB*, 3 (1970), 163–68.

———. "Dictionaries and the Semantic Analysis of Poetry." *SIGLASH Newsletter*, 7, No. 3 (June 1974), 5–8.

Stone, Philip J., Dexter C. Dunphy, Marshall S. Smith, and Daniel M. Ogilvie. *The General Inquirer: A Computer Approach to Content Analysis*. Cambridge, Mass.: MIT Press, 1966.

X. Stylistics: Studies of Form

Allais, Christiane, and Claude Allais. "A Method of Structural Analysis with an Application to *Les Liaisons dangereuses*." R.E.L.O. *Revue*, No. 2 (1968), pp. 13–33.

Bailey, Richard W., and Dolores M. Burton. *English Stylistics: A Bibliography*. Cambridge, Mass.: MIT Press, 1968.

Bailey, Richard W., and Lubomír Doložel, eds. *An Annotated Bibliography of Statistical Stylistics*. Ann Arbor: University of Michigan Department of Slavic Languages and Literature, 1968.

Brainerd, Barron. "Article Use as an Indicator of Style among English-Language Authors." *Linguistik und Statistik.* Ed. Siegfried Jäger. Braunschweig: Vieweg, 1972. Pp. 11–32.

————. "An Exploratory Study of Pronouns and Articles as Indices of Genre in English." *Language and Style*, 5 (1972), 239–59.

————. "On the Distinction between a Novel and a Romance: A Discriminant Analysis." *CHum*, 7 (1973), 259–70.

————. "On the Number of Words a Character Speaks in the Plays of Shakespeare." *CSHVB*, 4 (1973), 57–63.

————. "On the Relation between Types and Tokens in Literary Text." *Journal of Applied Probability*, 9 (1972), 507–18.

————. "Statistical Analysis of Lexical Data Using Chi-Squared and Related Distributions." *CHum*, 9 (1975), 161–78.

————. *Weighing Evidence in Language and Literature: A Statistical Approach.* Toronto: University of Toronto Press, 1974.

Bruno, Agnes M. *Toward a Quantitative Methodology for Stylistic Analyses.* Berkeley: University of California Press, 1974.

Burton, Dolores M. "Aspects of Word Order in Two Plays of Shakespeare." *CSHVB*, 3 (1970), 34–39.

————. "The Grammar of Shakespeare's Roman Plays: A Linguistic Approach to the Problem of Style." *Shakespeare Newsletter*, 15 (December 1965), 54.

————. *Shakespeare's Grammatical Style.* Austin: University of Texas Press, 1973.

Chatman, Seymour. "Stylistics: Quantitative and Qualitative." *Style*, 1 (1967), 29–43.

Cherubini, William. "The 'Goldenness' of Sidney's *Astrophel and Stella*: Test of a Quantitative-Stylistics Routine." *Language and Style*, 8 (1975), 47–59.

Cluett, Robert. "Arcadia Wired: Preliminaries to an Electronic Investigation of the Prose Style of Philip Sidney." *Language and Style*, 7 (1974), 119–37.

————. *Prose Style and Critical Reading.* New York: Columbia University Teachers College Press, 1976.

————. "Style, Precept, Personality: A Test Case (Thomas Sprat, 1635–1713)." *CHum*, 5 (1971), 257–77.

Dilligan, Robert. "*Ibant Obscvri*: Robert Bridges' Experiment in English Quantitative Verse." *Style*, 6 (1972), 38–65.

Donow, Herbert S. "Concordance and Stylistic Analysis of Six Elizabethan Sonnet Sequences." *CHum*, 3 (1969), 205–08.

————. "Prosody and the Computer: A Text Processor for Stylistic Analysis." *AFIPS Proceedings*, 36 (1970), 287–95.

Ducretet, Pierre R. "Quantitative Stylistics: An Essay in Methodology." *CHum*, 4 (1970), 187–91.

Ducretet, Pierre, and Marie-Paul Ducretet. *Candide de Voltaire: Etude Quantitative*. Toronto: University of Toronto Press, 1974.

Duggan, Joseph J. "Formulas in the *Couronnement de Louis*." *Romania*, 87 (1966), 315–44.

————. *The Song of Roland: Formulaic Style and Poetic Craft*. Berkeley: University of California Press, 1973.

Foley, John M. "Formula and Theme in Old English Poetry." *Oral Literature and the Formula*. Ed. Benjamin A. Stolz and Richard S. Shannon. Ann Arbor: Center for Coordination of Ancient and Modern Studies, 1976. Pp. 207–38.

Follett, Brian. "The Literary Computer: Hemingway on Line." *SIGLASH Newsletter*, 7, No. 4 (October 1974), 9–11.

Frautschi, Richard L. "Recent Quantitative Research in French Studies." *CHum*, 7 (1973), 361–72.

Green, Donald C. "Formulas and Syntax in Old English Poetry: A Computer Study." *CHum*, 6 (1971), 85–93.

Joyce, James. "Poetry Generation and Analysis." *Advances in Computers*. Ed. Morris Rubinoff and Marshall Yovits. Vol. 13. New York: Academic Press, 1975. Pp. 43–72.

Kline, Edward A. "Computational Stylistics." *Proceedings of the Second Indiana University Computer Network Conference on Instructional Computer Applications (March 7, 1975)*. Bloomington: Office of Information and Computer Services, Indiana University, 1975. Pp. 11–17.

Kroeber, Karl. *Styles in Fictional Structure: The Art of Jane Austen, Charlotte Bronte, George Eliot.* Princeton: Princeton University Press, 1971.

Leaska, Mitchell A. *Virginia Woolf's Lighthouse: A Study in Critical Method.* New York: Columbia University Press, 1970.

Leavitt, Jay, and J. Lawrence Mitchell. *Gap Recurrence: A Lexicostatistical Measure.* Technical Report 75–8. Minneapolis: University of Minnesota Department of Computer Information and Control Sciences, 1975.

MacFadden, Fred R., Jr. "Report on Opportunities for Teaching and Researching the Literature of Shakespeare Using the Computer." *CSHVB,* 4 (1973), 3–8.

Mansell, Darrell. "*The Old Man and the Sea* and the Computer." *CHum,* 8 (1974), 195–206.

"The Mathematics of Style." *Times Literary Supplement,* 22 October 1971, p. 1336.

Milic, Louis T. "The Computer Approach to Style." *The Art of Victorian Prose.* Ed. George Levine and William Madden. New York: Oxford University Press, 1968. Pp. 338–62.

———. *A Quantitative Approach to the Style of Jonathan Swift.* The Hague: Mouton, 1967.

———. *Style and Stylistics: An Analytical Bibliography.* New York: The Free Press, 1967.

Oakman, Robert L. "Carlyle and the Machine: A Quantitative Analysis of Syntax in Prose Style," *ALLC Bulletin,* 3 (1975), 100–14.

Packard, David W. "Computer Techniques in the Study of Minoan Linear Script A." *Kadmos,* 10 (1971), 52–59.

Pasta, Betty A. "Four Types of Computer-Aided Analysis." *Proceedings of the International Federation for Information Processing Congress 1974.* Ed. Jack L. Rosenfeld. Amsterdam and London: North-Holland, 1974. Pp. 837–41.

Ross, Donald, Jr. "Emerson and Thoreau: A Comparison of Prose Styles." *Language and Style,* 6 (1973), 185–95.

———. "Stylistic Contrasts in Yeats's Byzantium Poems." *Language and Style,* 8 (1975), 293–305.

Ross, Robert N. "The Coefficient of Concordance: A Mathematical Tool for Comparing Literary Texts." *Style*, 7 (1973), 1–20.

Rosslyn, Wendy. "COCOA as a Tool for the Analysis of Poetry." *ALLC Bulletin*, 3, No. 1 (1975), 15–18.

Saha, P. K. "A Linguistic Approach to Style." *Style*, 2 (1968), 7–31.

Sainte-Marie, Paule, Pierre Robillard, and Paul Bratley. "An Application of Principal Component Analysis to the Works of Molière." *CHum*, 7 (1973), 131–37.

Sebeok, Thomas A., ed. *Style in Language*. Cambridge, Mass.: MIT Press, 1960.

Sedelow, Sally Y. Rev. of *Toward a Quantitative Methodology for Stylistic Analyses*, by Agnes M. Bruno. *Style*, 10 (1976), 300–02.

———. *Stylistics Analysis: Report on the Third Year of Research*. Report TM-1908/300/00. Santa Monica: Systems Development Corp., 1967.

Sedelow, Sally Y., Martin Dillon, Gerald Fisher, Walter Sedelow, and Walter Smith. *Automated Analysis of Language Style and Structure—1969–70*. Document AD-711-643. Springfield, Va.: National Technical Information Service, 1970.

Smith, John B. "A Computational Analysis of Imagery in James Joyce's *A Portrait of the Artist as a Young Man*." *Proceedings of International Federation for Information Processing Congress 1971*. Ed. C. V. Freiman. Amsterdam and London: North-Holland, 1972. Pp. 1443–47.

———. "Computer Generated Analogues of Mental Structures from Language Data." *Proceedings of the International Federation for Information Processing Congress 1974*. Ed. Jack L. Rosenfeld. Amsterdam and London: North-Holland, 1974. Pp. 842–45.

———. "Image and Imagery in Joyce's *Portrait*: A Computer-Assisted Analysis." *Directions in Literary Criticism: Contemporary Approaches to Literature*. Ed. Stanley Weintraub and Philip Young. University Park: Pennsylvania State University Press, 1973. Pp. 220–27.

———. "Thematic Structure and Complexity." *Style*, 9 (1975), 32–54.

Tordeur, P. "Metrique et statistique." R.E.L.O *Revue*, No. 4 (1971), pp. 1–7.

Vanderbok, Judith A. "Developing a Quantitative Poetic: E. E. Cummings and His Sonnets." *SIGLASH Newsletter*, 9, No. 4 (September 1976), 2–9.

Wishart, David, and Stephen V. Leach. "A Multivariate Analysis of Platonic Prose Rhythm." *CSHVB*, 3 (1970), 90–99.

INDEX

Accumulator, 9. *See also* Processing
ADAGE graphics terminal, 167
AFFILI programs: establishing genealogy of texts, 136n
Ahnert, Heinz-Jörg, 136n
Aitken, A. J., 88, 91, 92, 175
ALGOL60, 49, 50
ALGOL68, 50; computers that run it, 55; features assessed, 57–60; program for Hopkins alliteration analysis, 57–62
Algorithm, 41–43; importance to literary problem solving, 64
Allais, Christiane, 167
Allais, Claude, 167
Allen, John R., 166n
Allwright, Christine, 181n
American Heritage Dictionary of the English Language, 90, 97
American Philological Association: Repository of Greek and Latin Texts in Machine-Readable Form, 16, 172–173
Andersson, P. L., 22n
Antony and Cleopatra (Shakespeare): stylistic analysis of, 84–85, 162–163
Aquinas, Thomas: concordance of, 36
Archives, text: in machine-readable form, 172–176; in various languages, 172–173, 174–176
Arnold, Matthew: concordance of, 31, 69
Arp, Dennis J., 150n
ARPANET computer network, 190
Assembler. *See* Assembly language
Assembly language, 49
Astrophel and Stella (Sir Philip Sidney): stylistic analysis of, 161
Austin, Warren B., 143
Authorship studies, 140–150; CONSTAT text analysis program, 183–184
Avram, Henriette D., 114n

Bacon, Francis, 5n

Bailey, Richard W., 35, 90, 91, 93, 96–97
Barnett, Michael P., 51n
BASIC, 50; features assessed, 52
Batch processing, 53
Baum, Frank, 152–153
Bayes Theorem: use in authorship studies, 141
Beckett, Samuel, 157
Bedford, Emmett G., 24n, 77n
Bender, Todd K., 34n, 71n, 85n, 168–169, 191–192
Beowulf: concordance of, 33–34, 73
Berry-Rogghe, Godelieve L. M., 74n, 178n
Bessinger, J. B., Jr., 33–34, 73
Bevan, E. Dean, 70n, 73
BIBCON concordance program, 80–81, 95
Bible, Revised Standard Version: concordance of, ix
Bibliography, automated, 97–110; choosing data structures for, 100–101; flow diagram of process, 98–99
Binary coding, 5–6
Bits, 5
Blake, William: concordance of, 75
Boolean operations, 109
Borden, George A., 179n
Brainerd, Barron, 159–160
Branching operation, 43
Brandwood, Leonard, 145
Bratley, Paul, 92n, 140n, 178n
Bridges, Robert: metrical analysis of, 168
Brinegar, Claude S., 141n
British Library: computerized catalog, 114
Brown, Peter J., 52
Brown University Standard Corpus of American English, 90, 159
Brunner, Theodore F., 22, 176
Bruno, Agnes M., 158n
Burton, Dolores M., 84–85, 162–163
Busa, Roberto, 36
Byron, Lord: concordance of, 76